AMERICAN HISTORY
THROUGH EARTH SCIENCE

American History Through Earth Science

Craig A. Munsart

1997
TEACHER IDEAS PRESS
A Division of
Libraries Unlimited, Inc.
Englewood, Colorado

*As this manuscript is being written,
my grandson Brandon is beginning to explore the world around him.
It is hoped, for the sake of all of us,
that those explorations will bring his and future generations
closer to a genuine understanding of,
and coexistence with, the earth sciences.*

TEACHER IDEAS PRESS
A Division of
Libraries Unlimited, Inc.
P.O. Box 6633
Englewood, CO 80155-6633
1-800-237-6124
www.lu.com/TIP

Production Editor: Kevin W. Perizzolo
Copy Editor: Jan Krygier
Proofreader: Natalie Jaro
Indexer: Nancy Fulton
Design and Layout: Pamela J. Getchell

Library of Congress Cataloging-in-Publication Data

Munsart, Craig A.
    American history through earth science / Craig A. Munsart.
    xxiv, 209 p. 22x28 cm.
    Includes bibliographical references and index.
    ISBN 1-56308-182-2
    1. Earth sciences--Study and teaching (Elementary)--United States.
2. United States--History--Study and teaching (Elementary)
3. Teaching--Aids and devices. 4. Activity programs in education--
United States.   I. Title.
QE47.A1M86 1997
550'.71'273--dc21   96-49617
                                                     CIP

CONTENTS

PREFACE

Since the habitation of North America people have had varying success in coming to terms with the earth sciences. Despite being labeled "primitive peoples" Native Americans respected and coexisted with the environment and natural forces. Although "modern society" has accomplished much, overconfidence has formed a foundation for unsuccessful efforts to control natural processes. As the population grows it develops cities on barrier beach environments, routinely places cities within river floodplains, enlarges cities into the paths of active debris flows being shed from mountain fronts, and develops planned communities on active faults; all ignore the earth sciences with predictable consequences. Humankind has developed a habit of placing itself in harm's way, then frantically looking for ways to extricate itself from impending, inevitable disaster. The old adage "An ounce of prevention is worth a pound of cure" applies today. It is much easier to avoid construction in a river's floodplain than it is to frantically sandbag failed levees as the water level rises above your chin. Today we are paying the price for more than 300 years of neglectful development.

OBJECTIVES

As Jahns (1967) writes,

> Today man is being more widely recognized as the kind of schizoid competitor he really is—imaginative, ingenious, resourceful, and remarkably courageous, but with distressing capacities for vastly increasing his own numbers, for enveloping himself with wastes of many kinds, and for making serious mistakes in dealing with his natural surroundings. (p. 69)

The lessons and activities in this book are intended to meet several objectives.

To Tie the Four Earth Science Disciplines Together

I have always believed that science disciplines cannot be isolated from one another; geology cannot be taught without some understanding of chemistry and physics just as biology studies the interactions between physical and chemical processes. The earth sciences are no different; they cannot be taught in isolation.

Conventionally, earth science consists of geology, oceanography, meteorology, and astronomy. Because these all interact to create and modify the earth around us, the premise of any earth science course should be to provide the student with a background to understand how all the processes within these four disciplines affect one another and the earth's population. Too often, however, during a 36-week school year the four disciplines are taught as four, discrete, 9-week minicourses, with few attempts at integration. At the end of the 36 weeks students' feedback is something akin to "So?"; they still don't know how the sciences they studied relate to one another, or to anything else. No, or little, effort is made to apply the knowledge gained over each 9-week study to the other 9-week studies.

The earth sciences cannot be separated from one another in the way they affect the earth. The El Niño phenomenon is a typical example:

1. Ocean warming in the Pacific changes weather patterns and ocean currents,

2. creating strong storms and rains along the California coast,

3. modifying the land by accelerating beach erosion (exacerbated by high tides created by the Moon) and

4. mud slides and debris flows from denuded hills,

5. blackened by fires,

6. nurtured by warm Santa Ana winds.

The processes may be separated by different names, but they are united in how they affect the earth and its inhabitants.

To Allow Students to Appreciate and Respect Natural Dynamic Systems

The seat belt caution "The life you save may be your own!" applies to an understanding of the earth's systems as well. In the future, many of the students involved in our classes may have the opportunity to vote on modifications to a river; or expansion of a city onto a floodplain, barrier island, or other precarious environment; or the location of a landfill. A fixed structure within a dynamic system does not fare well. As this is being written, the encampment of the French forces sent to maintain the peace in Bosnia has been destroyed by an overflowing river. Clearly, someone ignored the earth sciences. Sustaining golf courses, lawns, and decorative fountains in desert areas with increasing populations flies in the face of reason and would be difficult to justify to the inhabitants of the Sahel, where the (largely) natural process of desertification regularly kills thousands of people. A better understanding of natural processes might create a more informed citizenry and, perhaps, save a few lives in the process.

To Allow Students to Understand History Does Not Occur in a Vacuum

Factors involved in the sinking of the *Titanic* included glaciers, ocean currents, and injudicious navigation. The United States was inhabited by Asians because of a lowering of sea level due to glacial advances. Europeans settled in the eastern United States because of wind and ocean currents. In each case the former event occurred because the latter condition existed. The operations of the dynamic systems of the earth sciences not only *make* things happen, but *allow* things to happen. The global distribution of pollutants in the oceans and atmosphere today is dictated by the same systems that have existed for thousands of years.

To Allow Students to Understand They Can Often Avoid Putting Themselves at Risk

What recurs as a disconcerting theme in many of this book's chapters is the inability of common sense to dictate human behavior. As the second paragraph of the Declaration of Independence begins, "We hold these truths to be self-evident . . . ," so, too, the following earth science rules should be obvious, even to the layperson:

Don't build at the base of steep slopes covered with rocks.

Don't build in areas that have been flooded many times before by hurricanes, rivers, or tsunamis.

Don't build on the flanks of active volcanoes.

Don't build astride active fault zones.

Heed warnings of imminent danger.

Proceed slowly when piloting a large ship through an iceberg-filled ocean.

Don't build near the ocean on a sinking pile of sand.

One would think all of the above admonitions to be "self-evident"; unfortunately, such cautions have been, and continue to be, largely ignored. Several years ago I purchased a gasoline-powered chain saw. As I read the operating instructions I was amazed to see, "Do not attempt to stop the moving chain with your hand." How stupid, I thought, to even have to tell someone not to do that! After writing this book, I am convinced the chain saw warning needs to be printed much larger.

What makes a geologic *process* a geologic *hazard* is people. "From time to time some of the risks [hazards] are translated into disasters, either unavoidably or through the active cooperation of man" (Jahns, 1967, 69). The storm surge generated by a hurricane that floods a coastal area is a natural process. That same hurricane surge devastating a city built on a barrier island in its path is a geologic hazard. The process is the same; the hazard was created by humans. In our 300-year, headlong rush to inhabit the United States and take advantage of its abundant natural resources, we have largely ignored the processes that created it all. Volcanic eruptions from the crater of Diamond Head, Oahu, Hawaii millions of years ago were a geologic curiosity; similar eruptions today would be a catastrophe. People create such hazards and are then often shocked when nature takes its predictable course.

Unfortunately, many of the processes of earth science involve the loss of human life, largely because the ever-increasing population of the planet spends most of its time concerned with the gratifications of today rather than the consequences of tomorrow. High-rise beachfront condominiums, homes built on steep slopes in areas prone to earthquakes, and cities expanding within the floodplains of rivers all place inhabitants at risk. As a teacher and geologist I am chagrined that even a minimal knowledge of the earth sciences has not reached much of the population. Describing the needless deaths of tens of thousands of people while knowing they could have been saved merely by heeding a strong voice of reason is frustrating, to say the least. The saddest part of all is that such deaths, the result of a lack of recognition or respect for the earth sciences, will continue. The foolhardy will still want to have "hurricane parties" rather than evacuate in the face of an oncoming storm. Dwellings will continue to be built on unstable beachfronts. Residents in river floodplains will still complain about poor government response when their homes or crops wash away. Volcanoes, earthquakes, and tsunamis will still kill people despite increasing knowledge and early warnings. Students are often accused of ignoring warnings because of a feeling of invulnerability; too many adults carry that same feeling to their premature graves.

As we enter the twenty-first century an ever-expanding population confined to a relatively fixed land area with decreasing resources will be faced with an array of earth science problems of increasing severity: shortages of water, fuel, and mineral supplies; pollution and alteration of the natural environment (land, water, and air); and deterioration of soil nutrients essential to crop production. These problems were created by people and, with sufficient knowledge, may be solved by people. Those "people" are the students in our classrooms today.

In 1991 the National Center for Earth Science Education of the American Geological Institute proffered four interrelated goals considered essential to earth science education: (1) students need to become stewards of the earth; (2) students need to develop a deep aesthetic appreciation of the history, beauty, simplicity, and complexity of the earth; (3) students need to understand ways in which earth scientists investigate the earth; and (4) students need to understand essential earth science concepts. I would humbly propose a fifth goal: Upon meeting the first four goals, students need to effectively communicate the knowledge to those with less awareness of the earth sciences. If history has taught us nothing else, it provides substantial evidence that those of us with knowledge do a poor job of communicating with, convincing, and educating those without.

STANDARDS

As this is being written there is a growing movement within the educational community to implement standards in education. As its title implies, this book deals with subjects across disciplines and this necessarily involves content standards for many subjects. It is impossible here to complete an exhaustive compilation of the combinations and permutations among the activities in this book and the standards for the various disciplines involved. Instead, I would like to indicate generally how geography and science standards can be addressed with the activities that follow.

Geography

The National Geography Standards address such issues as

seeing the world geographically (maps and knowledge of the globe);

places and regions (physical and human characteristics of places);

environment and society (the interactions of human and physical systems);

natural systems (the physical processes that shape the earth's surface); and

uses of geography (applying geography to the past and the future).

An investigation of history suggests that the earth sciences provide the physical framework within which the subjects of the above standards are found. History is created by the interaction of people with each other and the world around them. The activities in this book encourage students to understand and appreciate those interactions, and to become involved in the processes that create them. By understanding those interactions, our students, soon to be active members of a voting citizenry, can be better prepared to deal with complex issues affecting the world in which we live.

Science

The National Science Standards encourage students to "combine processes and scientific knowledge as they use scientific reasoning and critical thinking to develop their understanding of science." The Standards address such issues as

unifying concepts and processes (system forms and changes);

science as inquiry (abilities and understandings of scientific inquiry);

physical science (properties of matter, energy, and motion);

life science (populations, ecosystems, and environments);

earth and space science (evolution, structure, and interaction of earth systems);

science and technology (understanding about science and technology);

science in personal and social perspectives (populations, resources, and environments; risks, hazards, and benefits); and

history and nature of science (nature of science and science as a human endeavor).

Although the standards vary slightly by grade level, the themes indicated above are consistent through the K-12 continuum. The activities in the chapters that follow allow students to appreciate the systems and processes that affect the earth's surface, upon which the population continues to expand. The interaction of that growing population with the dynamic systems of the earth will determine the fate of the planet and its inhabitants.

REFERENCES

American Geological Institute. *Earth Science Education for the 21st Century: A Planning Guide.* Alexandria, Va.: National Center for Earth Science Education, 1991.

Explorer. 17, no. 1 (January 1996). American Association of Petroleum Geologists, Tulsa, Oklahoma.

Jahns, Richard H. *Geologic Jeopardy in Limitations of the Earth: A Compelling Focus for Geology.* Austin, Tex.: Bureau of Economic Geology, University of Texas–Austin, 1967.

Kenney, Marianne, and Lori Morrow. *Mapping Out a Standards-Based Framework for Geography: The Colorado Geography Curriculum Framework.* Denver, Colo.: Colorado Department of Education, 1995.

National Science Education Standards. Washington, D.C.: National Academy Press, 1996.

ACKNOWLEDGMENTS

Any success this project may have is due, in part, to the people who generously donated their time and energy to help make this a better book. In the early stages, two former members of the Teacher Ideas Press staff, David Loertscher and my friend Suzanne Barchers, provided a great deal of encouragement and support. That support still exists, but they have both gone on to other pursuits. Consequently, the editorial baton was passed to Susan Zernial, who continued to provide constructive criticism and strong support through the completion of the manuscript. Public Affairs Offices of the U.S. Army Corps of Engineers at Galveston, Texas, and New Orleans, Louisiana, provided a great deal of information. Susann Powers of the U.S. Geological Survey Library in Denver ferreted out many obscure references and was very helpful during the preparation of chapter 2. Michael Crane of the National Ocean Survey, Washington, D.C., was very helpful during the preparation of chapter 3. Dr. Nicholas K. Coch, the only forensic hurricanologist I know (with my alma mater Queens College of the City University of New York), reviewed chapter 6 and was a valuable resource about hurricanes. Donald L. Murphy, Chief Scientist of the International Ice Patrol, provided details about the North Atlantic currents and reviewed chapter 7; Gerald Levine provided additional comments. James F. Lander, of the Cooperative Institute for Research in Environmental Sciences, Boulder, Colorado, reviewed chapter 8 and provided state-of-the-art information about tsunamis.

I am fortunate to have had three teaching colleagues review the entire manuscript. Nancy White, an earth science teacher at Lakewood High School and Richard Will, an earth science teacher at Columbine High School (both in Jefferson County, Colorado) were very helpful. In addition, Ruth Mitchell, a member of my school's science team, my friend and fellow IJAJ member, was thankfully "ruthless" in her corrections. I owe all of the above a great deal. They can be credited for improving this book. I alone accept the blame for any errors.

I would also like to acknowledge the staff of the Geology Department of Queens College of the City University of New York, many of whom I was fortunate enough to have had as instructors while I labored to complete the requirements for both undergraduate and graduate Geology degrees; specifically, in alphabetical order,

Dr. Eugene A. Alexandrov

Dr. Nicholas K. Coch

Dr. Robert M. Finks

Dr. David H. Krinsley

Dr. Peter H. Mattson

Dr. Andrew S. McIntyre

Dr. Walter S. Newman

Dr. William A. Thomas

and a special thanks to Leonard J. Cinquemani, a former classmate and longtime stalwart of the department whose middle initial I omitted from a memo almost 30 years ago. Without their efforts this book never would have become reality.

As this is being written the survival of that department (like much of public education, already faced with drastic budget cuts) is being threatened by the bureaucratic pundits who measure the value of education with an accounting ledger. It can be argued, by those shortsighted enough to think along such lines, that (1) a department member or former student saving lives or millions of dollars in a coastal community of South Carolina provides no "bottom-line" monetary reward for a publicly funded college in New York City, or (2) a former student teaching secondary students and other teachers about earth science is not enhancing the financial pockets of the institution.

As we enter a new millennium, such narrow, provincial thinking is absurd. The economy is global, the spread of disease is global, environmental concerns are global, waste disposal problems are global, energy issues are global, resource supply is global, food and water problems are global, and, certainly, the population problem on this planet is global. Adoption of a "what's in it for me" attitude created many of the problems that exist today and will certainly doom us all. An unfortunate aspect of education is that it is difficult to predict which of your students might be the one to discover the cure for a particular disease or develop a valuable substitute for fossil fuels ten years in the future, so we must teach them all! And, to improve the chances of such discoveries, we must teach more of them, not fewer.

INTRODUCTION

The events that constitute American History did not occur in a vacuum; they all took place in the context of the oceanographical, astronomical, meteorological, and geological processes that affected the landmass considered North America. The continent was first populated by Asians as a result of the Ice Age; the early European settlements of both the east and west coasts were largely dictated by ocean currents, which, in turn, were generated by the earth's rotation and dominating winds; the Pilgrims first landed on part of a terminal glacial moraine called Cape Cod, before continuing on to a glacial erratic called Plymouth Rock; the Donner Party endured catastrophic problems on the (appropriately named, nevada means "snowy") Sierra Nevada Mountains because of blizzards; exploration paths were determined by rivers; and railroad routes were dictated by terrain and the availability of fuel and water; the presence and subsequent absence of mineral resources both created and destroyed many settlements. Today, the launches of spacecraft from Florida are influenced by the earth's rotation and planetary phenomena. The earth sciences dictated much of what was created—and destroyed—in America's past.

The earth sciences describe phenomena that are mixed blessings. Volcanoes created the beautiful scenery and fertile soils of the Hawaiian Islands while at the same time forming the greatest natural hazard to their inhabitants. The same warm weather and tropical breezes enjoyed by the citrus-growing residents of Florida create the hurricanes that can destroy their homes. The natural highway of the Mississippi River, flowing south through the United States, that allowed much of the country to be explored in the first place has also become a source of disastrous floods.

COURTING DISASTER

Despite what they may believe, people everywhere in North America are vulnerable to some type of natural process that could place them at risk: flood, drought, heat, cold, earthquake, volcanic eruption, tornado, hurricane, landslide, erosion, deposition, sea level rise, land subsidence, and, as if processes generated near and on the planet's surface weren't bad enough, even impacts of extraterrestrial masses. These processes have all occurred and will, no doubt, reoccur.

Many such disastrous incidents (e.g., meteorite impacts) are unpredictable spatially or temporally; neither when nor where they might occur can be predicted. Some events can be generally defined spatially (oceanic events occur along the coast, earthquakes occur in areas of active faults, tornadoes occur in "Tornado Alley," volcanic eruptions occur in areas known to have active volcanoes), but the time of occurrence can be only predicted generally. Still others can be defined temporally; the event is known to occur within a narrow time frame, but the location is only vaguely known. For instance, hurricanes along the southeastern United States occur from June to October, tornadoes in the Midwest occur in late spring and early summer.

One of the most useful geologic concepts is called Uniformitarianism, which states that the geologic processes and systems that operate today are much the same as those that operated in both the near and distant past. Uniformitarianism applies to all geologic processes: glacial transport, deep sea sedimentation, sand dune construction, beach erosion, meteorite impact, volcanic eruptions, movement on fault lines, and river construction and destruction.

The dynamics of the earth sciences make all maps of the United States (and the rest of the world) continually obsolete. As the land surface rebounds from the weight of the glaciers and ice caps melt, relative sea level falls and rises, causing changes in the shape of the coastlines as well as surface elevations and ocean depths. Erosion constantly modifies coastlines, as well as the earth's topography. Climatic variation can rapidly increase the expanse of deserts. Major storms, like hurricanes, can do in a few hours what less violent erosional processes modify in years. Volcanoes can modify dramatically the earth's surface in short periods of time, destroying mountains as well as adding new islands. For example, the symmetrical peak of Mount St. Helens was destroyed in a few minutes and a new Hawaiian island is growing below the surface of the Pacific Ocean southeast of Hawaii as this is being written. Mass wasting processes such as landslides and mudflows move large amounts of materials from higher to lower elevations, sometimes in years, sometimes in minutes. Earthquakes rapidly move large land areas long distances in short time frames; portions of the San Andreas Fault moved 20 feet during San Francisco's 1906 earthquake. Magnetic North, that apparently immutable cartographic beacon, is actually quite variable. The magnetic "north" detected by compasses not only wanders in the northern part of the world but in the geologic past has regularly "flip-flopped" between the Northern and Southern Hemispheres.

Much of what we see as *terra firma* is really part of an active system in dynamic equilibrium. A beach appears to be merely an accumulation of sand adjacent to a body of water. The reality is that the sand forming that beach is always moving; some is being removed by wind and ocean currents while new sand is being added by those same two agents. Strong winter storms remove the sand while more placid currents during warmer weather allow sand to accumulate. This dynamic system works to maintain a beach while at the same time constantly moving the small components of the beach. The beach is always there but never in the same form. Similar systems operate for the huge landmasses of the earth's surface. Older rocks are removed at the leading edges of plates while new material is added at the trailing edges; Mount Everest is pushed ever higher as India and Asia collide at the same time that processes of erosion wear it away. Although there has been a Mississippi River flowing south through the center of the United States for tens of thousands of years, it is never the same river. The river changes course, cutting new channels, abandoning older ones, always widening and changing depths of the channels within which the water flows, and always carrying huge amounts of sediment toward the Gulf of Mexico.

Native Americans recognized the usefulness of teepees as structures within such transient environments; European settlers built cities. What common sense suggests, yet is apparently unnoticed by the majority of the population, is that locating permanent structures within such variable systems is absurd. Having placed structures within such systems, the next link in this concatenation of the bizarre seems to be to spend vast sums of money to protect the former from the latter. Two examples are the city of New Orleans, Louisiana, built within the transient delta complex of the Mississippi River, and the city of Galveston, Texas, built on a sinking barrier island.

Activity: Getting Them Hooked

With disaster as a backdrop, it's surprising (to me anyway) that many students are not excited by the announcement "Today we're going to study earth science!" They perceive the study of earth science as one of those abstract exercises involving memorization of obscure information having virtually no bearing on anything. In an attempt to overcome that initial reluctance I developed the following presentation while I was student teaching. With a sufficiently enthusiastic presentation (and enough props), students will quickly come to appreciate the role of the earth sciences in a grand enterprise of historic significance, like the construction of the Panama Canal (see also chapter 4).

This is a relatively short (20-30 minute) dynamic lecture/presentation during which the students should be both entertained and involved. It would be wonderful to distribute props among the class so that, as the presentation continues, students can add their own particular segments as needed. Unfortunately, when I have done so in the past, props have either disappeared or gotten damaged. A workable alternative is to distribute to the class index cards or larger signs containing the historic events described, keeping the props themselves accessible to you on a table where they are visible to the class. Additional props, such as character costumes or hats (e.g., Admiral Dewey, Teddy Roosevelt) and accents, can be used at the discretion of the more theatrical presenter (I am not!). As the presentation continues refer to the world map to show the spatial relationships.

The diverse collection of paraphernalia in the materials list below can ultimately relate how earth science can affect U.S. history, specifically the building of the Panama Canal. The continuous thread of earth science ties the following historic elements together:

the building of the Suez Canal

the opera *Aida*

Ferdinand De Lesseps

the sinking of the battleship *Maine*

the Panama Railroad

the building of the Panama Canal

Theodore Roosevelt

Admiral Dewey and the Battle of Manila

the Spanish-American War

the Eiffel Tower

the Statue of Liberty

the Brooklyn Bridge

the San Francisco 49ers

the discovery of gold in California and Alaska

the purchase of the U.S. Virgin Islands from Denmark

Time

+ approximately 20-30 minutes; determined by presenter

Materials

I have accumulated many of these over the past twenty-five years; substitutions are possible as needed.

+ set of event cards (one 4" x 6" card for each event listed under "Directions")
+ sand from Egypt
+ French francs (coins and bills)
+ Statue of Liberty replica
+ Eiffel Tower replica
+ picture of the Brooklyn Bridge
+ sand from Nome, Alaska
+ an object made of gold
+ football
+ anthracite coal from Fort Jefferson in the Dry Tortugas, Florida
+ railroad spike from the Panama Railroad (or equivalent)
+ plastic model of the cruiser *U.S.S. Olympia*
+ recording of triumphal march of Giuseppe Verdi's opera *Aida*
+ a phonograph, or tape or CD player to play the above recording
+ large world wall map or overhead map
+ small bell

Grouping

+ Entire class

Directions

1. Arrange the props on a table in front of the room, and review them with the students.

2. Before the presentation, prepare the following event cards (they can be rewritten or merely copied, cut out, and pasted onto 4" x 6" cards);

> Card 1 (1522). Spanish priest recommends Panama and Nicaragua as possible canal routes.
>
> Card 2 (1811). Alexander Von Humboldt recommends Nicaragua as the route with the fewest difficulties.
>
> Card 3 (1830). The need for a canal through Egypt to establish convenient communication between Europe and east Africa, as well as southern and southeastern Asia, was determined.
>
> Card 4 (1849). Travelers rush to California to seek their fortunes in newly discovered gold.
>
> Card 5 (1854). French entrepreneur Ferdinand De Lesseps promoted the relatively easy digging of the Suez Canal through the dry climate and soft sands of Egypt, connecting the almost tideless waters of the Mediterranean and Red Seas.
>
> Card 6 (1855). The first transcontinental railroad is completed across Panama. Gold seekers travel down the east coast, across Panama, and up the west coast.
>
> Card 7 (1869). The Suez Canal is completed.
>
> Card 8 (1869). The second transcontinental railroad is completed at Promontory Point, Utah.
>
> Card 9 (1870). President U. S. Grant promotes expeditions to investigate the building of a canal across Central America.

Card 10 (1871). Verdi's opera *Aida* is performed in Cairo to celebrate the opening of the Suez Canal.

Card 11 (1881). The French arrive in Panama to start construction of a sea-level canal.

Card 12 (1882). First excavations on French canal at Panama take place.

Card 13 (1886). Alexandre-Gustave Eiffel builds the structural framework for the Statue of Liberty.

Card 14 (1888). Alexandre-Gustave Eiffel plans the structural framework for the doors of the locks on the Panama Canal.

Card 15 (1889). Theodore Roosevelt recognizes the need for a Central American canal for U.S. interests.

Card 16 (1890). Alexandre-Gustave Eiffel builds his famous tower in Paris; it is the tallest structure in the world at the time.

Card 17 (1896). Gold is discovered in Alaska, sparking a second gold rush across the United States to Skagway and Nome.

Card 18 (1898). The battleship *Maine* leaves Tampa, Florida, obtains anthracite coal for fuel in the Dry Tortugas, and sails to Havana.

Card 19 (1898). Battleship *Maine* blows up in a Havana harbor.

Card 20 (1898). Spanish-American War begins.

Card 21 (1898). Admiral George Dewey, on board the cruiser *Olympia,* destroys the Spanish fleet in Manila Bay.

Card 22 (1898). The battleship *Oregon* rushes to the Atlantic Coast from San Francisco.

Card 23 (1901). The United States and Great Britain sign the Hay-Pauncefote Treaty giving the United States the right to build and operate a canal through Panama.

Card 24 (1903). The French sell their rights to build a canal through Panama (then part of Colombia) to the United States.

Card 25 (1903). The United States recognizes Panama's independence from Colombia. The U.S. cruiser *Nashville* is made available to defend Panama if needed.

Card 26 (1904). Americans begin excavation at Panama for a lock canal.

Card 27 (1910). Steel cables used in the building of the Panama Canal were provided by John Roebling and Sons, the same family that designed and built the Brooklyn Bridge in 1883.

Card 28 (1914). The Panama Canal opens.

Card 29 (1917). The United States purchases the Virgin Islands from Denmark to provide submarine protection for the Caribbean entrance to the Canal.

Card 30 (1980). One hundred forty years after the gold rush a football team named in its honor becomes a dynasty.

Card 31 (1999). Panama Canal operations and Canal Zone lands are set to be returned to Panama.

3. Distribute the event cards to the class. Have the class read the cards in sequence with the teacher providing props as needed. Allow the students to determine when props should be used.

4. As a card is read by a student, involve the prop. For instance, when Card 10 is read, play the overture for *Aida*. Point out the historic events on the world map as the process continues.

5. Depending on your theatrical range, prepare appropriate costumes for yourself, or involve the students by giving them cards in advance and asking them to prepare their own costumes.

Extension

Have the students construct a time line of the presentation and indicate what earth science aspect is involved at each step.

THE FORMAT OF THIS BOOK

As a classroom teacher I appreciate the need for teacher-friendly, classroom-ready materials. The activities described in this book include background text, time and material requirements, suggested student grouping, step-by-step instructions, sources of additional information, and references and extensions. For the most part, the illustrations are prepared as reproducibles. Some may need to be enlarged on a photocopy machine to 8½" x 11" size. Still other maps are necessarily much larger and are included as page-sized sections that will need to be taped together by students as part of the activity.

The required student materials include readily available supplies students might already have: rulers, protractors, transparent tape, colored markers or pencils, graph paper, and a calculator (recommended in some cases). Teacher needs include an overhead projector and a copying machine capable of enlarging.

The activities all presume students and teachers have a working knowledge of the earth sciences. The introductory text for each chapter and activity is designed to provide specifics of the chapter subject rather than a broad background of the generalities of the processes involved. For instance, Chapter 5, "Coal, Canals, and Black Bass," discusses flooding along a river in the Appalachian Mountains but does not describe river mechanics nor the geologic history of the area. Although the activities in this book can stand alone they will be more meaningful if applicable earth science concepts are taught first. The introductory text will provide general information and background, but is not intended to replace an introductory earth science course.

One final note. Since I became involved in earth science I have been amazed that it is treated as the "dummy science." Students with minimal, or no, science aptitude are encouraged to "Take earth science, it's easy." When I entered college (longer ago than I care to record here), geology was for science majors only. The department faculty were outraged subsequently when the administration told them that because too many nonscience majors were having trouble with chemistry, physics, and biology they would have to be allowed to take introductory geology to satisfy their science requirement. In many instances, earth science is still treated that way. In many high schools earth science is a required course. Yet, in the need to balance class enrollments with teaching staff, nonscience-trained teachers are often asked to teach earth science because "it's easy!" Recently, Robert Ballard commented that 85 percent of science teachers had not taken a college-level course in the subject they were teaching (*Explorer* 1996, 6). The teacher is often placed in an uncomfortable position at the same time the students are being shortchanged. The earth sciences are no less rigorous than chemistry, biology, and physics; they need to be given the same respect. If the earth's problems are to be addressed with any hope of solution, earth science classes need to be taught by someone other than the high school football coach with, possibly, one geology credit from fifteen years earlier, who happened to have a free period when the school schedule needed a science teacher. The academic program for Gifted and Talented students in a large Colorado school district requires participants to have life and physical sciences in middle school and biology, chemistry, or physics in high school. Students in normal academic course sequence are all required to take earth science in ninth grade. Apparently, it is not a science worthy of advanced students. There are indications that attitudes may be changing. In the National Science Standards announced in November 1995 the three main branches of science education listed are **earth science** (author's emphasis), physical science, and life science (*Explorer* 1996, 10). If the national standards can be translated from guidelines to reality, earth science education could be dramatically improved.

RESOURCES

The federal government is often maligned as being an invasive, nonfunctional bureaucracy. Without debating the merits of this view, that same "invasiveness" makes the government privy to an incredible amount of information, much of which is easily accessible to educators. A broad array of federal agencies, with extremely helpful staff members, is available and willing to provide information about many of the subjects discussed here. Amassing a comprehensive list of agencies is beyond the scope of this book, but a few are mentioned below. Details about the U.S. Army Corps of Engineers and the International Ice Patrol are given in the appropriate chapters. Additional information is available from the National Aeronautics and Space Administration (NASA), and the National Oceanographic and Atmospheric Administration (NOAA).

The United States Geological Survey (USGS) is an excellent source of a wide variety of earth science information (data are current as of October 1996). Some of the resources (such as those of the Geo-Center) are also available through USGS offices and Geo-Centers in Reston, Virginia, and Menlo Park, California.

Ask-A-Geologist

To obtain, within a day or two, answers to general questions about earth sciences:

ask-a-geologist@octopus.wr.usgs.gov

Astrogeology: General planetary information

U.S. Geological Survey
Regional Planetary Image Facility (RPIF)
2255 North Gemini Drive
Flagstaff, AZ 86001
(520) 556-7264

Core Information: Rock cores; collection of rock core, cuttings, and thin sections

Core Research Center
Building 810
Denver Federal Center
Box 25046, Mail Stop 975
Denver, CO 80225
(303) 202-4851

Core Information: Ice cores; ice cores taken from around the world stored and studied in a special facility; tours available

National Ice Core Laboratory
Building 810
Denver Federal Center
Box 25046, Mail Stop 975
Denver, CO 80225
(303) 202-4843

Earthquakes: Records and studies of earthquakes from around the world; tours available. The center is located on the campus of the Colorado School of Mines in Golden, Colorado, but uses the following address

National Earthquake Information Center
Building 810
Denver Federal Center
Box 25046, Mail Stop 967
Denver, CO 80225
(303) 273-8500 (tours)
(303) 273-8450 (fax)

General Education

The Geo-Center is an earth science education resource within the USGS Library, providing books, videos, CD-ROMs, and fossil resources free on loan. Susann Powers, USGS librarian, is an excellent resource.
The Geo-Center
Building 20
Denver Federal Center
Box 25046, Mail Stop 914
Denver, CO 80225
(303) 236-1015

To obtain fossil and mineral sets for teachers, contact:
Tom Michalski
Building 810
Denver Federal Center
Box 25046, Mail Stop 975
Denver, CO 80225
(303) 202-4851

Landslides: The Information Center is located in Golden, Colorado, but uses the Denver address

USGS National Landslide Information Center
Denver Federal Center
Box 25046, Mail Stop 966
Denver, CO 80225
1-800-654-4966

Maps and Publications: Excellent and relatively inexpensive publications

For maps, booklets, teacher's packets, and general interest publications:
U.S. Geological Survey
Building 810
Denver Federal Center
Box 25046, Mail Stop 306
Denver, CO 80225
(303) 202-4700

For computerized maps and data, aerial photography, satellite imagery, and computer programs:
U.S. Geological Survey
Earth Science Information Center (ESIC)
Building 810
Denver Federal Center
Box 25046, Mail Stop 504
Denver, CO 80225
(303) 202-4200

For your school to receive a 40 percent discount on maps (as of February 1, 1996), order five or more sheets of the same title and submit the order to:
USGS Information Services
Business Partner Program
P.O. Box 25286
Denver, CO 80225
(303) 202-4693

For information or help in ordering:
1 (800) USA-MAPS or
1 (800) HELP-MAP

Minerals Information Office

To obtain mineral-resource assessments, publications and periodicals, and address and reference lists:
(303) 236-5438

Volcanoes

Richard Moore
Central Region Representative
Building 20
Denver Federal Center
Box 25046, Mail Stop 903
Denver, CO 80225
(303) 236-5900

Water

To obtain a free set of colorful posters:
Water Resource Education
Steve Vandas
Denver Federal Center
P.O. Box 25046, Mail Stop 406
Denver, CO 80225

For water resource information from all states in the United States:
National Water Information Clearinghouse
U.S. Geological Survey
Mail Stop 423
12201 Sunrise Valley Drive
Reston, VA 22092
1 (800) 426-9000

World Wide Web

The U.S. Geological Survey has a site on the World Wide Web:

http://www.usgs.gov/

With the continual press for budget cutbacks, many federal agencies must reduce or eliminate certain services. Unfortunately, many of these cutbacks seem to be in the area of educational outreach. Therefore, be aware that these resources are always subject to change.

ONE

Inuit, Isostasy, and Mammals Long Gone

As far as we know, Earth is the only planet in the solar system that has liquid water. Water may look ordinary, but it is actually special stuff. It is the only compound on Earth that occurs naturally in three states of matter: gas (steam, as from geysers and volcanoes), liquid (oceans and streams), and solid (ice caps and glaciers). Although the state of matter may change, the quantity of water does not. Since its formation approximately 4.5 billion years ago Earth has held a relatively constant amount of water. The stream water in which dinosaurs made footprints 100 million years ago could be the same water with which you prepare your morning coffee; difficult to prove and more than a little disgusting, but possible.

The amount of water on Earth does not change. What changes is how that water is distributed on the planet. Table 1.1 lists the forms of water on earth and their average distribution. What should be obvious from the table is that any significant changes in water distribution must affect the two largest water sources: the oceans and the bodies of ice (caps and glaciers). These two sources account for more than 99 percent of the earth's water. Note that these percentages are necessarily estimates, for, as even a cursory study of the water cycle indicates, they are changing as you read this.

Table 1.1. The Earth's Water Distribution.

Type	% of Earth's supply
oceans	97.2
ice caps and glaciers	2.14
soil moisture and all groundwater	0.625
freshwater lakes	0.009
saltwater lakes and inland seas	0.008
atmospheric moisture	0.001
rivers	0.0001

Source: Raymond L. Nance, *Water of the World*. Washington, D.C.: U.S. Geological Survey, 1977, 11.)

Note: Percentages do not total 100 percent as these are estimates.

Activity: That's All There Is?

Table 1.1 indicates that the ever-increasing population of the earth must share a relatively miniscule amount of the total water available. This activity will allow the students to transfer the tabulated data to a graphic format.

Time

+ 30-45 minutes

Materials

+ table 1.1 (presented as overhead or written on the chalkboard)
+ graph paper (depicting ¼-inch squares; one 8½" x 11" sheet per student)
+ a straightedge
+ colored pencils
+ figure 1.1 (presented as an overhead)

Grouping

+ individuals

Directions

1. With table 1.1 visible to the class, discuss the data. The actual amount of water that is potable (drinkable) in its current form should seem very small compared with the total amount of water present on Earth. Students need to understand that it is critically important to avoid water pollution and waste to preserve this tiny, precarious supply.

2. Have students hold their graph paper with the short side across the bottom. Ask them to draw a rectangle 40 squares high and 25 squares wide. The rectangle will thus contain 1,000 squares. Figure 1.1 shows how it should look, but because it contains the solution do not show it to the students.

3. With each student having the appropriate-sized rectangle drawn on their graph paper, explain that they will transfer the tabulated data to a pictorial view. The data on table 1.1 are percentages— numbers out of 100. On their graph paper students will represent the same distribution using squares out of 1,000. From table 1.1 we know that the oceans contain 97.2 percent of the earth's water. This percentage can be thought of as 97.2 squares out of 100 squares, or 972 squares out of 1,000. Because the number of squares is being multiplied by 10, the decimal point is moved one place to the right to get the number of representative squares out of 1,000. Be certain students understand the numerical conversion before continuing.

4. Students should transfer the first three sources of water listed on table 1.1. These will total 99.975 percent of the earth's water supply; 999.75 squares of the 1,000 available squares will now be accounted for.

5. Once drawn, the areas for each type of water can be colored to distinguish them from one another more clearly. Use figure 1.1 as a reference for a completed grid.

Extensions

Earth's natural water distribution system is incredibly complex. Water moves vertically and horizontally in the atmosphere, in the oceans, and in the land masses. Although the general circulation pattern is fairly regular, aberrations such as El Niño create chaos. Use table 1.1 to review the hydrologic cycle to make certain students understand how Earth's natural water distribution system operates. Students can become involved in specific aspects of the system by studying, for example, the dustbowl conditions of the 1930s, alterations

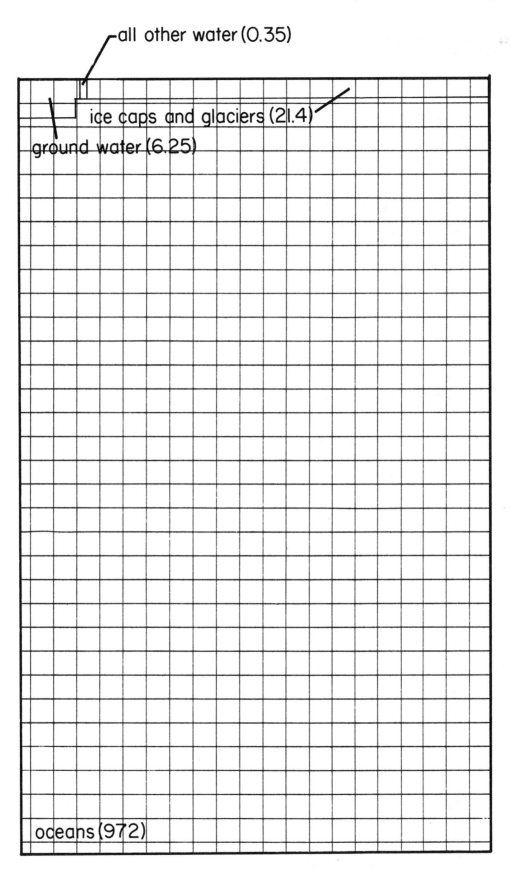

all other water (0.35)

ice caps and glaciers (21.4)

ground water (6.25)

oceans (972)

Fig. 1.1. Graphic Representation of the Distribution of the Earth's Water (Includes Solution for "Activity: That's All There Is?").

of drought with above-normal rainfalls in Southern California, or the Midwest floods of 1993.

Using paper gridded 10 squares to the inch, with a total of 10,000 squares, the percentages of distribution can be shown more accurately. More tangible methods can be used with a large container; provide each student with one small container of water at a time, with each small container representing one percent of the total.

Greenland and Antarctica account for approximately 96 percent of the earth's ice-covered land area; they also contain an incredible volume of ice. The ice on Greenland exceeds 3,000 meters (9,840 feet) in thickness. The ice on Antarctica is about 2,300 meters (7,544 feet) in thickness, and on Marie Byrd Land, in southwestern Antarctica, the ice is more than 7,400 meters (24,272 feet) thick. If all that ice were to melt, it is estimated that sea level could rise approximately 60 meters (200 feet; Leet and Judson 1971, 306). Conversely, in the past, when Earth's climate was much colder than it is today, ice covered a much greater portion of the earth than it does now, almost two and one-half times as much. The water that created that much ice had to come from somewhere. It came from the oceans, causing sea level to drop approximately 120 meters (394 feet; Leet and Judson 1971, 307). The sea level that we consider fixed today actually has a vertical range of more than 180 meters (590 feet) and at any particular time can be anywhere within that range. The change in sea level due to a change in the amount of water is called a *eustatic* sea level change. The actual "level" that is marked on maps today is merely a temporary and convenient reference point through which the sea surface has passed several times when going much higher or much lower. Topographic maps used to have a zero elevation of "mean sea level," which is now known as N.G.V.D. (National Geodetic Vertical Datum). A large body of evidence indicates that the climate is warming, global ice is melting, and sea level is on its way up. How far? No one knows.

On a worldwide average, over the last 600 million years sea level has risen approximately 1 millimeter per thousand years (Holmes 1965, 714). In local areas, and for relatively short periods of time, that number varies considerably:

- Along the U.S. Atlantic Coast since 1960 sea level has risen at a rate of approximate 2 feet (60 centimeters) per hundred years; prior to the 1920s it rose at a rate of only 3.5 inches (8.75 centimeters) per hundred years.

- Southern California has seen sea levels as high as 1.5 inches (4 centimeters) per hundred years.

- Near the mouth of the Mississippi River water levels have increased up to 3.28 feet (1 meter) per hundred years (estimated to double for the next century).

The worldwide average sea level rise is approximately 4-6 inches (10-15 centimeters) per hundred years (Williams, Dodd, and Gohn 1991, 8). Significant sea level rises would not be new. Dramatic evidence of such a rise is a cave in coastal France containing 27,000-year-old paintings that now lies 110 feet (33 meters) below sea level (Clottes and Courtin 1993, 64-70).

Although it would seem relatively easy to study changes in the level of the ocean, the problem is complicated by the fact that both the level of the water and the land (where most people live and work) are moving up and down. It's a little like attempting to determine the rise and fall of the tide while you are on a boat being loaded. As crustal plates move across the outer part of the earth, they change the shapes (vertically and horizontally) of the basins containing the water and, consequently, the level of the water within those basins. Not only do the plates of continental crust move laterally across the earth, but because they are floating on the denser material below, they can also move vertically, much like a raft in water with a weight on it (this self-leveling process is called *isostasy*). When the crustal plates have a large mass on them (such as occurred during continental glaciation), the plates are depressed into the material below, and to an observer riding on those plates sea level seems to rise (see fig. 1.2). When the mass is removed (the ice melts), the plates rise to their former level (or higher) and to that same observer sea level would seem to fall. As new sediment is deposited along coastal areas it is compacted over time, resulting in an apparent, or relative, **rise** in sea level. The vertical motion of the land creates an apparent or relative vertical motion of the water level. Such changes are known as *tectonic* sea level changes.

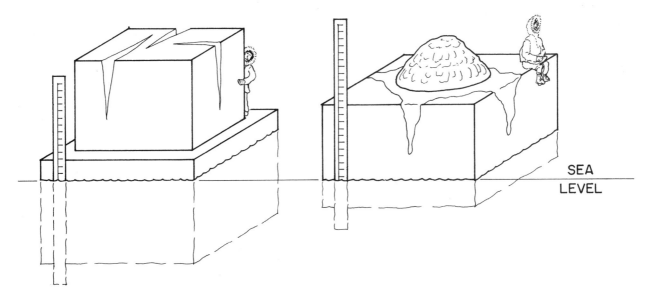

Fig. 1.2. Isostasy and the Difficulty of Observing Sea-level Changes As the Land Moves Up and Down.

Historic drops in sea level create large, new land areas. Australia and the chain of islands between it and the mainland of Asia were once almost a continuous land area (Luling 1979, 6); the Bahamas were once a wide plateau, not a group of isolated islands, and the Diomede Islands (between Alaska and Russia) were once isolated hills rising above a broad, flat plain, in places more than 1,000 miles wide. Now the Bering and Chukchi Seas are connected by the 55-mile (88 kilometer)-wide Bering Strait. At the time of the maximum drop in sea level the Bering and Chukchi Seas were separated by a 1,000-mile wide landmass called Beringia; a land bridge connected what is now Siberia and Alaska. The eastern end of the bridge, on what is now the Seward Peninsula in Alaska, has been named the Bering Land Bridge National Preserve and is administered by the National Park Service.

As sea level dropped 50,000 years ago, the newly emergent land areas provided opportunities for animals seeking new food supplies and for animals attempting to escape predation to move away from their original homes. Shortly after the seas disappeared, animal migrations began. Mammals migrated both east and west across the Bering Land Bridge, and humans following the animals they typically hunted migrated toward a generally unknown land area to the east eventually to settle both North and South America. Some North American mammals (camels and horses) traversed the bridge into Asia while new species, such as elephants, mammoths, bison, elk, reindeer, and musk ox, moved east to North America (Russell 1962; Flerow 1967; Pewe and Hopkins 1967; Repenning 1967; Vangengeim 1967; Claiborne 1973). Conflicting archaeological evidence suggests the oldest human sites in North America could be as old as 40,000 years (Kopper 1986, 33; Ballantine and Ballantine 1993, 35). DNA and language analysis also link Native Americans with Asian ancestors and suggest a series of migrations for different groups 15,000-30,000, 12,000, and 7,500 years ago (Ballantine and Ballantine 1993, 32). Some migrated east across North America and others south along the west coast to Central and South America.

Science, with all its searching for truth, can have the unfortunate effect of removing the wonder and magic from reality. Although the land bridge explanation seems to fit the archaeological and geological evidence, Native American legends offer alternatives. Here's one from a Northwest Coast Creation Story:

> Raven watched and listened intently as the clam slowly opened up. He was surprised and happy to see tiny people emerging from the shell. All were talking, smiling, and shaking the sand off their tiny bodies. . . . He had brought the first people to the world. (Ballantine and Ballantine 1993, 30)

Activity: How They Got Here

A hypothetical ocean depth survey was undertaken of the Bering Sea to determine where the Bering Land Bridge might have been. It is hoped archaeologists will use the survey as a starting point from which to search for artifacts left by the migrants from Asia to North America. Table 1.2 lists the survey lines, survey points, and depths (in meters) of the ocean bottom at each point. Lettered lines run south to north, numbered lines run west-southwest to east-northeast. Line locations are shown on Figure 1.3 (page 8). Students will (a) use data obtained from the survey to plot data points on the base map, (b) make a bathymetric map of the area by contouring the data from the survey, (c) determine the areal extent of a possible land bridge at various drops in sea level, and (d) make a sea-bottom profile to show what the land bridge looked like.

Time

+ 2-3 class periods

Materials (for each pair of students)

+ a copy of table 1.2
+ a copy of figure 1.3
+ a copy of figure 1.4 (A-H)
+ figure 1.5 (presented as an overhead or drawn on a chalkboard)
+ transparent tape that can be written on
+ scissors (1 or 2 per pair of students)
+ graph paper
+ pencils and erasers
+ colored pencils
+ atlases (or provide library time or assign map work as homework)

Grouping

+ pairs

Directions

1. Start the lesson by introducing the idea that when the Europeans arrived in North America the Native Americans already had a flourishing society. Ask the question, "Where did the Native Americans come from?" Students should already have a working knowledge of glaciation from previous lessons, but a quick review here might be useful. Introduce the concept of a land bridge to students.

2. Distribute copies of figure 1.4 (A-H), scissors, and tape. Tell the students they will need to tape the eight pieces of the figure together to form the base map depicted in figure 1.3. Show them figure 1.5 as a guide. Students should trim the pieces of figures 1.4 (A-H) carefully along the lines shown and tape them together.

3. Tell the students about the survey that recorded sea-bottom data between Asia and North America to possibly locate the Bering Land Bridge. Distribute table 1.2 to the students. Have them look at the table and their assembled figure 1.4 to understand where the data came from and how the two will be used.

4. Students will need to transfer the depth from each data point on table 1.2 to the map (see fig. 1.4) and then contour the map in meters below N.G.V.D. using a 10-meter contour interval. A solution is shown as figure 1.6.

5. Once the map is completed students should prepare a north-south profile (at the longitude of their choice) going down to at least 200 meters below sea level. The profile should cross either the Asian or the North American landmass and not pass through the Bering Strait. The profile should be made two ways: one with no vertical exaggeration and the second with a vertical exaggeration of 20 times. Profile examples are given on figure 1.7, shown with two different vertical exaggerations.

Text continues on page 17.

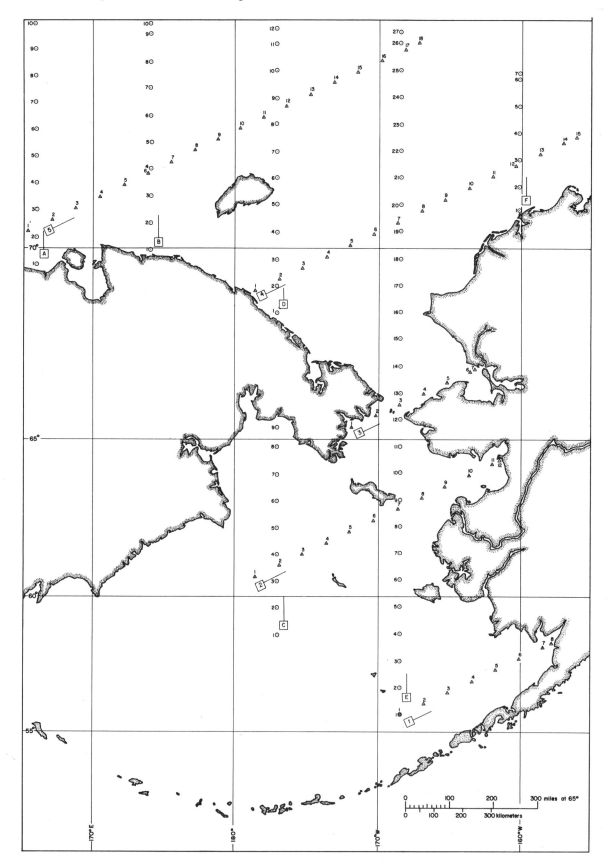

Fig. 1.3. Base Map Depicting Land Areas and Survey Lines ("Activity: How They Got Here").

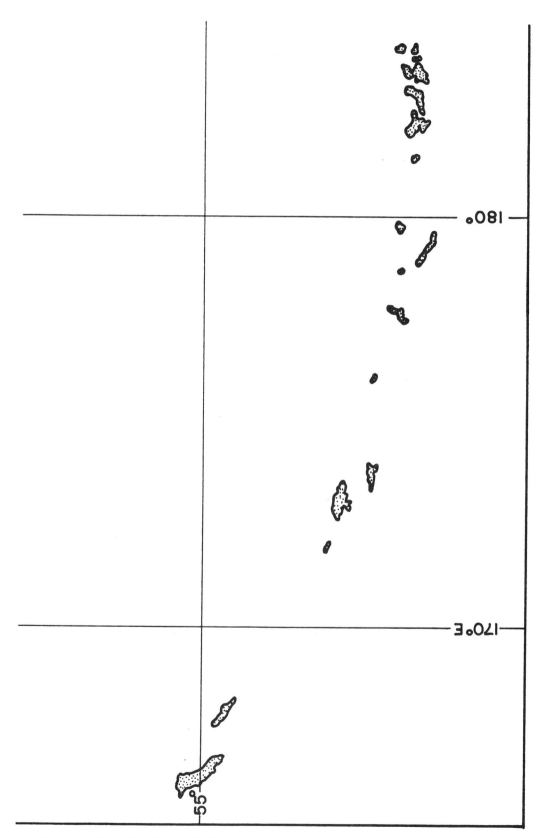

Fig. 1.4A. Base Map Sections (A-H).

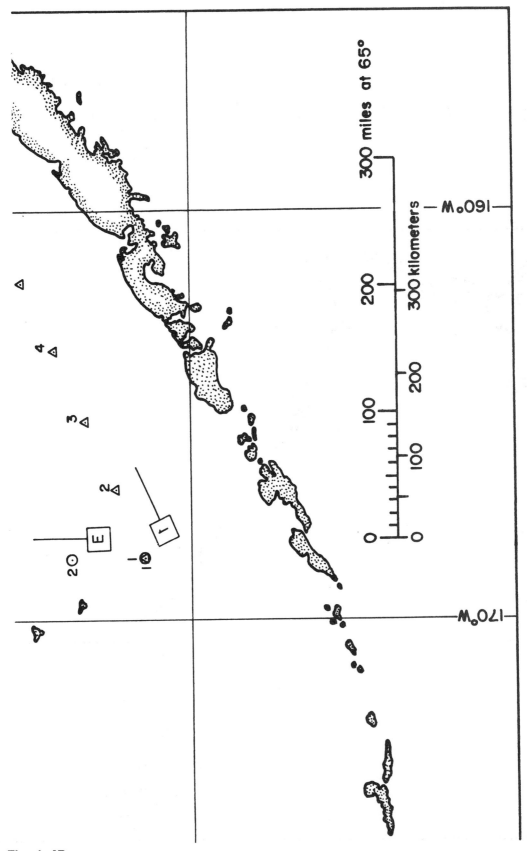

Fig. 1.4B.

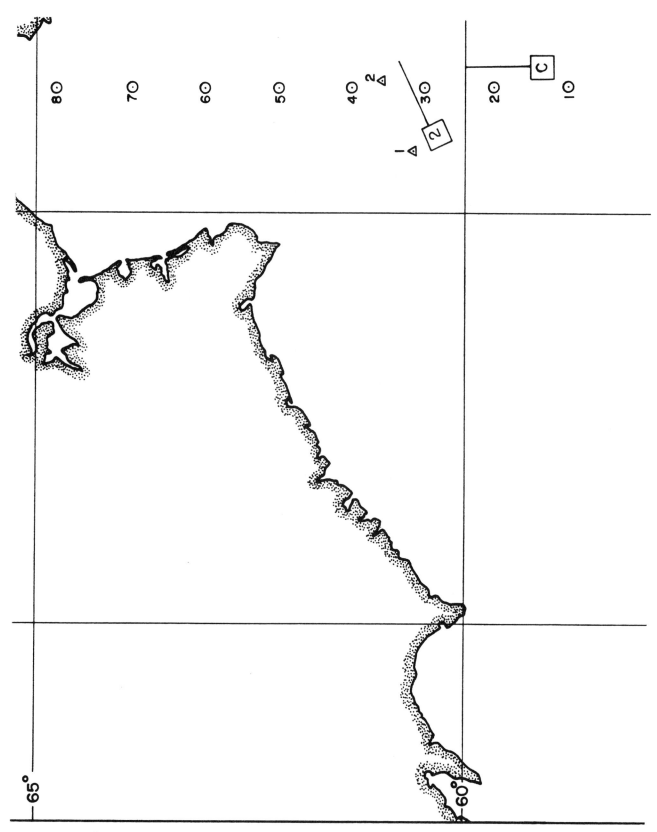

Fig. 1.4C.

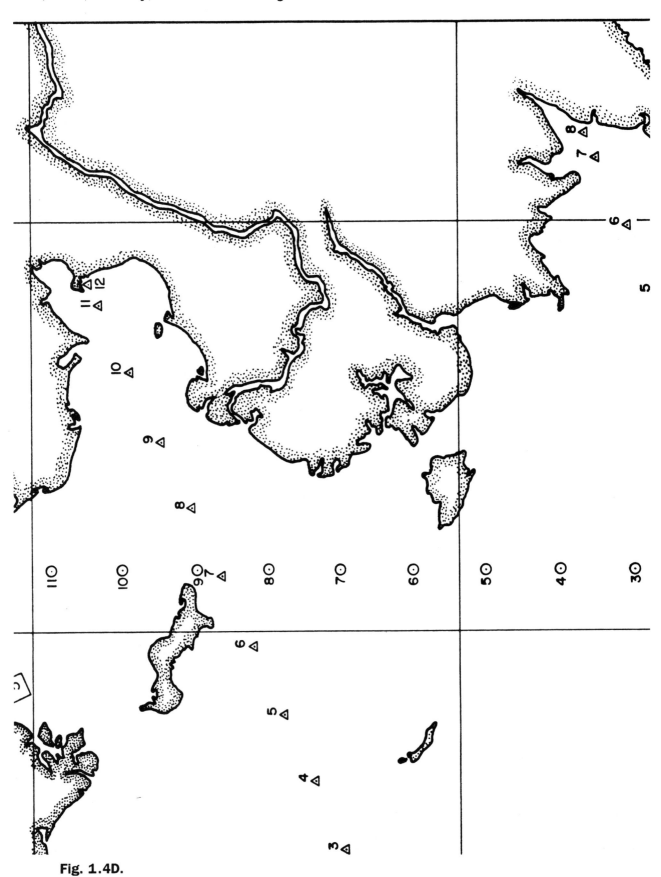

Fig. 1.4D.

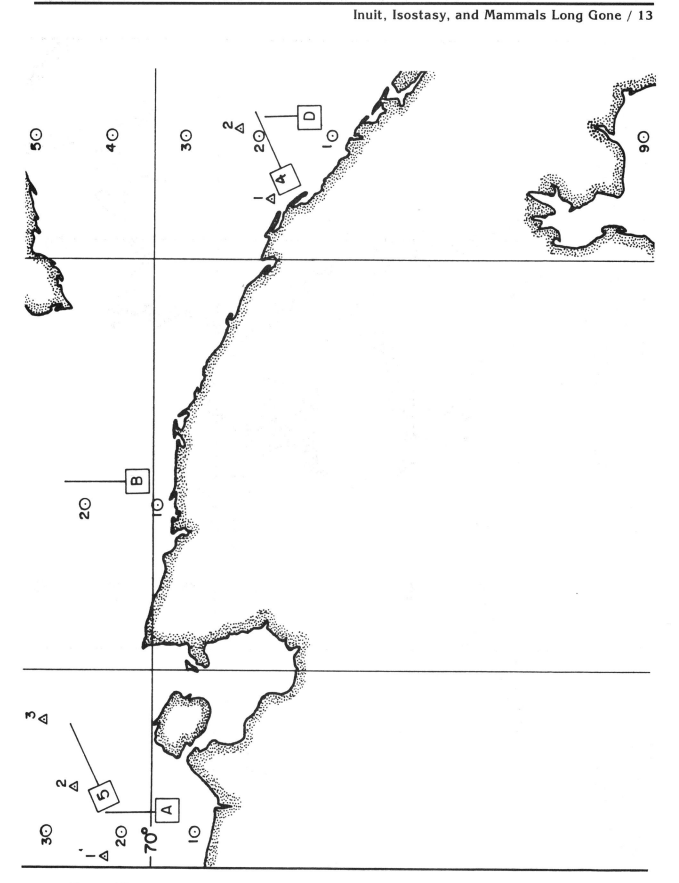

Fig. 1.4E.

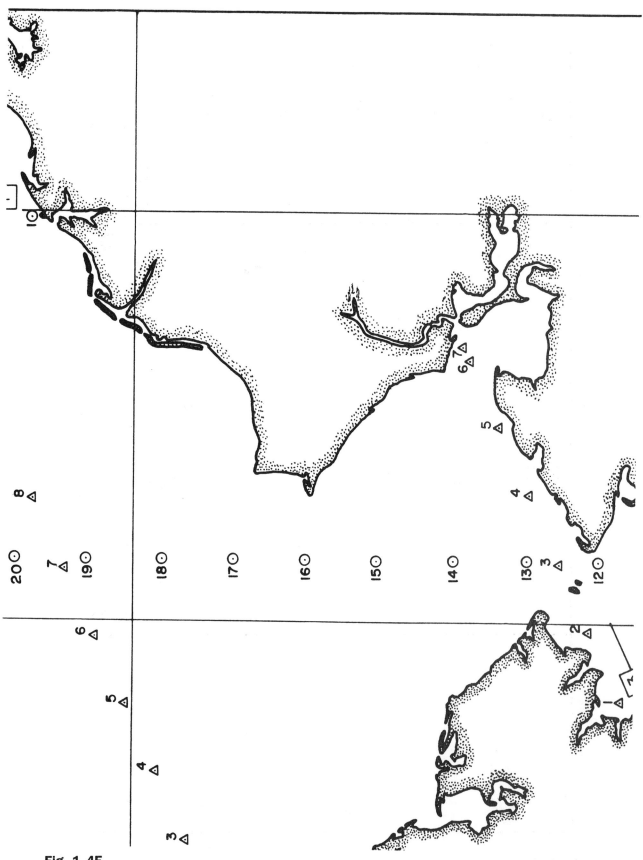

Fig. 1.4F.

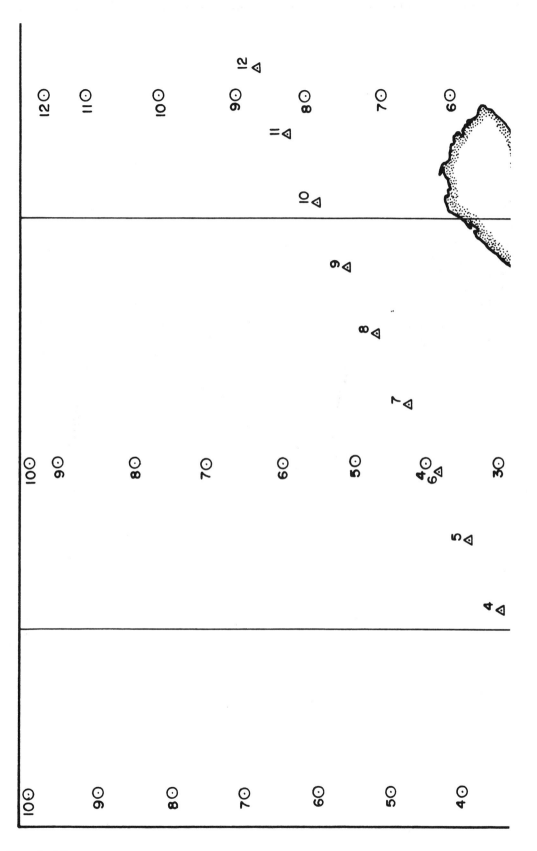

Fig. 1.4G.

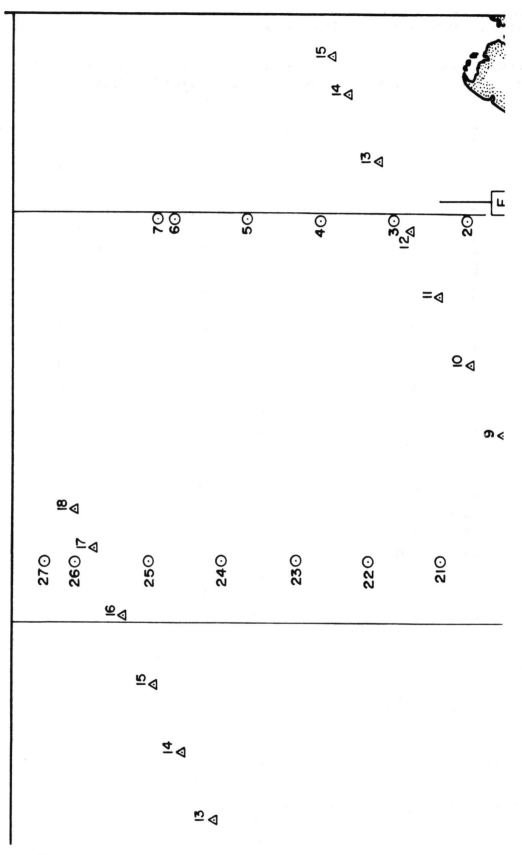

Fig. 1.4H.

Table 1.2. Survey Data (North-South Lines).

Survey Line	Survey Point	Depth (meters)	Survey Line	Survey Point	Depth (meters)	Survey Line	Survey Point	Depth (meters)
A	1	6	B	1	4	C	1	1000
	2	15		2	13		2	190
	3	21		3	16		3	149
	4	32		4	21		4	127
	5	40		5	26		5	99
	6	43		6	32		6	91
	7	41		7	40		7	79
	8	41		8	50		8	55
	9	48		9	79		9	30
	10	67		10	91			
D	1	20	E	1	200	F	1	10
	2	52		2	120		2	48
	3	52		3	80		3	35
	4	52		4	55		4	42
	5	50		5	40		5	75
	6	13		6	38		6	180
	7	42		7	31		7	240
	8	62		8	30			
	9	90		9	30			
	10	120		10	36			
	11	160		11	41			
	12	270		12	50			
				13	53			
				14	41			
				15	50			
				16	56			
				17	53			
				18	49			
				19	41			
				20	40			
				21	47			
				22	58			
				23	62			
				24	78			
				25	98			
				26	170			
				27	280			

Table 1.2. Survey Data (East-West Lines). (*continued*)

Survey Line	Survey Point	Depth (meters)	Survey Line	Survey Point	Depth (meters)	Survey Line	Survey Point	Depth (meters)
1	1	200	2	1	240	3	1	10
	2	130		2	130		2	20
	3	90		3	93		3	51
	4	66		4	73		4	10
	5	54		5	51		5	9
	6	52		6	38		6	12
	7	19		7	30		7	9
	8	4		8	27			
				9	16			
				10	19			
				11	12			
				12	4			
4	1	30	5	1	17			
	2	52		2	18			
	3	55		3	19			
	4	51		4	18			
	5	47		5	19			
	6	37		6	19			
	7	42		7	23			
	8	49		8	27			
	9	41		9	35			
	10	41		10	43			
	11	39		11	63			
	12	35		12	82			
	13	42		13	103			
	14	110		14	118			
	15	210		15	118			
				16	115			
				17	150			
				18	230			

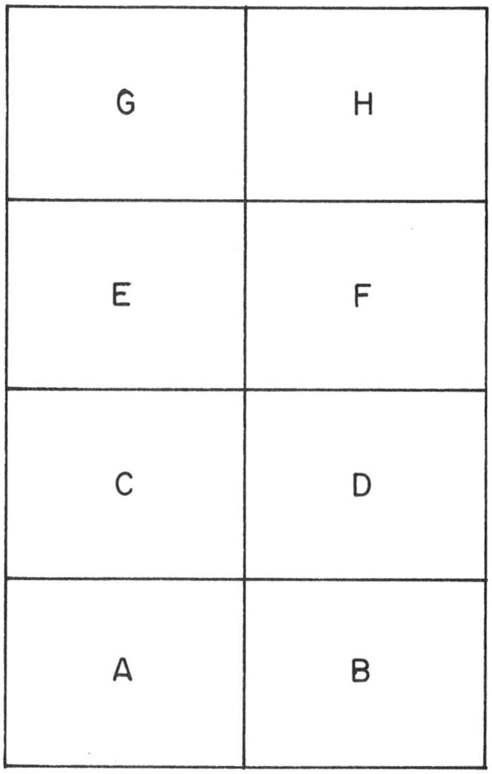

G	H
E	F
C	D
A	B

Fig. 1.5. Template for Assembly of Figure 1.4 (A-H).

6. It is estimated that the maximum lowering of sea level during the Pleistocene was approximately 120 meters. Given sea level drops of 30, 70, and 120 meters students should color the land bridge on their bathymetric maps at each of those sea level drops. For example, if yellow were used for 30 meters, everything higher than 30 meters should be colored yellow (including what is land today). The yellow would then be the area of the land bridge if sea level dropped only 30 meters. The yellow should also be transferred to the completed profile. Two other colors would then be used on the same map, one for 70 meters (30 down to 70 meters would have the second color) and the other color for 120 meters. At the conclusion of the coloring a broad, fairly level plain would be delineated which could have been used as a migration path by both people and animals; the Bering Land Bridge. All three colors should also be on the profile.

7. Names have been omitted purposely from the base map. Using various library sources students should now locate the following place-names and add them to the base map:

Alaska
Alaska Peninsula
Aleutian Islands, Alaska
Anadyrskiy Gulf, Russia
Bering Sea
Bering Strait
Bristol Bay, Alaska
Chukchi Sea
Chukotsky Peninsula, Russia
Cook Inlet
Diomede Islands
Kotzebue Sound, Alaska

Nome, Alaska
Norton Sound, Alaska
Nunivak Island, Alaska
Point Barrow, Alaska
Pribilof Islands
Siberia
St. Lawrence Island
St. Matthew Island
Seward Peninsula, Alaska
Wrangell Island, Russia
Yukon River, Alaska

Extension

Many of the place names listed above represent people who played significant roles in Alaska's past. Investigate such notables as Bering, Cook, Seward, and Pribilof to discover their importance in Alaska's history.

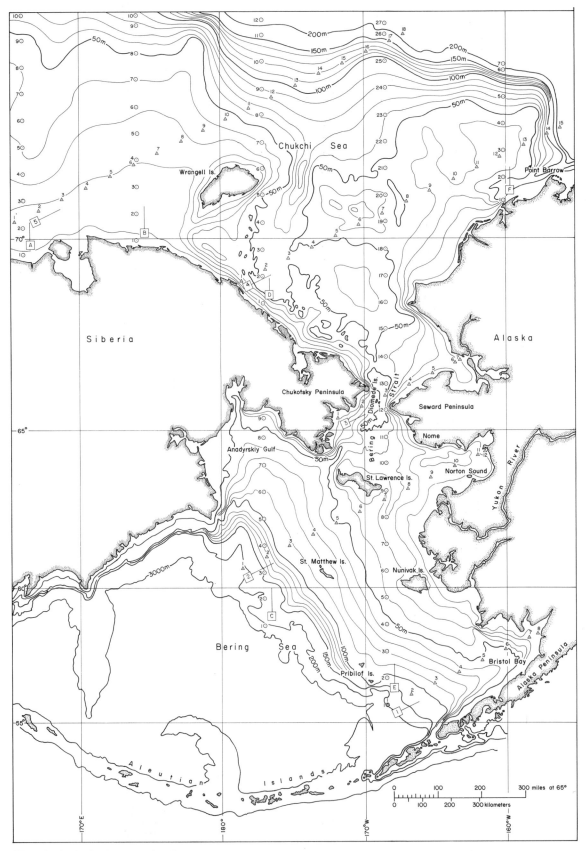

Fig. 1.6. Solution to the Bathymetric Map Exercise for the Bering Land Bridge.

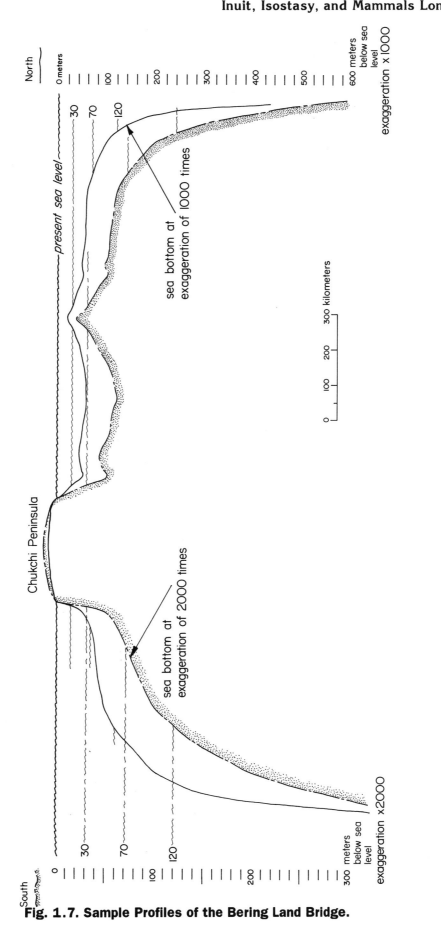

Fig. 1.7. Sample Profiles of the Bering Land Bridge.

Activity: What Might Happen

By observing major cities built near shorelines it is tempting to conclude that shorelines are fixed in their positions. Although the structures of the cities may be fixed, the shorelines are certainly not! Actually, North America can be considered a very large island. As such, it is not surprising that initial settlements occurred in coastal areas. The same is true even today. According to results of the 1990 U.S. Census, seven of the eight largest metropolitan areas (by population) in the United States are adjacent to oceans (the eighth is Chicago, adjacent to the Great Lakes; Williams, Dodd, and Gohn 1991, 2). If sea level were to rise even a few feet, many of these cities would face disaster. Cities like New Orleans, already below the level of the Mississippi River, would be inundated (unless the Army Corps of Engineers acted very quickly). Low-lying cities like Miami and Houston would also be submerged, their tall buildings becoming artificial islands. Conversely, if another ice age were to occur and sea level were to fall 328 feet (100 meters), the results would be different but equally disastrous. Cities like New York and Boston, with harbors adjacent to a broad continental shelf, would suddenly find themselves many miles away from the ocean. The barrier beaches that now protect many shorelines would be merely long, sandy hills high above the water. Cities along the west coast, where the shoreline drops off rapidly to 100 meters, would be perched high on a relatively steep slope above the sea.

Obtain the topographic maps of a major coastal city near where you live, or one of your choice; these can be obtained locally or through the U.S. Geological Survey (see page xxiii). If the climate were to become so warm that all the world's ice melted, it is estimated that sea level would rise approximately 60 meters (200 feet). What effects would that have on the city you have selected? Would it be possible to move critical facilities, or would the city have to be abandoned completely? What if sea level were to rise only half that much (30 meters or 100 feet)? The rise would likely occur over several thousands of years so there would be plenty of time available for adjustments. Examine the effects of even a small rise in sea level, perhaps 10 feet (3 meters), on a city like New Orleans, Louisiana; or Atlantic City, New Jersey; other vulnerable areas such as the Outer Banks of North Carolina (see Chapter 6).

As a footnote to this chapter, today's technology may be replacing the land bridge of thousands of years ago. As early as 1969 feasibility studies for a bridge connecting Siberia and Alaska were being financed. In 1994 the project received a new impetus because of the development of oil and natural gas reserves in Siberia and potential markets in North America. A second proposal linking Asia and North America involves construction of a tunnel beneath the Bering Strait as part of a worldwide railroad service called WorldLink (Tope 1994, 58).

REFERENCES

Ballantine, Betty, and Ian Ballantine, eds. *The Native Americans*. Atlanta, Ga.: Turner, 1993.

Claiborne, Robert. *The First Americans, The Emergence of Man*. New York: Time-Life Books, 1973.

Clottes, Jean, and Jean Courtin. "Neptune's Ice Age Gallery." *Natural History* 102 (1993): 64-70.

Coachman, L. K.; K. Aagaard; and R. B. Tripp. *Bering Strait: The Regional Physical Oceanography*. Seattle: University of Washington Press, 1975.

Flerow, C. C. "On the Origin of the Mammalian Fauna of Canada." In *The Bering Land Bridge*, edited by David M. Hopkins, 271-80. Stanford, Calif.: Stanford University Press, 1967.

Holmes, Arthur. *Principles of Physical Geology*. New York: Ronald Press, 1965.

Leet, Don, and Sheldon Judson. *Physical Geology*. Englewood, N.J.: Prentice-Hall, 1971.

Luling, Virginia. *Aborigines*. London: MacDonald Educational Limited, 1979.

Kopper, Philip. *The Smithsonian Book of North American Indians*. Washington, D.C.: Smithsonian Books, 1986.

Nance, Raymond L. *Water of the World*. Washington, D.C.: U.S. Geological Survey, 1977.

National Park Service. *Bering Land Bridge National Preserve*. Washington, D.C.: U.S. Government Printing Office, 1992.

Pewe, T. L., and David M. Hopkins. "Mammal Remains of Pre-Wisconsin Age in Alaska." In *The Bering Land Bridge*, edited by David M. Hopkins, 245-65. Stanford, Calif.: Stanford University Press, 1967.

Repenning, Charles A. "Palearctic-Nearctic Mammalian Dispersal in the Late Cenozoic." In *The Bering Land Bridge*, edited by David M. Hopkins, 288-311. Stanford, Calif.: Stanford University Press, 1967.

Russell, Loris S. "Mammalian Migrations in the Pleistocene." In *Problems of the Pleistocene Epoch and Arctic Area*, edited by G. R. Lowther, 48-55. Montreal: McGill University, 1962.

Tope, Gregory. "Alaska-Siberia Bridge." *Popular Mechanics* 171 (1994): 56-58.

Vangengeim, E. A. "The Effect of the Bering Land Bridge on the Quaternary Mammalian Faunas of Siberia and North America." In *Bering Land Bridge*, edited by David M. Hopkins, 281-87. Stanford, Calif.: Stanford University Press, 1967.

Williams, S. Jeffress; Kurt Dodd; and Kathleen Krafft Gohn. *Coasts in Crisis*. U.S. Geological Survey Circular 1075. Washington, D.C.: U.S. Government Printing Office, 1991.

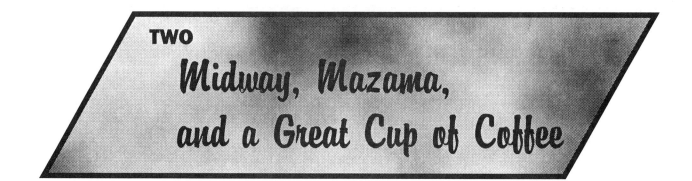

TWO

Midway, Mazama, and a Great Cup of Coffee

Living *near* a potentially destructive volcano can provide a certain, usually unwelcome, sense of adventure. Living *on* an active volcano can make one's day-to-day existence precarious to say the least. Yet millions of Americans do both. Volcanoes are associated with all manner of geologic phenomena considered incompatible with the human life form: earthquakes, lava flows, pyroclasts, mudflows, landslides, and *nueé ardentes*. Like many geologic agents considered destructive, however, volcanic eruptions have a positive side: New materials added to the earth's surface by eruption created the fertile soils that attracted inhabitants to the area in the first place. For instance, such soils, combined with local weather characteristics, allow the area around Kona, Hawaii, to produce the only coffee in the fifty states. Minerals are often mobilized into ores by the heat and pressure associated with volcanism. Copper deposits in the Keweenaw Peninsula of Michigan and some gold deposits of Colorado can be traced to volcanic origins. Pumice is used as a building material and abrasive, and weathered volcanic material, such as bentonite, is used as a drilling lubricant and sealer. Interestingly, in certain areas of the country where bentonite is abundant in the soils, building construction is adversely affected by bentonite's ability to swell dramatically when wet.

Volcanic island chains of the United States played a significant role during World War II in the battle plans of both the United States and Japan. The United States's involvement in the Pacific began with Japanese attacks on Pearl Harbor and Midway in the central part of the ocean. In the early 1940s aviation technology had not yet developed an airplane that could fly nonstop across the Pacific. Thus the strategic value of the Aleutian Islands was recognized early in World War II, and the islands were fortified by military forces of the United States. The Aleutian Islands provided a made-to-order series of stepping stones eastward from Japan to the northwestern United States. Shortly after the attack on Pearl Harbor the Japanese established bases on the islands of Kiska, Aggatu, and Attu. The first enemy air attack on North America occurred when bombers from Japanese aircraft carriers attacked U.S. naval facilities at Dutch Harbor, on the island of Unalasaka, in the Aleutians on 3 June 1942 (Miller 1947, 510). The defense of those islands by military forces of both the United States and Canada against the Japanese was exacerbated by the rugged terrain created by the volcanoes and the horrendous weather of the high northern latitudes. By August 1943 the Japanese recognized their positions were untenable, and the first American territory captured by the Japanese was reclaimed (Miller 1947, 613).

24

At times in the geologic past volcanoes affected broad areas of what is now the United States. Many areas, such as Maine, South Carolina, New York, Virginia, Missouri, and Nebraska are not associated with active volcanoes today, but were affected in the past. Some of the most unique scenery in the country is a result of volcanism: the Cascade Mountains of Washington and Oregon; the Aleutian Islands, Alaska; Devils Tower, Wyoming; Capulin Mountain National Monument, New Mexico; Devils Postpile, California; Crater Lake, Oregon; Shiprock, New Mexico; Craters of the Moon, Idaho; and the Hawaiian Islands.

Approximately 10 percent of the world's 1,500 geologically recent volcanoes are located in the United States. The United States ranks third in number of volcanoes with a history of recent (past 10,000 years) eruptions (behind Indonesia and Japan). Recent activity has been located only west of the Rocky Mountains and, as Steinbrugge (1982) writes, "Most of . . . [those] . . . have the potential to erupt in the future" (259). Areas of recent volcanism in the United States can be separated as follows:

The Cascade Range of Oregon and Washington. Sixteen volcanoes, all potentially active

The Aleutian Arc of southwestern Alaska. More than 70 active volcanoes, 36 eruptions since 1760

The Hawaiian Islands. Five volcanoes active on Hawaii, one on Maui

The Mono Basin of California. More than 20 explosive eruptions in the past 10,000 years

The Basin and Range Volcanic Field of California, Nevada, and New Mexico. Scattered eruptions; last one in 1850

The Snake River Plain of Idaho and Wyoming. Occasional fissure eruptions

Two types of active volcanoes are found in the western United States. Volcanoes of the Aleutian Islands and Cascade Mountains, along the Pacific Rim, are completely different from those of the Hawaiian Islands, in the central Pacific. Both the Aleutian and Cascade volcanoes are formed as the North American Plate overrides an oceanic plate. The volcanoes created are called composite volcanoes (or stratovolcanoes) because they form in alternating layers of ash, lava, and other ejected materials fused by the heat. Rock types associated with such volcanoes include andesites and rhyolites. The mountain itself is steep-sided and is the classic type of most well-known volcanoes such as Mount Etna in Sicily, Mount Vesuvius in Sicily, Mount Fuji in Japan, and Mount Rainier in Washington (Coch and Ludman 1991, 116). Eruptions are often explosive, sending ejected materials high into the atmosphere, affecting areas hundreds and thousands of miles away.

By contrast, the volcanoes of Hawaii have broad, relatively flat slopes. They are formed completely of lava from eruptions and, because of their shape, are called shield volcanoes. Shield volcanoes are the largest volcanoes on Earth. The Island of Hawaii is formed of five shield volcanoes reaching from the ocean floor 19,680 feet (6,000 meters) below sea level to more than 13,120 feet (4,000 meters) above sea level, a total height exceeding Mount Everest. As opposed to the large amounts of explosively ejected materials from composite volcanoes, shield volcanoes are characterized by large volumes of lava. Shield volcanoes are associated with the ocean basins and oceanic plates, and the associated rock type is almost exclusively basalt.

In 1975 the U.S. Geological Survey considered Mount St. Helens the Cascade Range volcano most likely to erupt. On 18 May 1980, after two months of steam eruptions and small earthquakes, the mountain fulfilled the prophesy and erupted explosively, killing approximately 60 people and sending ash around the world. It was one of the most well-documented eruptions. Sharing some of the many photographs, posters, videos, and slides taken of the eruption can help students appreciate the awesome power and beauty of volcanic processes.

The Cascade Mountains have an explosive history. Some 6,800 years prior to the Mount St. Helens eruption an estimated 10.1 cubic miles (42 cubic kilometers) of materials (approximately 52 times more than that spewed by Mount St. Helens) were ejected when Mount Mazama, a 12,000-foot peak in Oregon, literally blew its top to form Crater Lake. A Native American legend described the eruption:

> Fleeing in terror before it, the People found refuge in the waters of Klamath Lake. As the men prayed to the Chief of the Above World for safety, they realized only a living sacrifice would turn away the wrath of fire. Two medicine men . . . jumped in the pit of fire. When the morning sun rose, the high mountain was gone. The Chief of the Above World quartered the fallen chief and cast the head into the fire pit. Today it lies where it fell and strangers call it Wizard Island. The bereaved people . . . shed their tears for the fate of their chief. We know those tears as Crater Lake. (Warfield, Jullerat, and Smith 1982, 36)

Activity: How Do We Compare?

As impressive and frightening as the eruption of Mount St. Helens appeared, it was quite small compared with other historic volcanic eruptions in the United States and worldwide. Table 2.1 lists various volcanic eruptions around the world by year of eruption and volume of material ejected from the volcano. By placing the data on a bar graph students can appreciate the relative sizes of some eruptions in the United States compared with those elsewhere in the world.

Table 2.1. Dates of Eruption and Volumes of Ejected Material from Some Worldwide Volcanoes.

Name	Date of Eruption	Ejected Volume	
		cu. miles	cu. km.
Mt. Mazama, Oregon	5000 B.C.E.	10.1	42.1
Mt. Vesuvius, Italy	79	0.9	3.8
Mt. Fuji, Japan	1707	0.5	2.1
Mt. Tambora, Indonesia	1815	7.3	30.4
Mt. St. Helens, Washington	1850	0.2	0.8
Krakatoa, Indonesia	1883	4.4	18.3
Mt. Katmai, Alaska	1912	3.0	12.5
Bezymianny, Kamchatka	1956	0.2	0.8
Mt. St. Helens, Washington	1980	0.2	0.8

Time

+ less than 1 class period

Materials

+ copy of table 2.1 for each student
+ graph paper
+ colored pencils or markers
+ pictures (textbooks, posters, color slides, videos) of Mount St. Helens

Grouping

+ individuals

Directions

1. The eruption of Mount St. Helens was the largest recent volcanic eruption in the United States and probably one of the best documented eruptions in the world. Show pictures of the eruption to students so they can appreciate the release of energy and volume of material produced.

2. Distribute copies of table 2.1 to the students. Review the data with them. A cubic mile (4.168 cubic kilometers) of material is a huge volume; 147,197,952,000 cubic feet (4,168,182,000 cubic meters). A fraction of a cubic mile is a large volume; multiple cubic miles are almost unimaginable.

3. Ask the students to prepare a bar graph, placing volume of eruption on the y-axis (write cubic kilometers on the left and cubic miles on the right) and date of eruption on the x-axis. Dates of eruption should become younger as you move to the right. To make the graph easier to plot and more dramatic ask students to hold the graph paper with the long side as the y-axis and scale the graph so it fills the page.

4. Have students complete the bar graph. Figure 2.1 represents the completed graph.

Extension

The eruption of Mount Mazama approximately 7,000 years ago ejected more than fifty times more material than the most recent Mount St. Helens eruption. In the past 7,000 years considerable human development has occurred in the Pacific Northwest despite the fact that the volcanoes have become no less active. The eruption of Mount St. Helens was devastating; an eruption with power similar to that of Mount Mazama would have annihilated much of the Pacific Northwest.

Have the students review the Cascade Mountains of Washington and Oregon in relation to major cities such as Seattle, Portland, and Vancouver (B.C.) and major rivers such as the Columbia and Fraser. Much of the area's electricity is generated using hydroelectric power from dams along rivers such as the Columbia. Commercial enterprise of the area depends on transportation by air as well as water. What would happen to the infrastructure of the area after a choking ashfall resulting from a gigantic eruption similar to that of Mount Mazama? Inhabitants might have difficulty sustaining themselves in the area and might have even more trouble attempting to leave. How could survivors endure without transportation and electricity? How could emergency services function? What effect would wind direction have? Which direction would be least harmful?

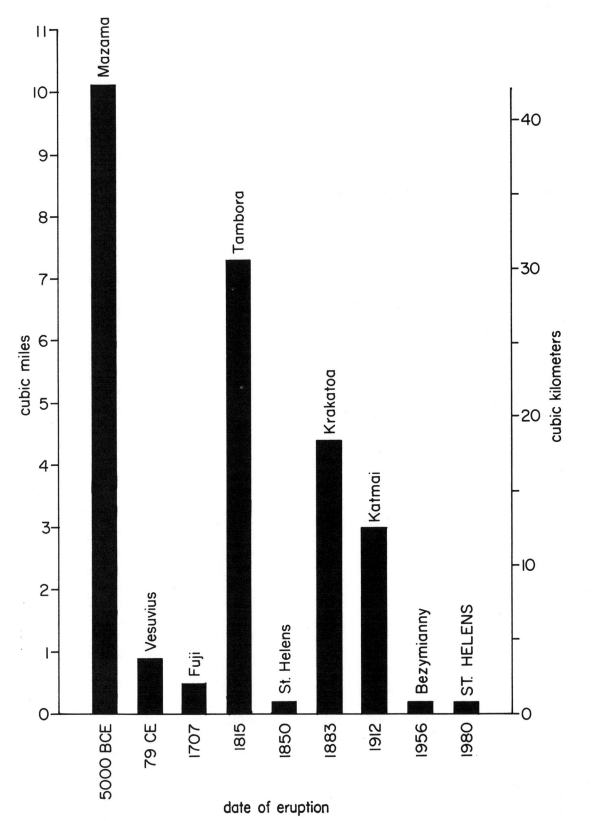

Fig. 2.1. Comparisons of Volumes of Ejected Materials from Some Major Worldwide Volconic Eruptions.

Note: Adapted from Bruce L. Foxworthy and Mary Hill, *Volcanic Eruptions of 1980 at Mount St. Helens: The First 100 Days*. Geological Survey Professional Paper 1249. Washington, D.C.: U.S. Government Printing Office, 1982.

Activity: Where Did It All Go?

Many visitors to Mount St. Helens today purchase small vials of ash from souvenir stands along Highway 504, on the way to Mount St. Helens National Volcanic Monument. Those willing to get out of their car to "feel" and really appreciate the scenery can walk barefoot in the same ash alongside the highway, in the bed of the North Fork Toutle River. When the mountain erupted the ashfall was widespread. In this three-part activity students will see (a) how quickly the ash from the May 18th eruption moved vertically into the atmosphere, (b) how quickly the ash dispersed downwind, toward the east, and (c) how the ash thickness was distributed.

Part A

Students can get a sense of the explosive energy of Mount St. Helens by completing a graphic representation of how quickly ejected material rose into the atmosphere after the eruption.

Time

+ less than one class period

Materials

+ a copy of table 2.2 for each student (duplicate on card stock and laminate for durability)
+ a copy of figure 2.2 for each student (enlarged to 11" x 17")
+ calculator (recommended)

Grouping

+ individuals

Directions

1. Distribute table 2.2 to all students. Table 2.2 lists minutes after the 8:32 A.M. eruption of May 18 and altitude above sea level of the ejected material from Mount St. Helens. Review the table with the students to be certain they understand the information provided.

2. Provide one copy of figure 2.2 for each student. Explain how the information from table 2.2 will be plotted onto the graph in figure 2.2.

Table 2.2. Rise of the Ejected Material from the May 18th Eruption of Mount St. Helens.

Minutes After Eruption	Altitude (feet)	Minutes After Eruption	Altitude (feet)
0	0	16	78,000
2	5,500	18	79,500
4	12,000	20	81,000
6	21,000	22	83,000
8	37,000	24	84,500
10	55,000	26	86,500
12	72,000	28	88,200
14	76,000	30	90,000

From *American History Through Earth Science.* © 1997 Craig A. Munsart. Teacher Ideas Press. (800) 237-6124.

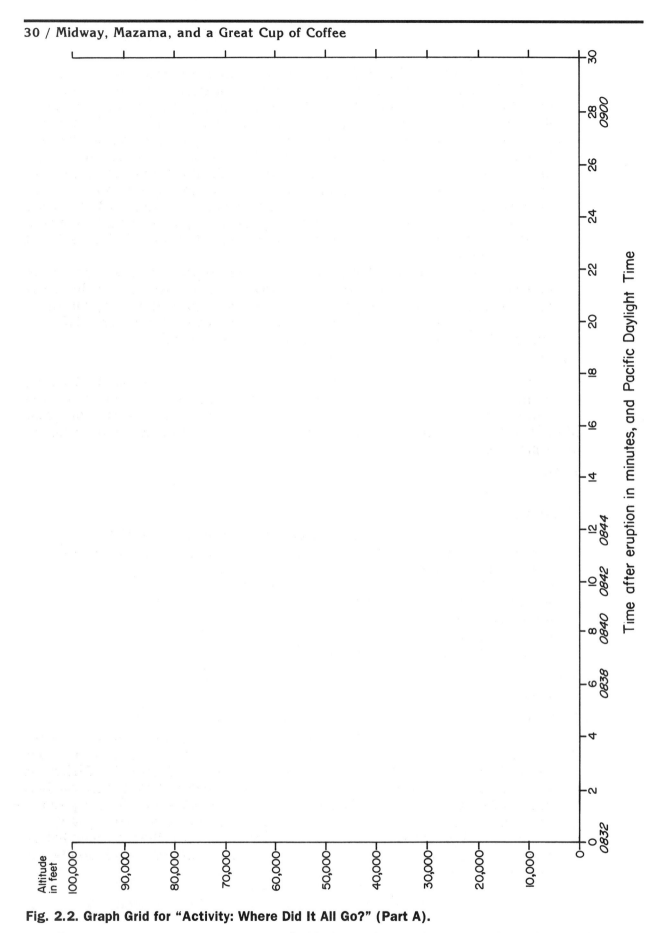

Fig. 2.2. Graph Grid for "Activity: Where Did It All Go?" (Part A).

3. Have students plot the data. Figure 2.3 is a completed graph.

4. Based on their plotted graphs have students calculate the upward velocity between 6-8 minutes and 8-10 minutes (Answer: approximately 97 mph). To convert to kilometers per hour multiply miles per hour times 1.6. Ask students to place their answers on the graph in the appropriate location. As a check for the students the two calculations should be the same. The elapsed time is known and the elevation change is known. Dividing the distance by the time a velocity in feet per minute can be determined. Hint: 88 feet per minute = 1 mile per hour. Repeat the activity for 14-16 minutes and 22-24 minutes (Answer: approximately 11 mph). Students will determine the velocity of downwind dispersals in the next part of the activity.

5. There are two different slopes to the graph. Ask the students to explain why. Vertical velocities of the lower part are due primarily to the high vertical ejection energy from the volcano. As ejecta rose, the high-velocity upper level winds of the atmosphere moved the material laterally (the next part of this activity will examine those winds).

Part B

In the Mount St. Helens eruption, once the ash plume reached above approximately 40,000 feet (12.2 kilometers) high, winds rapidly dispersed the ash towards the east. In the following activity students will contour the progress of the front of the ash plume as it moves downwind and calculate the velocity of its progress.

Time

+ 1-2 class periods

Materials

+ a copy of figure 2.4 for each student (enlarged to 11" x 17")
+ a copy of table 2.3 for each student (duplicated on card stock and laminated for durability)
+ atlases for each student (or provide library time)
+ calculator (recommended)
+ pencils for contouring
+ pen or thin marker
+ a copy of figure 2.5 for reference

Grouping

+ individuals

Directions

1. Distribute figure 2.4 to each student. Explain that this is a map of the area over which the ash plume from the May 18th eruption of Mount St. Helens spread the morning after the eruption. Mount St. Helens is represented by a triangle. Geographic reference cities (all with zero ashfall) are represented by an open square. Cities that provide data for progress of the ash plume are represented by a filled-in circle or the open square.

2. Distribute table 2.3 to students. Table 2.3 lists cities represented by filled-in circles in figure 2.4. The table also shows the time at which the ash plume reached that city.

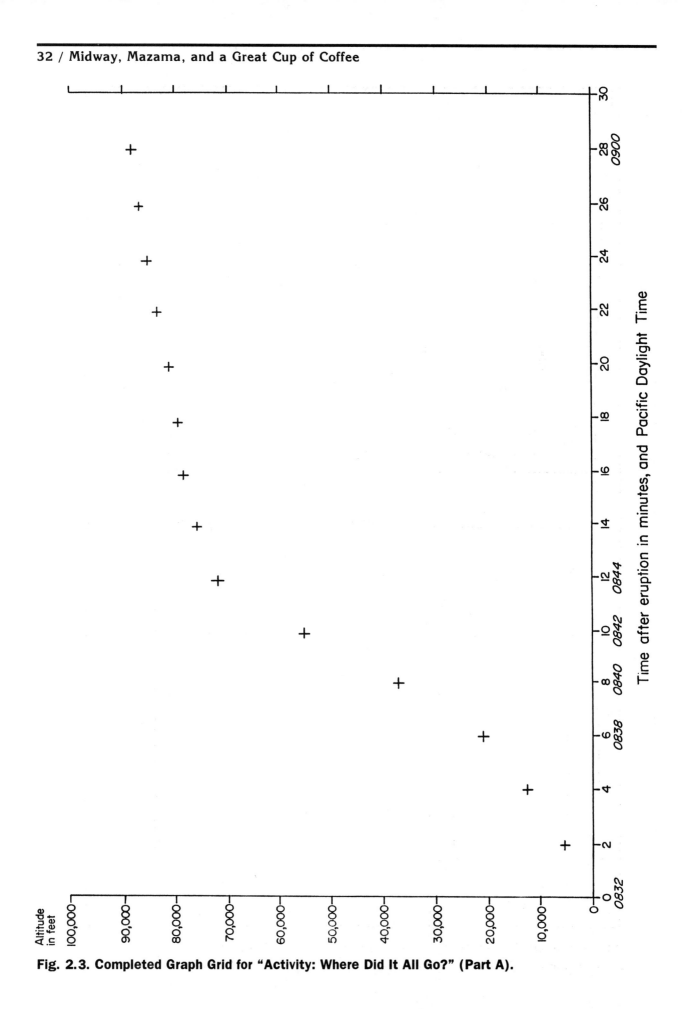

Fig. 2.3. Completed Graph Grid for "Activity: Where Did It All Go?" (Part A).

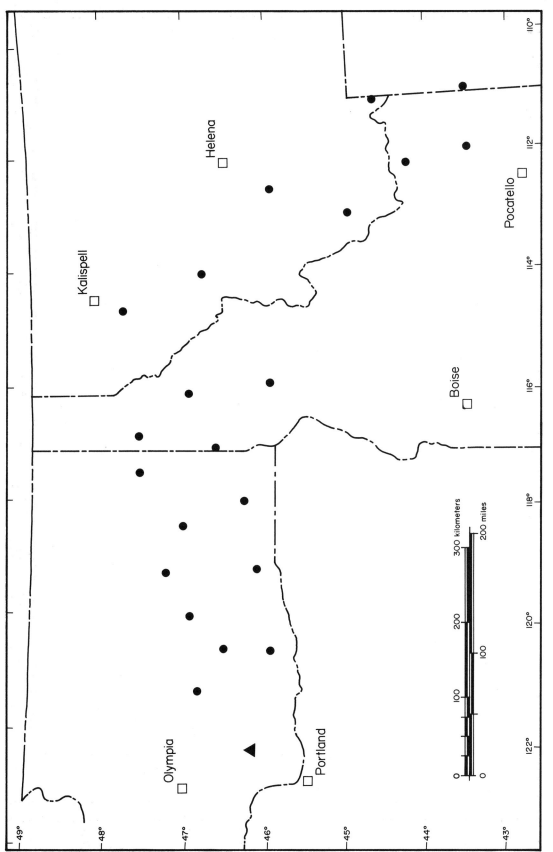

Fig. 2.4. Base Map for "Activity: Where Did It All Go?" (Part B).

Table 2.3. Downwind Progress of Ash Front from the May 18th Eruption of Mount St. Helens. Eruption occurred at 0832.

State	City	Time of Ash Front May 18, 1980	Minutes Since Eruption	Hours Since Eruption	Distance from Mt. St. Helens kilometers	miles	Velocity to City kph	mph
Idaho	Clarkia	1245						
	Coeur D'Alene	1220						
	Dubois	1630						
	Hapster	1245						
	Idaho Falls	1735						
	Moscow	1155						
	Pocatello	1830						
Montana	Butte	1605						
	Grant	1535						
	Lone Pine	1430						
	Missoula	1445						
	West Yellowstone	1730						
Washington	Dayton	1115						
	Gooseprairie	1015						
	Moses Lake	1100						
	Pasco	1040						
	Ritzville	1120						
	Spokane	1145						
	Trout Lake	0935						
	Vantage	1035						
	Yakima	0945						
Wyoming	Jackson	1745						

From American History Through Earth Science. © 1997 Craig A. Munsart. Teacher Ideas Press. (800) 237-6124.

3. What students must do:
   a. Match the cities in table 2.3 with the filled-in circles on the map and write in the city name in pen or marker.
   b. Write the time of the ash front arrival on the map in pen or marker next to the city name. Do the same for the cities shown by open squares as well.
   c. Ask students to contour the front of the moving ashfall by time. Figure 2.6 is the completed map.
   d. Remind students that the eruption occurred at 8:32 A.M. (0832). Knowing the time of the eruption and the time of the ash front arrival at a city makes it possible to determine the travel time of the ash front. Students should fill in the column "minutes since eruption."
   e. Convert minutes to hours (and hundredths of an hour). Remember to remind students that there are 60 minutes in an hour (many students seem to believe there are 100 minutes in an hour).
   f. Using the scale on the map students should determine the distance from Mount St. Helens to the data city (in kilometers and miles).
   g. Knowing the distance and the number of hours makes it possible to calculate the velocity of the ash as it moved downwind (in kilometers per hour and miles per hour).

$$\text{velocity} = \frac{\text{distance}}{\text{time}}$$

   h. Show the students the profile of wind velocity (figure 2.5). Do their numbers agree with the velocity indicated? Discuss why or why not.
4. Table 2.4 shows answers for selected cities.
5. Knowing the velocity of the ash students can calculate its travel time around the world. Have students research the circumference of the earth and calculate how long it would take for the ash to travel around it. (Equatorial circumference is 24,901 miles or 39,842 kilometers. At 70 mph the ash would take 355.6 hours or 14.8 days to complete a circle. Kilometer calculations would produce identical times.) Note: After the eruption the ash was tracked east across New England and the North Atlantic Ocean, eventually returning over western North America in early June (Sarna-Wojcicki et al. 1981, 580). Comparisons can be made with the more recent eruption of Mt. Pinatubo in the Philippines.

Part C

At high altitude the ash from the eruption moved tens of thousands of kilometers. On the earth's surface the ash moved hundreds of kilometers and covered the ground with varying thicknesses of choking, caustic, abrasive, sky-darkening ejected material. The ash caused unemployment, as well as damaging timber, fisheries, strawberry crops, vehicles, sewage systems, and homes. When combined with water the ash formed devastating mudflows. During the first nine hours of the eruption an estimated 540 million tons of ash covered more than 22,000 square miles (Tilling 1985, 17). When the air had cleared of ash it could be seen that 1,313 feet (400 meters) from the top of Mount St. Helens was gone, spread eastward over much of Washington and Idaho as granular fallout from the volcano. In this part of the activity students will draw a cross section east from the volcano to show the ash distribution.

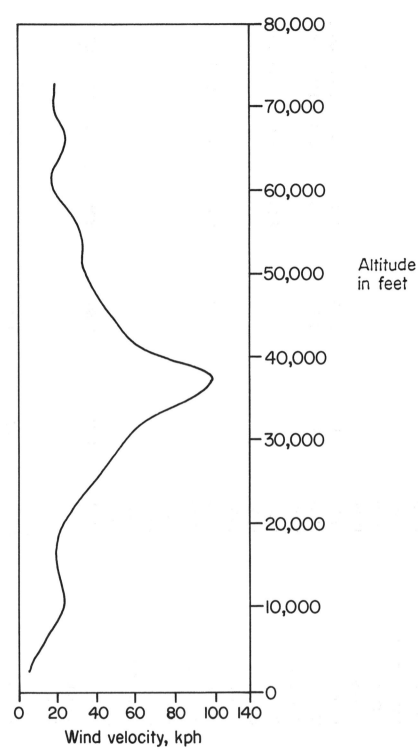

Fig. 2.5. Vertical Profile of Wind Velocities Near Mount St. Helens at the Time of the May 18th, 1980, Eruption.

Note: Adapted from Andrei M. Sarna-Wojcicki, Susan Shipley, Richard B. Waitt, Jr., Daniel Dzurisin, and Spencer H. Wood, "Areal Distribution Thickness, Mass, Volume, and Grain Size of Air-Fall Ash from the Six Major Eruptions of 1980." In *The 1980 Eruptions of Mount St. Helens*, U.S. Geological Survey Professional Paper 1250, edited by Peter W. Lipman and Donal R. Mullineaux. Washington, D.C.: U.S. Government Printing Office.

Table 2.4. Downwind Progress of Ash Front from the May 18th Eruption of Mount St. Helens.

State	City	Time of Ash Front May 18, 1980	Minutes Since Eruption	Hours Since Eruption	Distance from Mt. St. Helens kilometers	miles	Velocity to City kph	mph
Idaho	Clarkia	1245						
	Coeur D'Alene	1220						
	Dubois	1630						
	Hapster	1245						
	Idaho Falls	1735	543	9.05	1000	625	110.5	69.1
	Moscow	1155	203	3.38	400	250	118.3	73.9
	Pocatello	1830						
Montana	Butte	1605	452	7.53	880	550	116.9	73.0
	Grant	1535						
	Lone Pine	1430						
	Missoula	1445	373	6.22	630	394	101.3	63.3
	West Yellowstone	1730						
Washington	Dayton	1115						
	Gooseprairie	1015						
	Moses Lake	1100						
	Pasco	1040						
	Ritzville	1120	168	2.80	305	190	108.9	67.9
	Spokane	1145						
	Trout Lake	0935						
	Vantage	1035						
	Yakima	0945	73	1.22	137	86	112.3	70.5
Wyoming	Jackson	1745						

From *American History Through Earth Science.* © 1997 Craig A. Munsart. Teacher Ideas Press. (800) 237-6124.

Time

+ 1 class period

Materials

+ visual aids of ash from Mount St. Helens falling— samples of the ash would be great!
+ a copy of table 2.5 for each student
+ graph paper
+ figure 2.5 from part B (as completed by students)
+ a copy of figure 2.6 for each student
+ a copy of figure 2.7 for each student
+ a copy of figure 2.8 for each student

Grouping

+ individuals

Directions

1. Distribute a copy of table 2.5 to each student. The table lists distance from the volcano, grain size, and thickness of ashfall along a line going east from Mount St. Helens through Ritzville, Washington, to Missoula and almost to Helena, Montana, a distance of just over 700 kilometers.

Table 2.5. May 18, 1980 Eruption of Mount St. Helens Ashfall Amounts and Particle Grain Size.

Distance from Volcano (km)	Ash Thickness (cm)	Particle Size (mm)
0	0	–
12	20	–
25	16.0	–
50	9.9	6.0
100	3.4	0.35
150	1.6	0.10
200	1.7	0.080
250	3.7	0.060
300	4.9	0.038
350	4.4	0.037
400	2.9	0.043
450	1.5	0.045
500	0.8	0.044
550	0.5	0.041
600	0.4	0.037
650	0.3	0.031
700	0.3	0.025

2. Have the students refer to their completed figure 2.6 to ensure they are familiar with the geography and the line of cross section or see figure 2.6.

3. Explain to the students that they will first be preparing a cross section of the ashfall thickness based on the data in table 2.5. Figure 2.7 should be used for plotting the cross section.

4. Before beginning the cross section discuss with students what it might look like. A good first guess might be a wedge shape, thickest at the volcano and tapering eastward to zero.

5. Have the students prepare the cross section on figure 2.7 with the ash thickness data from table 2.5, using an "X." Draw a best-fit line through the data points with short dashes. Figure 2.8 shows the completed graph.

6. Discuss how the completed section is different from the guess. At Ritzville approximately 5 centimeters of ash accumulated, 3 centimeters more than what might have been anticipated. The reason for the thickening is unclear. One suggestion is that the ash plume reached above the high-altitude, high-velocity wind layer and rapidly settled out over Ritzville. Ask students for their ideas.

7. Material ejected from a volcano, much like sediment carried by a stream, is sorted by the medium through which it travels. Large material is deposited near the source and successively smaller sizes are deposited as the distance from the source increases. There are many complicating factors (such as shape, density, or composition), but in general this can be considered a process of size sorting known as *sedimentary differentiation*. To see how this process operated at Mount St. Helens, refer back to table 2.5, which lists particle size of the ash. By plotting size data on figure 2.7 students can see how the particle size related to the ash thickness and distance from the source.

8. Discuss with the class what the particle size distribution might be away from the volcano. Ask them to predict what the distribution might be.

9. Have students plot the particle sizes from table 2.5 on cross section 2.7 using a circle and dot for each data point. Show a best-fit line using long dashes. Figure 2.8 shows the completed graph. Once again, the anomaly at Ritzville is obvious. Nothing in the grain size distribution indicates that ash at Ritzville should be thicker than the surrounding area.

Extension

Sedimentary differentiation is similar to the process by which wheat is separated from the chaff or the way gold is separated from other minerals in a miner's flume. The process can be demonstrated in the classroom using a mixture of various-sized particles of similar materials (such as different sizes of sand and gravel) and running water. By running the water over a stream table or a slightly tilted tray covered with the unsorted material students can observe how finer-grained material is carried farther from the source. Similar tests can be done with mixtures of lighter materials such as tapioca, sawdust, flour, and using a hair dryer.

Text continues on page 43.

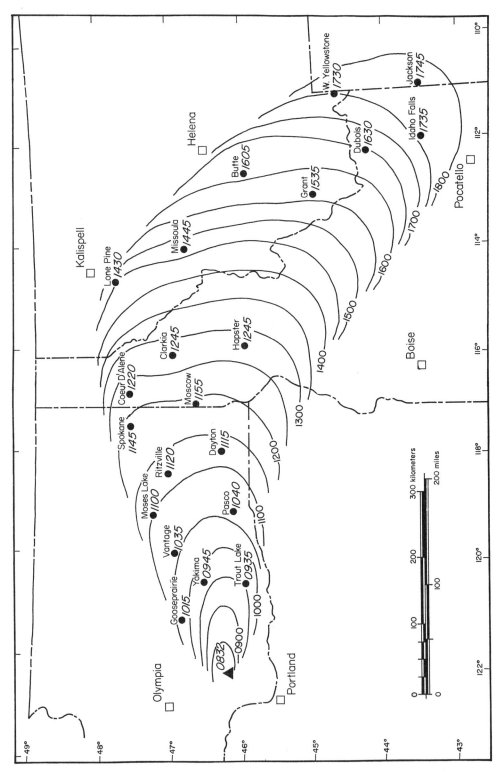

Fig. 2.6. Completed Base Map for "Activity: Where Did It All Go?" (Part B).

Note: Adapted from Andrei M. Sarna-Wojcicki, Susan Shipley, Richard B. Waitt, Jr., Daniel Dzurisin, and Spencer H. Wood, "Areal Distribution Thickness, Mass, Volume, and Grain Size of Air-Fall Ash from the Six Major Eruptions of 1980." In *The 1980 Eruptions of Mount St. Helens*, U.S. Geological Survey Professional Paper 1250, edited by Peter W. Lipman and Donal R. Mullineaux. Washington, D.C.: U.S. Government Printing Office.

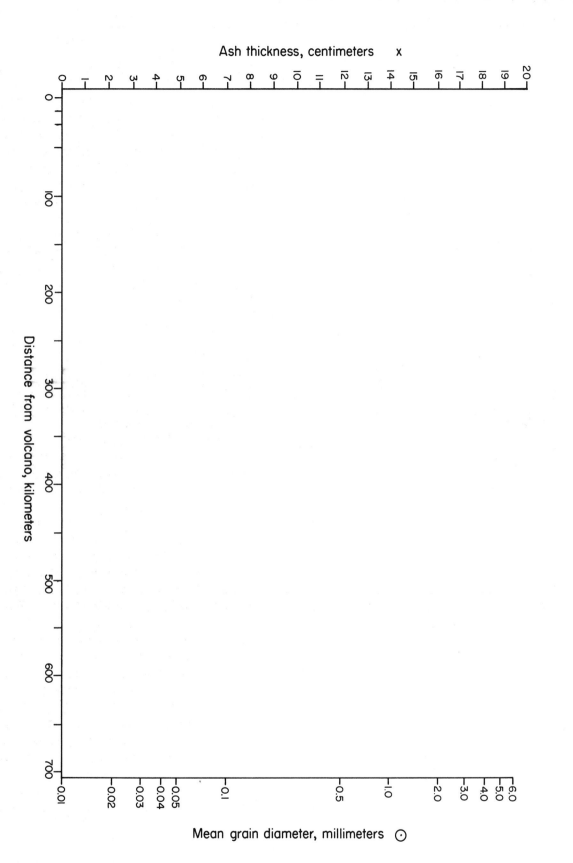

Fig. 2.7. Graph Grid for "Activity: Where Did It All Go?" (Part C).

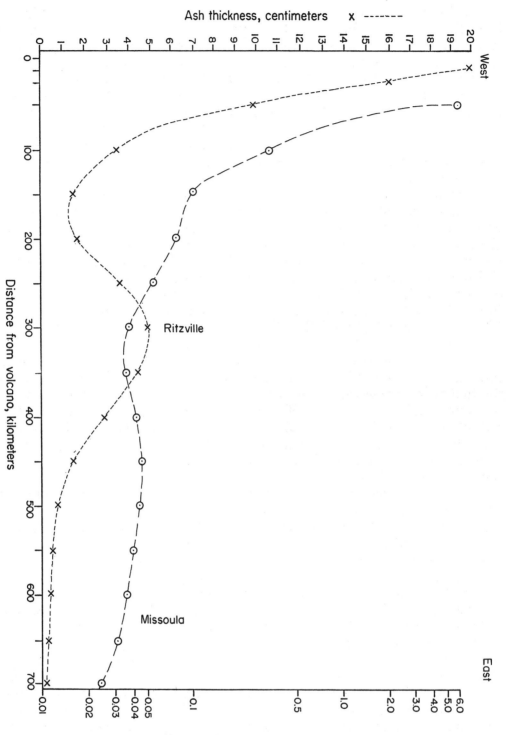

Fig. 2.8. Ash Thickness and Grain Size Downwind from Mount St. Helens: Completed Graph Grid for "Activity: Where Did It All Go?" (Part C).

Note: Adapted from Andrei M. Sarna-Wojcicki, Susan Shipley, Richard B. Waitt, Jr., Daniel Dzurisin, and Spencer H. Wood, "Areal Distribution Thickness, Mass, Volume, and Grain Size of Air-Fall Ash from the Six Major Eruptions of 1980." In *The 1980 Eruptions of Mount St. Helens*, U.S. Geological Survey Professional Paper 1250, edited by Peter W. Lipman and Donal R. Mullineaux. Washington, D.C.: U.S. Government Printing Office.

In the short term the Mount St. Helens eruptions were certainly a disaster. Over the long term, however, the eruptions and destruction became a working research laboratory for Cascade volcanoes, alerted residents to a geologic hazard, enriched soils over a large area, and became a new and unique tourist attraction for Washington, attracting more than 2 million visitors each year. The eruptions of Mount St. Helens provided important information about future eruptions— and there will be more, based on the intermittent eruptive history of volcanoes in the Cascades. As Foxworthy and Hill (1982, 116) state, "The question of greatest interest concerning the future of Mount St. Helens probably is, 'Will Mount St. Helens continue to erupt?' The answer is, 'Yes.' " Next time there should be more accurate predictions, fewer surprises, and, it is hoped, no victims.

Half an ocean away from Mount St. Helens, another type of volcano has attracted interest for hundreds of years. The Pearl Harbor of early Hawaii consisted of three large saltwater lakes protected from the sea by a narrow, shallow entry built up naturally by coral. It was known to the Hawaiians as *wai momi*, or water of pearl (Albright 1988, 57). Although the Hawaiian island of Oahu was a large volcano projecting above the sea, its last eruption was approximately 3.5 million years earlier, and thus it was considered safe. The British Navy became the first European visitors to Pearl Harbor in 1786. By 1825, a naturalist aboard the HMS *Blonde* recognized the military potential of the area: "It would form a most excellent harbor as inside there is plenty of water to float the largest ship and room enough for the whole Navy of England" (Lott and Sumrall 1977, 3). In 1840, a worldwide naval expedition performed the first technical work by the U.S. Navy: the preparation of a survey and chart of Pearl Harbor. In the 1860s, United States naval officers saw excellent potential on the site for a coaling station needed to refuel military ships in an area devoid of coal for thousands of miles in any direction. In addition, the narrow entrance and shallow draft of the harbor provided excellent natural protection both from the sea and enemies. The rights to establish a coaling station were awarded to the United States in 1887. After dredging and other site preparations, the harbor was officially opened on 14 December 1911. Unfortunately, in December 1941 the harbor's shallow draft provided a false sense of security to the ensconced U.S. Pacific Fleet. The Japanese military knew what the American military did not: A channel with a 40-foot depth would not stop aerial torpedoes (Albright 1988, 44).

By the 1840s geologist James Dwight Dana, while traveling with the worldwide U. S. Exploring Expedition, recognized the chronological sequencing of islands in many of the linear Pacific island chains: older to the northwest, younger to the southeast (Appleman 1985, 106). Although the Hawaiian Islands may be the best known, they are not the only Pacific island chain to share a linear, parallel west-northwest and south-southeast trend, resulting from motions of the Pacific Plate. Thousands of miles to the south-southeast lay the Marquesas Chain, Society Chain, Gambier Chain, and Cook Austral Chain, all with the youngest island on the southeastern end, parallel to one another and to the Hawaiian Island Chain (Morgan 1973, 659; Appleman 1985, 110-11).

Many of these chains were critical to human migration east across the Pacific Ocean. The human and wild animal migrations from Asia to North America traversed the Bering Land Bridge approximately 50,000 years ago. A similar migration from southeast Asia began more than 70,000 years ago, arriving 20,000 years later in Australia. By 2000 B.C.E. migrations east from Australia extended past the Solomon Islands, by 1500 B.C.E to Fiji, by 1000 B.C.E. to Tonga, by 1 P.E. to Samoa, by 500 P.E. to the Marquesas Island Chain, and by 1000 P.E. to the Hawaiian Island Chain (McEvedy and Jones 1979, 322).

Two incidents in the central Pacific dramatically affected the history of the United States. Both involved the Empire of Japan and the Republic of the United States. Both involved the attempted destruction of the capital ships of the U.S. Pacific Fleet. Both involved a linear chain of volcanic islands in the Pacific Ocean— the Hawaiian Islands. The attack on Pearl Harbor and the attack on Midway Island were the Japanese attempts to eliminate a potential threat to their expansion plans. The Americans were there because the island chain offered a defensive outpost and fueling station for the ships of the fleet. But why were the islands there?

Traditionally, the origin of these island chains is considered one of the many separate pieces of evidence that helps confirm the theory of plate tectonics. Consider a steam locomotive generating puffs of smoke as it moves along a straight section of track. If those puffs could somehow be frozen in the sky they would form a straight line, with puffs separated by a certain distance; the slower the train, the closer the puffs. Now imagine a spot in the upper portion of the earth's mantle that periodically squirts magma up into the Pacific Plate as that plate moves toward the west-northwest. Those squirts become frozen on the plate as a series of volcanic islands in a line, forming island chains. The spots that squirt the material are called hot spots or mantle plumes. More than thirty years ago Morgan (1973, 661) suggested that such plumes were the driving force for plate motions. For explanatory purposes, this is an oversimplification of a complex process, the details of which are poorly understood. As early as 1849, the Hawaiian Island Chain was considered a composite of two, parallel trends of volcanic eruptions (Ihinger 1995, 1038). Recent studies suggest the islands are the result of a complex interaction between hot material in the mantle and the overlying plate.

The process continues as you read this chapter. Just as older islands are found to the northwest of the Hawaiian Island Chain, newer islands are being formed to the southeast. Loihi Seamount, 17 miles (28 kilometers) southeast of the Island of Hawaii and 3178 feet (969 meters) below the Pacific Ocean surface, will likely be the next Hawaiian Island (Malahoff 1987, 133).

Activity: Midway Is Midway

Approximately six months after naval forces of Japan destroyed the warships of the U.S. navy at Pearl Harbor, naval forces of the United States destroyed four aircraft carriers of the Japanese navy at the Battle of Midway (Keegan 1989, 210). The two battles occurred 1,240 miles (2,000 kilometers) apart along an island chain with a coherent geologic history. Enough data are available to study the progressive formation of the Hawaiian Island Chain in detail. By examining the dates of the last known eruptions of the islands it is possible to

a. determine the direction of motion of the Pacific Plate over the hot spot,

b. determine the velocity of the plate as it moves over the hot spot, and

c. make a prediction about when the next island may appear at the southeast end of the chain.

Time

> + 1 class period

Materials

> + copies of figure 2.9 (A-C) (one for each student)
> + calculator (recommended)
> + copies of table 2.6 (one for each student)
> + protractor
> + transparent tape

Grouping

> + individuals

Directions

1. Discuss the concept of hot spots with students, using the information on page 49 as a guide.

2. Distribute figure 2.9 (A-C) to the students. Before proceeding have the students tape all three sections together to make a continuous map. This is a map of the Hawaiian Island Chain, from Loihi Seamount southeast of the Island of Hawaii, west-northwest to the Kanmu Seamount (also the southern end of the Emperor Seamounts).

3. Distribute table 2.6 to students. Table 2.6 lists the locations and names of various islands and seamounts in the Hawaiian Island Chain, and times of the last known eruptions in millions of years. Discuss the difference between islands and seamounts. Imagine that a volcanic eruption starts on the seafloor, more than 15,000 feet (4,573 meters) below the sea surface. As the lava erupts it builds up to create a mound, then a hill, then a mountain. If that mountain does not reach the sea surface it is called a seamount. If it extends above the sea surface it is an island. The mountain of Mauna Loa on Hawaii rises more than 32,000 feet (9,756 meters) above the seafloor, making it higher than Mount Everest; however, only 14,000 feet (4,268 meters) of its total height projects above the ocean.

4. Discuss the numbers on the table with the class. What kinds of conclusions can you draw from these numbers? In which direction do the islands get younger? Are the eruptions over, or are they likely to continue? If so, where and when? Some of the students may have been to Hawaii and may be familiar with the newer islands that tourists usually visit (Hawaii, Oahu, Maui, Kauai), but most people are unaware of how far the chain extends to the west-northwest. If students have visited the islands ask them to describe the differences between Kauai and Hawaii; the former is the Garden Isle and the latter has active volcanic eruptions. Why?

Text continues on page 49.

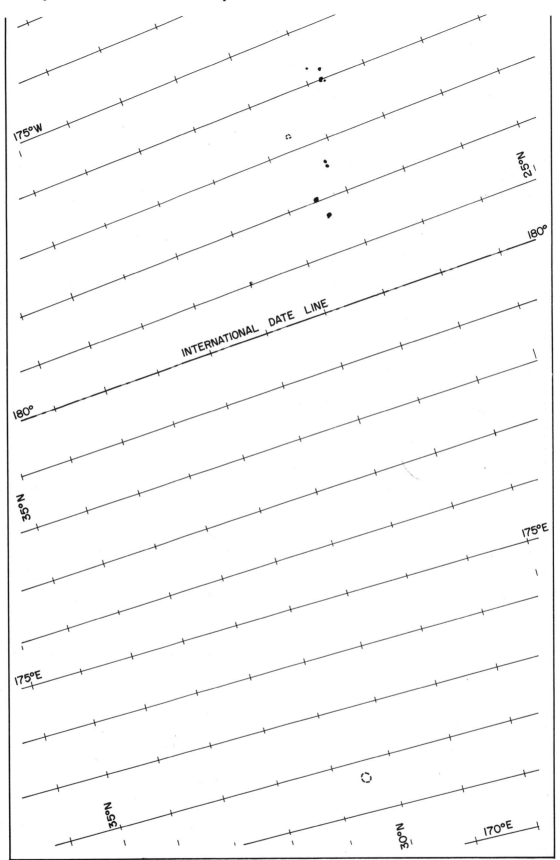

Fig. 2.9A. Base Map for "Activity: Midway Is Midway" (Parts A-C). Western section.

From *American History Through Earth Science.* © 1997 Craig A. Munsart. Teacher Ideas Press. (800) 237-6124.

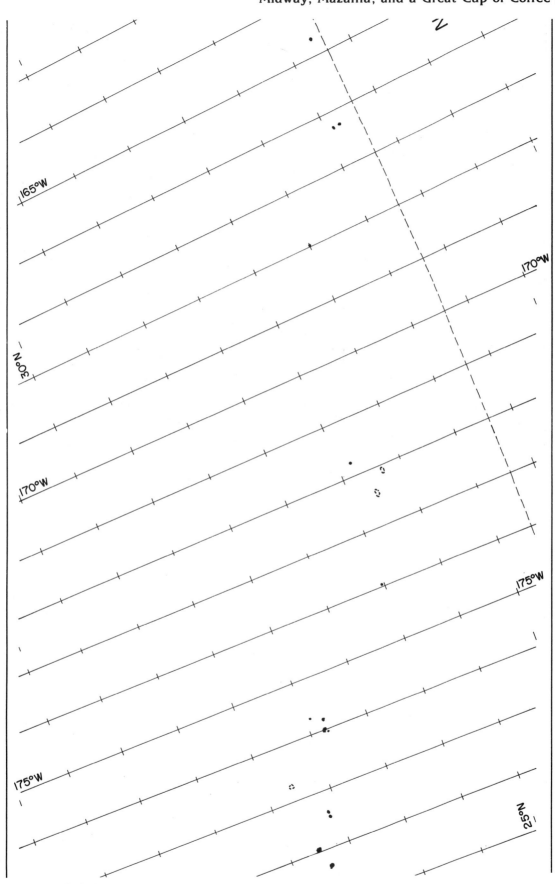

Fig. 2.9B. Center section.

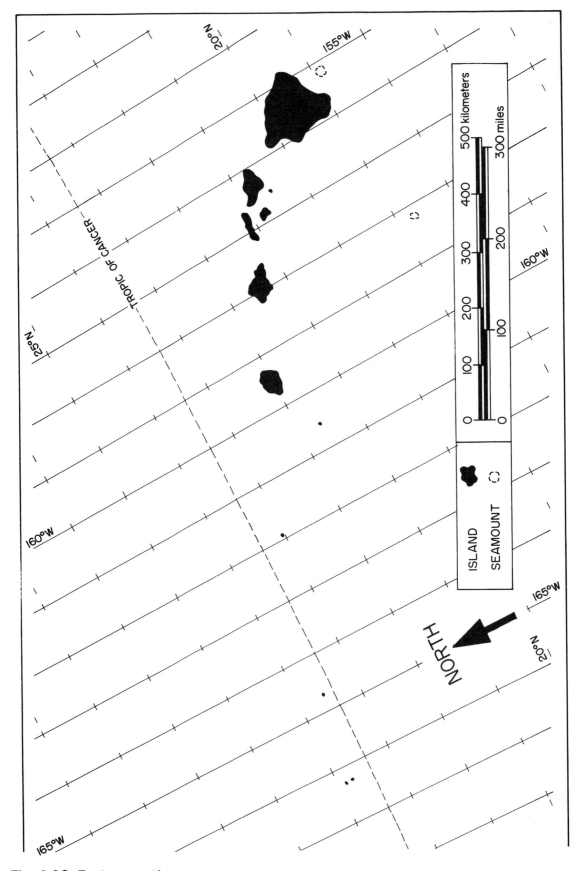

Fig. 2.9C. Eastern section.

Table 2.6. Hawaiian Island Hot Spot Data.

Island Name	Location longitude	latitude	Distance from Loihi (km)	Most Recent Major Eruption (mya)	Plate Movement in cm per Year
Kanmu Seamount	171°40'E	30°25'N		38.0	
Midway Island	177°25'W	28°08'N		16.2	
Necker Island	164°38'W	23°35'N		10.0	
Nihoa Island	161°55'W	23°02'N		7.2	
Kauai Island	159°28'W	22°02'N		5.1	
Oahu Island	158°02'W	21°28'N		3.7	
Molokai Island	157°00'W	21°06'N		1.8	
Maui Island	156°30'W	20°45'N		1.3	
Hawaii Island (Kilauea)	155°35'W	19°45'N		0 (now)	
Loihi Seamount	155°12'W	18°50'N		0.3	
Average					

5. Using the data in table 2.6 and figure 2.9 students will need to do the following:

a. Locate and label the islands and seamounts on the map.

b. Measure the distance between a given island and the Loihi Seamount in kilometers and fill it in on the table.

c. Calculate the plate movement in centimeters per year using the date of the recent eruption as the time the island was over the hot spot and the measured distance. Use the following formula:

$$\frac{\text{distance from Loihi Seamount (in kilometers)}}{\text{date of more recent eruption (millions of years)}} = \text{velocity of plate movement}$$

Convert the kilometers to centimeters and millions of years to years to determine the answer in centimeters per year. Complete the calculations for all islands and seamounts until table 2.6 is completed. Table 2.7 is the completed version of table 2.6.

6. The Pacific Plate moves northwest between 2 inches (6 centimeters) per year and 15 centimeters (6 inches) per year, most frequently between 3 inches and 4 inches (8 centimeters and 10 centimeters) per year. Compare those rates with the rates obtained by your students. Discuss possible errors with your students— errors in measurement of distance, errors in age dating of last eruption. Perhaps, at the last eruption, the island was not over the hot spot? Perhaps the hot spot theory is incorrect, and there are other factors at work? Perhaps there is more than one hot spot? Ask students to continue the map to the southeast. What will the Hawaiian Island Chain look like 10 million years from now?

Extensions

Northwest of the Hawaiian Islands, a chain of submerged mountains continues toward the north as the Emperor Seamounts. The two chains are separated by a significant directional change, or bend, that occurred approximately 43 million years ago. The Hawaiian Island Chain trends North 68° West; from approximately 32° North Latitude northward, the Emperor Seamounts trend North 10° West. From Kanmu northward, names and ages of some of the seamounts are Koko Seamount, 48 million years; Ojin Seamount, 55 million years; Nintoku Seamount, 56 million years; and Suiko Seamount, 65 million years (Clague and Dalrymple 1987, 5). At the northern end of the Emperor Seamount trend the Meiji Guyot is approximately 73 million years old. As the chain continues toward the north it subducts (dives under) into the Aleutian Trench so that ages exceeding 73 million years are not found. However, by locating the seamounts on a map students can continue this activity toward the north to see if the rate of plate movement has changed. In addition there is a significant change in the line of the two volcanic chains. The Emperor Seamounts are much more north-south than the Hawaiian Islands. What might account for such a change?

Visit the library to research other island chains in the Pacific similar to the Hawaiian Island Chain. Have the students learn more about them to see if they are similar to the Hawaiian Islands in topography, geology, agriculture, and culture.

Table 2.7. Completed Version of Hawaiian Island Hot Spot Data.

Island Name	Location		Distance from Loihi (km)	Most Recent Major Eruption (mya)	Plate Movement in cm per Year
	longitude	latitude			
Kammu Seamount	171°40'E	30°25'N	3700	38.0	9.74
Midway Island	177°25'W	28°08'N	2500	16.2	15.43
Necker Island	164°38'W	23°35'N	1100	10.0	11.00
Nihoa Island	161°55'W	23°02'N	800	7.2	11.11
Kauai Island	159°28'W	22°02'N	600	5.1	11.76
Oahu Island	158°02'W	21°28'N	400	3.7	10.81
Molokai Island	157°00'W	21°06'N	300	1.8	16.77
Maui Island	156°30'W	20°45'N	200	1.3	15.38
Hawaii Island (Kilauea)	155°35'W	19°45'N	0	0 (now)	–
Loihi Seamount	155°12'W	18°50'N	-28	0.3	–
Average					12.60

Encourage students to model the hot spot-island generation process, either as an animation project on the computer or as a physical model using either map or cross-sectional views.

Constant monitoring of active volcanoes may, one day, provide detailed predictions of forthcoming eruptions. Years before it happened scientists knew Mount St. Helens was going to erupt. In 1975 three scientists predicted an eruption before the end of the century. They reinforced that prediction with a subsequent report three years later. Other predictions outline areas of the United States that may be subject to potentially dangerous volcanic activity. Not surprisingly, they are the same areas that have been subject to recent volcanic activity. There is still no way, however, to predict the size, location, duration, or long-term behavior of a volcano (Tilling 1985, 36). Even with more accurate predictions, populations and property would still be at risk. Areas like the Hawaiian Islands would be difficult to evacuate, and property could not be protected. In Vestmannaeyjar, Haimaey, Iceland inhabitants successfully sprayed lava with water to prevent its advance (McPhee 1989, 95). It would be foolhardy, however, to rely routinely on such efforts as protection from the dangers of volcanoes.

RESOURCES

Volcano World on the World Wide Web

http://volcano.und.nodak.edu/

The U.S. Geological Survey publishes several brochures about volcanoes that are of general interest. Some of the titles dealing with volcanoes are *The Interior of the Earth*; *Monitoring Active Volcanoes*; *Natural Steam for Power*; *Volcanic Hazards at Mt. Shasta, California*; *Volcanic Seismic Hazards of Hawaii*; and *Volcanoes of the U.S.* Class sets are sometimes available. Obtain free brochures from the following address:

U.S. Geological Survey
Branch of Distribution
Denver Federal Center
P.O. Box 25286
Denver, CO 80225

In addition, the U.S. Geological Survey publishes a bimonthly magazine called *Earthquakes and Volcanoes*. It contains articles as well as a listing and description of earthquakes that occurred since publication of the previous issue. More information is available from the following:

Earthquakes and Volcanoes
U.S. Geological Survey
Denver Federal Center
Mail Stop 967
Denver, CO 80225
(303) 273-8408
(303) 273-8450 (fax)

REFERENCES

Albright, Harry. *Pearl Harbor: Japan's Fatal Blunder*. New York: Hippocrene Books, 1988.

Appleman, Daniel E. "James Dwight Dana and Pacific Geology." In *Magnificent Voyagers*, edited by Herman J. Viola and Carolyn Margolis, 88-117. Washington, D.C.: Smithsonian Institution Press, 1985.

Brantley, Steven R. *The Eruption of the Redoubt Volcano, Alaska, December 14, 1989 and August 31, 1990*. U.S. Geological Survey Circular 1061. Washington, D.C.: U.S. Government Printing Office, 1990.

————. *Volcanoes of the United States*. Washington, D.C.: U.S. Geological Survey, 1994.

Clague, David A., and Brent G. Dalrymple. "The Hawaiian-Emperor Volcanic Chain." In *Volcanism in Hawaii*. U.S.G.S. Professional Paper 1350, edited by Robert W. Decker, Thomas L. Wright, and Peter H. Stauffer, 5-54. Washington, D.C.: U.S. Government Printing Office, 1987.

Coch, Nicholas K., and Allan Ludman. *Physical Geology*. New York: Macmillan Publishing Company, 1991.

Corcoran, Thom. *Mount St. Helens: The Story Behind the Scenery*. Las Vegas, Nev.: KC Publications, 1985.

Drummond, Kenneth J. "Plate Tectonic Map of the Circum-Pacific Region," map to accompany. *Tectonostratigraphic Terranes of the Circum-Pacific Region*, edited by David G. Howell. Houston, Tex.: Circum Pacific Council for Energy and Mineral Resources, 1995.

Foxworthy, Bruce L., and Mary Hill. *Volcanic Eruptions of 1980 at Mount St. Helens: The First 100 Days*. Geological Survey Professional Paper 1249. Washington, D.C.: U.S. Government Printing Office, 1982.

Hays, W. W., ed. *Facing Geologic and Hydrologic Hazards*. Geological Survey Professional Paper 1240-B. Washington, D.C.: U.S. Government Printing Office, 1981.

Ihinger, Phillip. "Mantle Flow Beneath the Pacific Plate: Evidence from Seamount Segments in the Hawaiian-Emperor Chain." *American Journal of Science* 295 (1995): 1035-57.

Keegan, John. *The Price of Admiralty.* New York: Viking Penguin, 1989.

Lott, Arnold S., and Robert F. Sumrall. *Pearl Harbor Attack: An Abbreviated History.* Annapolis, Md.: Leeward Publications, 1977.

Malahoff, Alexander. "Geology of the Summit of Loihi Submarine Volcano." In *Volcanism in Hawaii.* U.S.G.S. Professional Paper 1350, edited by Robert W. Decker, Thomas L. Wright, and Peter H. Stauffer, 133-45. Washington, D.C.: U.S. Government Printing Office, 1987.

McEvedy, Colin, and Richard Jones. *Atlas of World Population History.* New York: Facts on File, 1979.

McPhee, John. *The Control of Nature.* New York: The Noonday Press, 1989.

Miller, Francis Trevelyan. *History of World War II.* Washington, D.C.: Community Home Sales, 1947.

Morgan, W. Jason. "Convection Plumes in the Lower Mantle." In *Plate Tectonics and Geomagnetic Reversals,* edited by Allan Cox, 659-61. San Francisco, Calif.: W. H. Freeman, 1973.

Sarna-Wojcicki, Andrei M.; Susan Shipley; Richard B. Waitt Jr.; Daniel Dzurisin; and Spencer H. Wood. "Areal Distribution, Thickness, Mass, Volume, and Grain Size of Air-Fall Ash from the Six Major Eruptions of 1980." In *The 1980 Eruptions of Mount St. Helens, Washington.* U.S. Geological Survey Professional Paper 1250, edited by Peter W. Lipman, and Donal R. Mullineaux, 577-600. Washington, D.C.: U.S. Government Printing Office, 1981.

Steinbrugge, Karl V. *Earthquakes, Volcanoes and Tsunamis.* New York: Skandia America Group, 1982.

Tilling, Robert I. *Eruptions of Mount St. Helens: Past, Present, and Future.* Washington, D.C.: Superintendent of Documents, 1985.

Warfield, Ronald G.; Lee Juillerat; and Larry Smith. *Crater Lake, The Story Behind the Scenery.* Las Vegas, Nev.: KC Publications, 1982.

Wright, Thomas L., and Thomas C. Pierson. *Living with Volcanoes.* U.S. Geological Survey Circular 1073. Washington, D.C.: U.S. Government Printing Office, 1992.

THREE
Coriolis, Columbus, and Waterlogged Derelicts

It is generally agreed that the first human settlers of North America were likely nomadic hunters from Arctic Asia, with no writing skills or calendars and only limited geographic and medical knowledge. The Mayan calendar began on 12 August 3113 B.C.E. (Heyerdahl 1971, 258). Across the Atlantic Ocean in Egypt, the first dynasty of the Pharaohs began between 3200 and 3100 B.C.E. Both the Mayan and Egyptian civilizations at that time included individuals who could read and write; demonstrate mathematical, astronomical, and geographical knowledge; construct pyramids for worshipping the sun; demonstrate mummification skills; and perform cranial surgery without killing the patient. Was it merely coincidence that the two civilizations, separated by a vast ocean, reflected the same level and degree of skills? Or was there a relationship between the two civilizations? If the latter, how did the Egyptians travel to southern North America and Central America? In 1970 winds, along with the Canary and North Equatorial currents, pushed archaeologist Thor Heyerdahl 3,270 miles (5,232 kilometers) across the Atlantic Ocean, averaging 57 miles (91 kilometers) a day from Morocco to Barbados, in a boat made of papyrus reeds. Did he prove that the Egyptians played an early role in the settlement of the Americas? No. All he was trying to find out was if a reed boat could make the journey to America. It could.

That Central and South America, the Caribbean, and southern North America were settled by southern Europeans was largely due to a fortuitous combination of vertical and horizontal circulation of the atmosphere, counterclockwise rotation of the earth (the Coriolis effect), density currents in the ocean, wanderlust, greed, and ignorance of what lay on the other side of the ocean. Like their counterparts searching for a northern passage to China, the sailors of the tropical Atlantic Ocean were seeking a route to the wealth-laden "Indies" (meaning all of Eastern Asia made famous by Marco Polo; Hale 1966, 52). The rotation of water in the North Atlantic appears as motion in a generally circular, clockwise pattern called the North Atlantic Gyre. In reality, because of differences in the density of the types of water involved (cold fresh, warm salty, cold salty, warm fresh), the circular pattern is more like a series of overlapping spirals.

55

Leaving Spain or Portugal, ships would be carried south and southwest by the Canary Current, west by the North Equatorial Current and the tradewinds, north and east by the Gulf Stream, and finally eastward and home by the North Atlantic Drift. (See fig. 3.1.) Christopher Columbus used these currents in four voyages between 1492 and 1502. In 1497 Amerigo Vespucci sailed westward across the Atlantic, following the Loop Current and the Gulf Stream up through the Gulf of Mexico and along the southeastern coast of what is now the United States before returning to Europe. His reports of a new continent inspired publisher Martin Waldseemuller to call the continent "America" on new maps. Giovanni da Verrazano made the complete circuit in 1524, discovering New York Harbor, where one of the longest suspension bridges in the world honors his name. After stopping at several Caribbean islands British settlers eventually founded the colony at Jamestown, Virginia, in April 1606 (Dabney 1971, 3). Hundreds of years of Spanish influence in the New World were made possible by the North Atlantic Gyre, including settlements in the Caribbean and protective fortresses in San Juan, Puerto Rico and St. Augustine, Florida (Arana and Manucy 1977, 10). More recent voyages by Heyerdahl and Callahan demonstrated that the currents and winds have not changed. (See fig. 3.1.)

Currents such as the Gulf Stream affected more than early explorations and discoveries. In the 1770s Postmaster Benjamin Franklin, concerned that westbound mail between Europe and the United States took longer than eastbound mail, had a chart of the Gulf Stream printed so that ships carrying mail to and from England could take advantage of its flow and improve mail service to the United States (Stommel 1958, 4).

Activity: Current-Driven Hulks

In this activity students will plot the surface currents of the North Atlantic Gyre using four abandoned hulks or ghost ships and one recent drifting vessel. During the late stages of the nineteenth century, floating wooden vessels abandoned by crews (known as derelicts) became frequent navigation hazards in the North Atlantic Ocean. In 1893 more than 418 different derelicts were reported. Derelicts were created by severe storms, leaking hulls, collisions, mutiny, disease, or shipboard disasters such as fire. Their positions were reported and plotted on Pilot Charts for distribution to navigators. The predecessor of the Coast Guard— the Revenue Service— removed many derelicts by towing them, ramming them, burning them at sea, or torpedoing them (Richardson 1985). Many, however, remained afloat for several years, moved by the ocean currents. Because they represented a potential menace to shipping, the derelicts were reported, tracked, and now provide a means to determine the pattern of current motion.

Time

+ 2 class periods

Materials (for each student)

+ a copy of tables 3.1, 3.2, 3.3, 3.4 and 3.5
+ a copy of figure 3.2
+ a straightedge (ruler or triangle)
+ pencil and eraser
+ colored pencils or thin markers
+ transparent tape (that can be written on)
+ scissors

Grouping

+ individuals

Directions

1. Explain to the students what derelicts are and that the major causes of movement of these hulks are the surface ocean currents.

2. Distribute a copy of tables 3.1, 3.2, 3.3, 3.4 and 3.5 to each student. Review the tables with the class, explaining the tables represent when a derelict was observed by another ship, and the longitude and latitude of that observation.

3. Distribute a copy of figure 3.2 (A-B) to each student. Explain that it is a base map of the North Atlantic Ocean with longitude and latitude markings along the margins. Before beginning the activity, have the students use transparent tape to put the two pieces of the map together. If using clear tape that can be written on, put tape on the front side. For all other kinds of tape put the tape on the back.

4. Using table 3.1 and a pencil, have students plot the track of the schooner *Twenty-One Friends*. Once the track is completed and checked, students can outline it with a colored pencil or marker. Explain that the track was created as the ship was moved by currents across the Atlantic for about eight months. Based on the track of the derelict, have the students indicate the current directions with a long arrow of the same color as the track.

5. Repeat the process with tables 3.2, 3.3, 3.4, and 3.5, using a different color for each track.

6. At the conclusion of the activity draw arrows on the map to indicate the clockwise rotation of the water currents that constitute the North Atlantic Gyre. On the completed map have the students label the following: Azores Islands, Cape Verde Islands, Canary Islands, North Equatorial Current, Gulf Stream, Canary Current, and North Atlantic Drift. Figure 3.2 shows the completed tracks with the currents.

7. Compare the rotation of the gyre to the tracks of the historical explorations from southern Europe to see the influence of the gyre on early sailing routes.

Text continues on page 62.

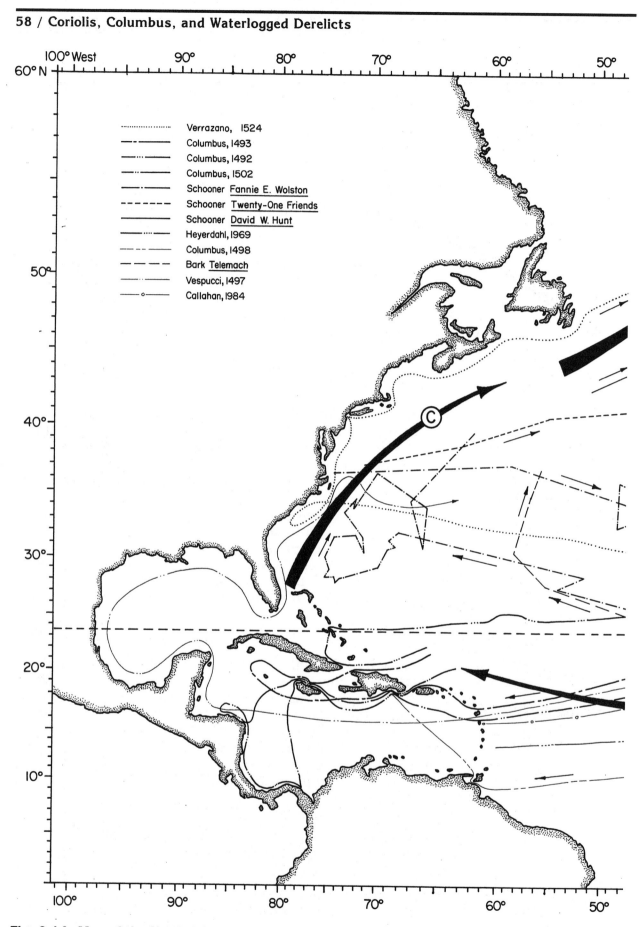

Fig. 3.1A. Map of the North Atlantic Showing Routes of Exploration (A-B).

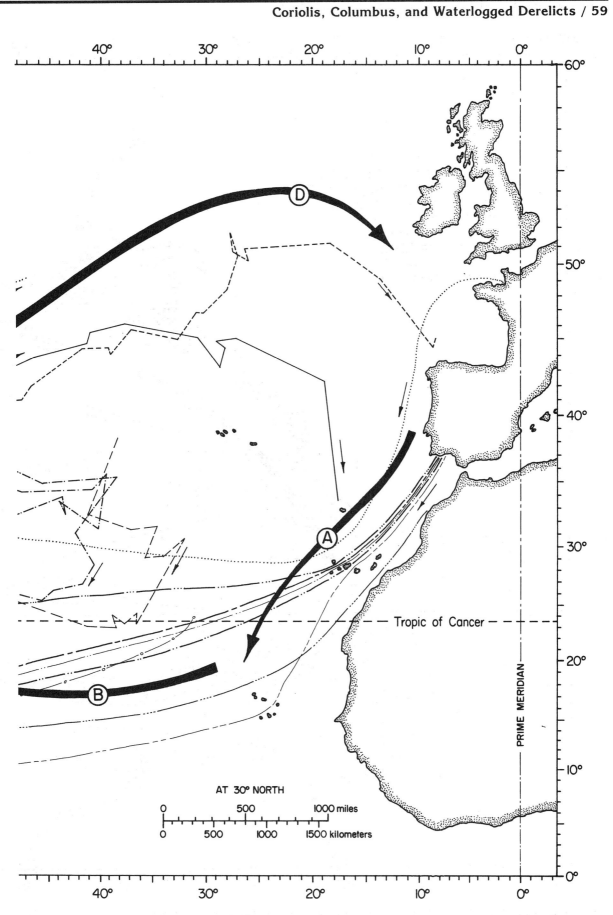

AT 30° NORTH

| 0 | 500 | 1000 miles |

| 0 | 500 | 1000 | 1500 kilometers |

Tropic of Cancer

PRIME MERIDIAN

Fig. 3.1B.

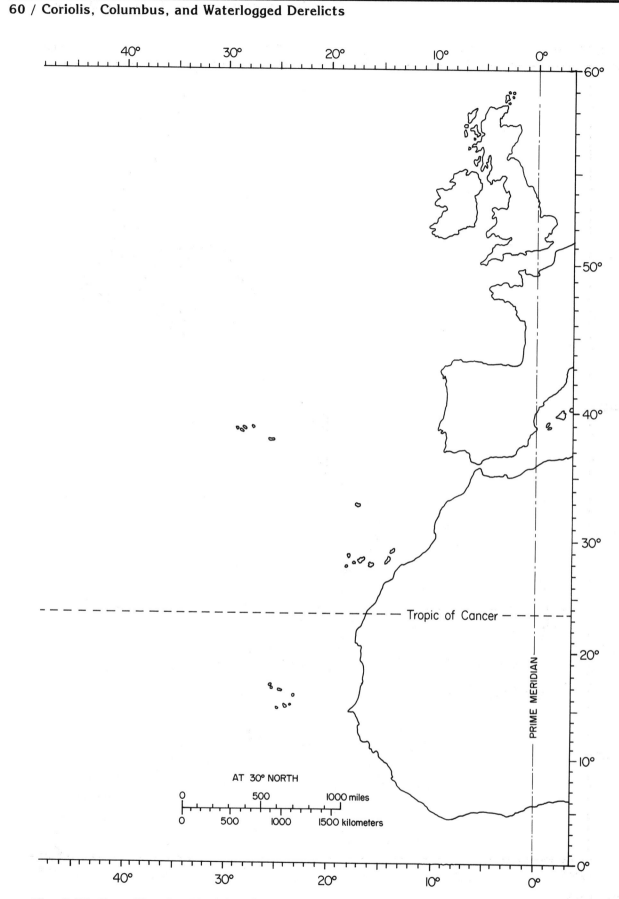

Fig. 3.2A. Base Map for "Activity: Current-Driven Hulks" (A-B).

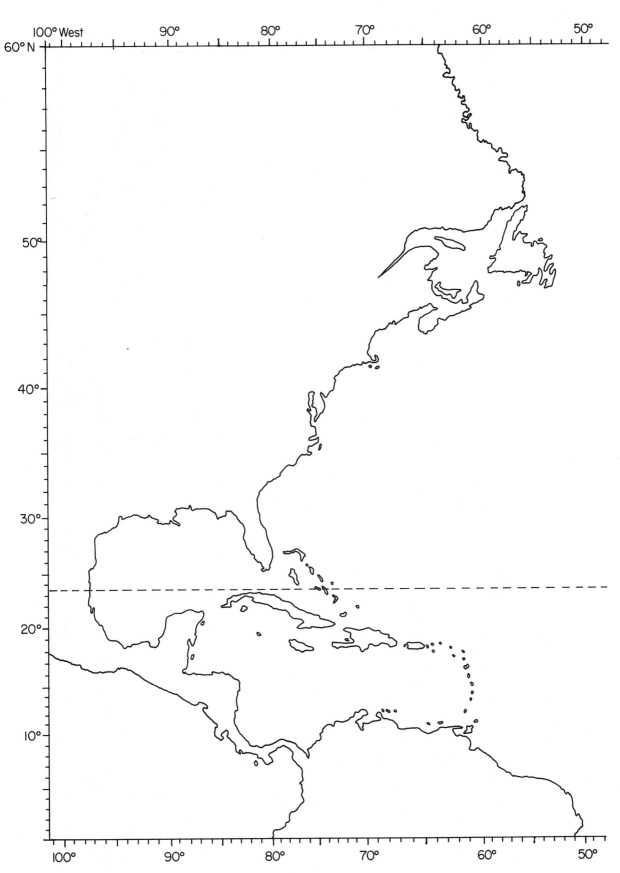

Fig. 3.2B.
From *American History Through Earth Science.* © 1997 Craig A. Munsart. Teacher Ideas Press. (800) 237-6124.

Table 3.1. Positions of the Schooner *Twenty-One Friends*. (Built in 1872 in Mays Landing, New Jersey. Length, 108 feet; weight, 221 gross tons. Drifted 3,525 miles in 255 days.)

Observation	Date	West Longitude Degrees ° Minutes '	North Latitude Degrees ° Minutes '
1	3-24-1885	71°10'	37°00'
2		66°50'	37°50'
3		63°10'	38°30'
4		59°00'	39°40'
5		55°00'	40°35'
6		51°30'	40°50'
7	4-28-85	47°35'	41°00'
8		46°50'	42°00'
9		44°50'	43°00'
10		42°00'	44°30'
11		39°10'	44°30'
12		39°00'	44°00'
13		37°00'	45°55'
14		34°50'	45°30'
15	6-30-85	32°50'	45°00'
16		31°00'	47°55'
17		30°20'	47°50'
18		28°10'	48°30'
19		27°00'	50°30'
20	8-8-85	28°00'	51°50'
21		27°30'	50°50'
22		26°00'	50°20'
23		26°30'	51°00'
24		22°00'	51°10'
25		18°20'	51°20'
26		17°20'	50°50'
27		16°00'	50°10'
28		13°30'	49°10'
29		10°50'	46°50'
30		08°40'	44°30'
31	12-2-85	08°30'	45°00'

Table 3.2. Positions of the Schooner *Fannie E. Wolston*. (Built in 1882 in Bath, Maine. Length, 120 feet; weight, 295 gross tons. Drifted 8,965 miles in 1,100 days.)

Observation	Date	West Longitude Degrees ° Minutes '	North Latitude Degrees ° Minutes '
1	10-15-1891	74°30'	36°40'
2		58°30'	37°10'
3		47°40'	34°20'
4		41°00'	34°30'
5	6-13-92	39°30'	35°50'
6	7-14-92	40°20'	31°30'
7		43°00'	33°00'
8		44°00'	34°00'
9		43°20'	34°00'
10		43°50'	32°30'
11		44°20'	33°30'
12		48°30'	32°30'
13		48°10'	36°00'
14		45°40'	35°00'
15	12-26-92	38°30'	35°30'
16		42°30'	31°05'
17	4-7-93	40°50'	28°40'
18		41°50'	27°00'
19		44°40'	26°30'
20	5-18-93	45°50'	25°20'
21		54°00'	27°30'
22		51°30'	28°30'
23		68°00'	32°00'
24		69°00'	31°30'
25		68°20'	31°00'
26		69°00'	30°40'
27		70°00'	29°20'
28		73°30'	28°20'
29		74°20'	28°00'
30		74°30'	28°30'
31		75°10'	28°35'
32		75°00'	29°10'
33		75°10'	30°00'
34		74°20'	31°45'
35		72°00'	31°55'

From *American History Through Earth Science.* © 1997 Craig A. Munsart. Teacher Ideas Press. (800) 237-6124.

Table 3.2. Positions of the Schooner *Fannie E. Wolston*. (Built in 1882 in Bath, Maine. Length, 120 feet; weight, 295 gross tons. Drifted 8,965 miles in 1,100 days.) (*continued*)

Observation	Date	West Longitude Degrees ° Minutes '	North Latitude Degrees ° Minutes '
36		71°00'	30°30'
37		71°20'	31°40'
38		73°20'	33°30'
39		72°00'	34°40'
40		72°10'	33°55'
41	10-21-94	70°00'	36°40'
42		65°50'	34°00'
43		66°00'	31°50'
44		66°05'	31°00'
45		67°00'	34°20'
46		62°00'	39°40'

Table 3.3. Positions of the Schooner *David W. Hunt*. (Built in 1881 in Bath, Maine. Length, 135 feet; weight, 349 gross tons. Drifted 4,800 miles in 347 days.)

Observation	Date	West Longitude Degrees ° Minutes '	North Latitude Degrees ° Minutes '
1		51°10'	41°50'
2	5-12-1889	47°00'	43°30'
3		41°55'	44°20'
4		41°30'	45°00'
5	6-4-89	38°20'	45°50'
6		31°20'	44°50'
7	7-5-89	29°10'	42°55'
8		28°40'	44°10'
9		29°30'	44°40'
10		27°40'	44°50'
11	9-3-89	19°00'	42°00'
12	11-12-89	17°30'	33°30'

Table 3.4. Positions of the Bark *Telemach*. (Built in 1873 in Grinstad, Norway. Length, 141 feet; weight, 623 gross tons. Drifted 3,150 miles in 551 days.)

Observation	Date	West Longitude Degrees ° Minutes '	North Latitude Degrees ° Minutes '
1	10-13-1887	38°50'	37°50'
2		41°20'	32°00'
3		37°20'	30°50'
4		34°55'	31°00'
5		35°55'	28°30'
6		34°00'	28°40'
7	3-25-1888	32°10'	30°10'
8		36°30'	22°40'
9		36°40'	23°50'
10		37°45'	22°40'
11		39°00'	23°30'
12		38°10'	22°20'
13	6-23-88	41°00'	22°30'
14		55°10'	26°50'
15	10-15-88	58°20'	29°30'
16		55°50'	36°00'

Table 3.5. While sailing from England to Antigua in 1984 Steven Callahan's small sailboat suffered severe damage northwest of the Cape Verde Island. The boat drifted along the North Equatorial Current.

Observation	Date	West Longitude Degrees ° Minutes '	North Latitude Degrees ° Minutes '
1	2-4-1984	31°00'	23°50'
2	7	31°10'	22°10'
3	11	32°50'	21°00'
4	13	34°00'	20°40'
5	15	34°45'	20°30'
6	19	36°00'	20°10'
7	20	36°50'	20°00'
8	23	38°10'	19°30'
9	28	39°40'	19°00'
10	3-4	41°00'	18°30'
11	7	42°30'	18°00'
12	10	44°10'	17°40'
13	13	45°30'	17°00'

Table 3.5. While sailing from England to Antigua in 1984 Steven Callahan's small sailboat suffered severe damage northwest of the Cape Verde Island. The boat drifted along the North Equatorial Current. (*continued*)

Observation	Date	West Longitude Degrees ° Minutes '	North Latitude Degrees ° Minutes '
14	16	47°10'	16°20'
15	19	48°10'	16°10'
16	24	49°50'	16°00'
17	27	51°20'	15°50'
18	29	52°30'	15°40'
19	4-2	53°30'	15°45'
20	5	54°30'	15°50'
21	7	55°30'	15°50'
22	10	56°40'	15°50'
23	12	57°40'	15°50'
24	14	58°40'	15°50'
25	17	60°00'	15°50'
26	20	61°20'	15°55'

Extensions

The wind and ocean currents that promoted the explorations of North America are also responsible for carrying dust from the Sahara Desert to the Caribbean and hurricanes from the Cape Verde Islands along the west coast of Africa to the Caribbean and the southeastern United States. Ask students to research the progress of a hurricane, from its inception as a tropical depression to its powerful, full-blown assault on the United States. Have them relate its progress to the currents of the water masses over which it travels.

"Ghost ships" or derelicts have provided many of the legends involving the Devil's (or Bermuda) Triangle off the southeastern U.S. coast. Military aircraft and modern vessels have also disappeared. Have groups of students research such airplane and ship stories and debate the existence of the Triangle before the class with the class acting as jury. Many publications on this topic exist, and agencies such as the U.S. Coast Guard can provide additional information.

REFERENCES

American Heritage Pictorial Atlas of United States History. New York: American Heritage, 1966.

Arana, Luis Rafael, and Albert Manucy. *The Building of the Castillo de San Marcos.* St. Augustine, Fla.: Eastern National Park and Monument Association, Castillo de San Marcos National Monument, 1977.

Callahan, Steven. *Adrift: Seventy-Six Days Lost at Sea.* Boston: Houghton Mifflin, 1986.

Dabney, Virginius. *Virginia, the New Dominion.* Garden City, N.Y.: Doubleday, 1971.

Hale, John R. *Great Ages of Man: The Age of Exploration.* New York: Time, 1966.

Hammond's Historical Atlas. Maplewood, N.J.: Hammond, 1960.

Heyerdahl, Thor. *The Ra Expeditions.* Garden City, N.Y.: Doubleday, 1971.

MacLeish, William H. *The Gulf Stream.* London: Hamish Hamilton, 1989.

Mayor, Adrienne. "Derelict Ships." *Mariner's Weather Log* (National Oceanographic Data Center, Washington, D.C.) 36 (1992):4-10.

Richardson, P. L. "Drifting Derelicts in the North Atlantic 1883-1902." In *Essays on Oceanography,* Progress in Oceanography, Volume 14, edited by J. Crease, W. J. Gould, and P. M. Saunders, 463-83. Oxford: Pergamon Press, 1985.

Richardson, Philip L. "Derelicts and Drifters." *Natural History* 94 (1985):6.

Stommel, Henry. *The Gulf Stream.* Berkeley, Calif.: University of California Press, 1958.

Villiers, Captain Alan. *Men, Ships and the Sea.* Washington, D.C.: National Geographic Society, 1973.

FOUR

Snakes, Sea Level, and the Battleship <u>Maine</u>

From the time of the Aztec civilization at Tenochtitlan, Mexico, more than 750 years ago, exploration and settlement of North America has involved canals. Canals have been built to drain swamps as well as to serve military and commercial needs. Some, like the Harlem River in New York, were merely minor modifications of existing waterways. Others, like the Panama Canal, required herculean effort and several decades to build an artificial waterway through the mountains and jungles of the geologic spine of the Americas.

The story of the Panama Canal begins in 1502, when Christopher Columbus established the city of Porto Bello on Panama's Caribbean Coast and followed an alligator-filled river across the narrow strip of land. He failed to reach the Pacific but named the river after its reptilian inhabitants, the Chagres (Latham 1964, 16). Perseverance by the Spaniards searching for the Pacific Ocean and for gold led them to both. One of the Spaniards, Vasco Nuñez de Balboa, became the first European to reach the Pacific Ocean in 1515, but despite the promise of riches from King Ferdinand, political infighting among the local Spanish military conspired against Balboa. He was beheaded in 1517. By 1533 Porto Bello was the main port from which gold and silver were shipped from Peru to Spain, across Panama along a road built by forced native labor called El Camino Real.

Students of North American history have already learned that the first transcontinental railroad was formed when 690 miles (1,110 kilometers) of the Central Pacific connected with 1,086 miles (1,747 kilometers) of the Union Pacific at Promontory Point, Utah, north of the Great Salt Lake on 10 May 1869. Well, not exactly. On 28 January 1855, a 47 mile (76 kilometer), single-track railroad was completed from Colon, on the Caribbean Sea, to Panama City, on the Pacific Ocean, creating the first Transcontinental Railroad. Although the overland stage route from New York to California was quicker (35-45 days), it was replaced by a longer, but more convenient, steamship-train-steamship route down the east coast, through Panama and up the west coast: a combination of the Pacific Mail Steamship Company and the Panama Railroad (Riegel 1964, 13). Even after a transcontinental railroad was completed through the United States, the route through Panama offered strong competition (ironically, the owner of the Pacific Mail Steamship Company also owned the Union Pacific Railroad—its chief competitor [Riegel 1964, 207]). The Panama Railroad still runs today within an almost dilapidated right-of-way, a single-track, swaying shadow of its former glory 150 years ago.

As soon as the geography of Central America was known, it became clear that a canal could be built someday to connect the Atlantic and Pacific Oceans across the relatively narrow strip of land separating the two. That it would be built was obvious to even a casual observer; where, how, and by whom were less well defined. A comprehensive history of the canal is not appropriate for this chapter; however, in *The Path Between the Seas* (Touchstone Books, 1977) David McCullough does an excellent job of detailing the canal's history. For reader background a brief summary of the three major concerns follows.

Where. Although the planners of the canal considered several initial sites, they narrowed the choice to two: the Isthmus of Panama (originally part of Colombia) and a site through Nicaragua. After many comprehensive surveys, debates, and analyses the former was chosen (Isthmian Canal Commission 1904, 71-111). The latter involved a longer canal (more than twice as long as Panama) connecting rivers and various lakes through terrain containing volcanoes with a recent history of eruption and earthquakes.

How. The big "how" was whether to build a sea-level canal like that recently completed at Suez or an elevated canal with locks. Proponents of the former cited the success at Suez and the lower costs. Proponents of the latter cited tidal differences between the Atlantic and Pacific ends of the canal, topography, difficult rock conditions, flooding problems of the Chagres River, and poisonous sea snakes (which had no natural enemies in the Atlantic). The idea of constructing tunnels as part of the Panama route was also considered but eventually abandoned.

By Whom. A French company, flush from success at Suez and still under the dynamic direction of Ferdinand De Lesseps, started the Panama Canal but went bankrupt trying to complete it. Years later, after some creative international political manipulation and strong direction, President Theodore Roosevelt spearheaded U.S. completion of the effort. Under a 1978 treaty, the canal and adjoining lands will be returned to Panama on 31 December 1999.

Ferdinand De Lesseps became a financial success and a national hero after the completion of the Suez Canal. Twenty-five years later he died penniless and in disgrace, beaten and demoralized by the attempted canal at Panama. The reason? He ignored the earth sciences. The climate, rivers, topography, tides, and geology of Panama combined to vanquish the man who successfully dug a ditch through the sands of Egypt. At Panama, only a short section of the 45 mile (72 kilometer) passage from the Atlantic to the Pacific Oceans is actually a canal; the remainder is really a flooded portion of the Chagres River. Rather than reduce the level of the land to that of the sea, the plan executed by the United States was to raise the level of the water by 85 feet (25.9 meters) using three locks at either end. It was the same plan that many of De Lesseps's advisors wanted to implement in Panama. They were ignored, a sea-level canal was started, and the French effort died several miles into the Panamanian jungle. Shortly after entering the canal from the Caribbean, a vestige of the failed French effort can be seen leading off to the right, heading into the dense Panamanian rain forest.

A comparison of the two canals (see table 4.1) indicates just how badly success at Suez prepared the Compagnie Universelle du Canal Interoceanigue (the French agency responsible for canal design) for the forthcoming debacle at Panama.

Table 4.1. A Comparison of the Suez and Panama Canals.

Characteristic	Suez	Panama
tidal difference	minimal to none	up to 21 feet
topography	flat	mountainous
maximum elevation	50 feet	350 feet
climate	dry, desert	heavy seasonal rains
ground material	sand and sandstone	jungle, fractured volcanic rock
floods	none	often, Chagres River
diseases	cholera	yellow fever, malaria
required excavation	estimated 90,000,000 cubic yards	262,000,000 cubic yards*
cost	estimated $80 million	$639 million

*Note: This is for the canal as built. The French, sea-level canal would have required much more excavation.

Nicholas-Joseph-Adolphe Godin de Lèpinay was Chief Engineer with the French Department of Bridges and Highways at the time and, in 1879, assessed the differences between Suez and Panama as follows:

> At Suez there is a lack of water, the terrain is easy, the land nearly the same level as the sea; in spite of the heat it is a perfectly healthy climate. In tropical America, there is too much water, the terrain is mostly rock, the land has considerable relief, and finally the country is literally poisoned. (McCullough 1977, 80)

Lèpinay's plan was ignored by De Lesseps but became the foundation for the plan successfully executed by the Americans; dams and lakes to harness the Chagres River, provide water and electricity, and minimize excavation.

The French effort had two strikes against it from the beginning. It was underfinanced, with equipment and human resources inadequate for the job at hand. Add to it the lack of respect for the earth sciences, and any umpire would have said, "S-t-e-e-r-i-k-e T-h-r-e-e, you're outta there!" On 4 February 1889, the Compagnie Universelle du Canal Interoceanique ceased to exist (McCullough 1977, 203).

Figure 4.1 (A-B) presents maps of the French and American canal plans, respectively. The former is the plan for the French sea-level canal, generally following the route of the Chagres River, crossing it and diverting it as necessary. The American lock canal plan (B), includes dams at the east and west ends of the canal and upstream on the Chagres to control floods and provide water and electricity for canal operation. The dams also created lakes that minimized excavations, and the locks provided control of the tidal differences. While transiting the canal today it is easy to get the feeling it is more natural than human made.

Although a long list of requirements existed, three primary obstacles had to be overcome for the successful construction of a canal in Panama: (a) regulation of the Chagres River; (b) completion of a cut through the Cordillera, the mountain spine (continental divide) of Panama; and (c) sanitation and improvement of working conditions in the hostile climate (Hunter 1899, 7). Because of the terrain, digging more than 40 miles (64 kilometers) of the sea-level canal envisioned by the French would have required removal of extraordinary amounts of geologically complex rock formations that form the structural spine of Central America. The amount of excavation of the sea-level canal was estimated at 157 million cubic yards (120 million cubic meters). Imagine an area the size of a football field covered by a pile of rock almost 17 miles (27.3 kilometers) high. As it turned out, even this enormous number was too conservative an estimate; 96 million cubic yards (73 million cubic meters) were removed from the Culebra Cut alone. Final estimates for the completed canal were 262 million cubic yards (200 million cubic meters) removed (McCullough 1977, 611). Remember that football field? The amount of material actually removed would have covered it with a pile of rock almost 28 miles (45 kilometers) high!

Activity: How Long?

Figure 4.2 is a cross section through the Culebra portion of the excavation for the canal. It shows the tremendous amount of material that needed to be removed in this one area. It also shows the successive excavations by the various canal-building entities. Although it appears on this drawing that only a small volume remained to be removed, that volume was much greater because landslides from the slopes of the areas already removed kept filling in the excavation as it was deepened, a mass wasting process that requires constant dredging, even today, to maintain the channel. For the canal as a whole, the French excavated far less material than their plans required. In this one area, however, they did an excellent job and accelerated the American effort.

In this activity students will graph the annual excavations for six years, determine an average, and, from that average, estimate how long the excavation of a sea-level canal would have taken and when the excavations for the canal might have been completed.

Text continues on page 74.

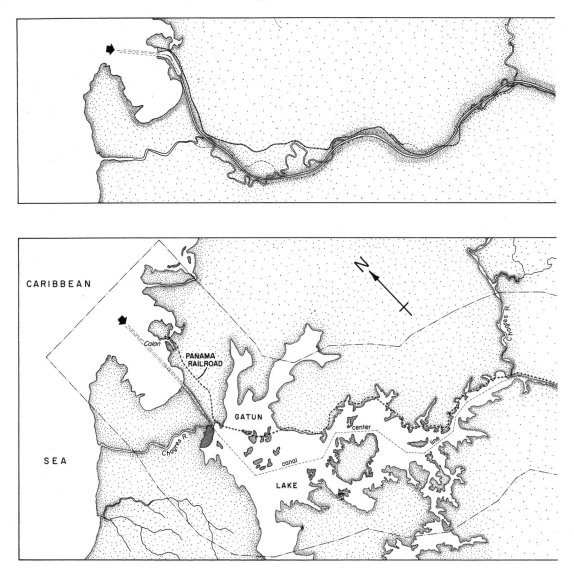

Fig. 4.1. Maps Comparing the French Plan for a Sea-Level Canal (A) with the American Plan for a Lock Canal (B) Through Panama. Striped Areas on (B) Are Locations of Dams.

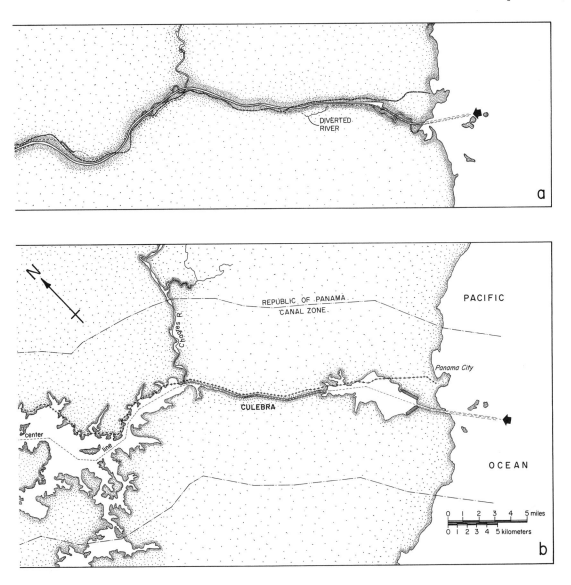

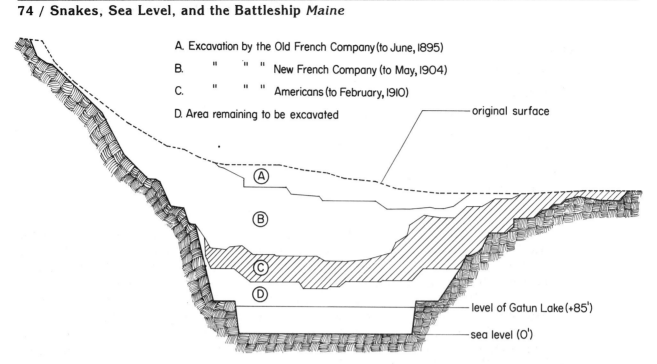

Fig. 4.2. Cross Section of Excavations Through the Culebra Cut During Various Stages of Construction.

Note: Adapted from Charles S. Small, *Rail to the Diggings*. Railroad Monographs. Denver, 1981, 25.

Table 4.2. Excavations at Panama, by Year.

Year	Number of Cubic Yards Excavated by Year	Cumulative Yards Excavation (cu yds)
1895	481,000	481,000
1896	910,000	1,391,000
1897	1,248,000	2,639,000
1904	243,504	2,882,504
1905	912,054	3,794,558
1906	2,673,545	6,468,103
1907	15,700,000	22,168,103
1908	37,000,000	59,168,103

Time

+ 1 class period

Materials

+ a copy of table 4.2 for each student
+ graph paper
+ two colored pencils for each student

Grouping

+ individual

Directions

1. Distribute copies of table 4.2 to students. Discuss the numbers on the table with the students. Data on the table are presented in two groups. Excavations during the years 1895-1897 were made by the French. Excavations during the years 1904-1908 were made by the Americans.

2. Ask students to set up their graphs listing years across the x-axis and yards excavated on the y-axis. Students will be projecting the year of completion of the canal and the number of yards to be removed (262 million), so it is important that room be left on the x- and y-axes for data beyond those given in the table.

3. Students should select a color to plot the French excavations. After plotting the three data points ask students to draw a best-fit line. The best-fit line will provide each student with a way of estimating the amount of excavation each year after 1897. Students will need to determine the amount of excavation for each year after 1897 and add those annual values until they reach 262,000,000—the total amount removed for the canal. Because each student will draw a slightly different best-fit line, answers will vary from student to student.

4. Discuss the results with the class. Were the French doing a good job? As a stockholder in the Compagnie Universelle du Canal Interoceanique would you have invested more money in the effort in 1897, if asked?

5. Ask students to continue the process *on the same graph* with the data from 1904-1908. Using a different color draw a new line plotting the additional data. Using that new line, project when the 262 million-cubic-yard excavation would have been completed. The first ship made a transit of the canal on August 15, 1914. How close were the student estimates? How would the best-fit line have to be modified to allow for a completed excavation before the first transit?

Extension

Many computer graphing programs can generate best-fit lines for the data supplied. Have students compare the answers they obtained by hand with those generated by the computer; compare and discuss differences.

In 1898 the military necessity of a trans-isthmus canal was dramatically reinforced when the battleship *Maine*, sent to Cuba as a sign of friendship with Spain, exploded in the harbor of Havana, Cuba, on 16 February. To protect United States' interests in the area, the battleship *Oregon* was ordered to Havana from San Francisco. The *Oregon* left San Francisco on 19 March and rushed around Cape Horn, arriving near Cuba 67 days later. In the middle of her transit (on 21 April), and encouraged by yellow journalism, Congress declared war against Spain, and the Spanish-American War was on (Legrand 1989, 518). It was clear to even a casual observer that a quicker military response was necessary to protect American interests on both coasts; a canal through Panama could provide that quick response.

If the *Oregon* had traveled from San Francisco all the way to New York the trip would have taken an estimated 73 days. In 1899 similar comparisons were made for sailing ships (steamships were only beginning to replace sailing ships for commerce) from San Francisco to New York. Although the range was from 118 to 169 days, largely depending on the season, the average length of the trip was 140 days. In 1851 the new clipper ship, *Flying Cloud* set a record, making the trip from New York to San Francisco in just under 90 days. The same trip through the then-being-planned Panama Canal would take only 59 days. The savings to a shipowner were calculated at $3,625 per trip based on operating costs of $75/day, a toll at $1/ton for a 2,000-ton ship, and a $450 towage fee (Isthmian Canal Commission 1904, 568-69).

Activity: There's Got to Be a Better Way

In the following activity students will compare the route the *Oregon* took with a route through the canal (as if that same trip were being made today) and calculate the speed of the *Oregon* in the process.

Time

+ 1 class period

Materials

+ a copy of figure 4.3 for each student (enlarged to 11" x 17") and made as an overhead

Grouping

+ individuals

Directions

1. Display figure 4.3 to the class on an overhead. Tell the students the story of the battleship *Oregon*. The dashed line is the route the *Oregon* took in 1899. The dotted line is the route the *Oregon* could have taken if the Panama Canal was available at the time. For reference, *A* is San Francisco; *B* is Cape Horn; *C* is Miami, Florida; *D* is Havana, Cuba; and *E* is the Panama Canal.

2. Explain to the students that they must first determine the speed of the *Oregon*, then calculate how many days the trip from San Francisco to Miami would have taken at the calculated speed if the Panama Canal was available.

3. Students should first measure along the dashed line, using the scale on the map, to determine the "around the Horn" distance (in both miles and kilometers) from San Francisco to Miami. The trip took the *Oregon* 67 days. Knowing the distance and the time (students should convert days to hours) the speed can be calculated in both miles per hour and kilometers per hour.

Fig. 4.3. Comparison of the Two Possible Routes Taken by the Battleship *Oregon*.

From *American History Through Earth Science.* © 1997 Craig A. Munsart. Teacher Ideas Press. (800) 237-6124.

4. Students should now measure the distance through the canal (if it had existed) along the dotted line. Using the speed determined in step 3, students can now estimate the time it would have taken for the *Oregon* to complete its trip through the (future) canal. Such a reduction in travel time not only created a military benefit to the canal but also a commercial one as it reduced both the operating time and costs for ships in transit. Prior to the building of the canal New York manufacturing firm analyzed its shipping routes as follows:

> It costs about $8 per ton to ship from New York to the Hawaiian Islands around the Horn (4-5 months), $12 per ton to send the freight by way of Panama [railroad] and San Francisco to Honolulu (3 months) and about $19 per ton to ship across the United States by rail to San Francisco or Vancouver and thence to Honolulu (at least 2 months). (Isthmian Canal Commission 1904, 572)

5. Other North American canals were built for many reasons, including the same ones that spurred the construction of the Panama Canal: trade, military needs, need for draining an area of water, or shorter routes of communication. Some of North America's major canals (many other smaller canals also exist) are:

Ala Moana Canal, Hawaii

Beaumont-Port Arthur Ship Canal, Texas

Cape Cod Canal, Massachusetts

Erie (New York State Barge) Canal, New York

Illinois Waterway, Illinois

Lake Washington Ship Canal, Washington

New Orleans, Industrial Canal, Louisiana

St. Lawrence Seaway Canals, Canada and United States

Sault St. Marie, Michigan

Welland Canal, Ontario, Canada

Ask the students to research canals in your area, those above, canals along major rivers, or canals in cities of North America. Do the canals still exist, or were older canals abandoned? What was the impact of that canal to the local area? What was the impact to a wider area? The Erie Canal, for example, provided a local communication pathway and opened much of the upper midwestern United States to exploration and settlement. If the canals were abandoned, what caused their demise?

Extension

At the turn of the century the overseas commercial trade of the United States involved products moving to all coastal areas of the country from worldwide sources. The following list provides information about the movement of imports and exports prior to the building of the Panama Canal. Students can study the movement on a world map before and after the canal was built, or individual students can research a single product from a country and report to the class on its worldwide uses and transport.

EXPORTS

cotton to China and Japan (approximately 60 percent by rail from southern states to Pacific ports, the rest by ship from New Orleans, Galveston, Pensacola)

manufactured cotton textiles to Asia from ports in the northeastern United States

iron and steel manufactured products from the midwestern United States (shipments from Chicago often sent to New York, then by ship to Panama, across isthmus by rail, then transshipped to South American ports or around Cape Horn)

barley and redwood from California to eastern states

fruit and agricultural products (including wine) from California to eastern cities, and eastern South America and Europe

Pacific coast fisheries shipping products to the east coast

coal to the Pacific Northwest (some coal was available in the Pacific Northwest, but much better coal was available from the east to supply the Pacific coast. The U.S. Navy rated the fueling ability of coals, from best to worst, as follows: West Virginia and Wales, Alabama, Australia, Washington, and British Columbia [Isthmian Canal Commission 1904, 547])

IMPORTS

nitrate fertilizer from Chile to ports in the southern United States

wool from Australia to New England textile mills

silk supplies from Asia to New England

tea imports from Asia to northeastern states

chinaware to northeastern cities

Activity: We've Got It All!

Canal operations are remarkably simple. Water supplied by the abundant rainfall fills the locks as a ship is raised. When a ship is lowered the water empties from the locks to the oceans at either end. Each transit requires 52 million gallons. The abundant water also generates hydroelectric power for canal operations.

A successful lock canal, such as that at Panama, had three critical elements; a short distance between the Atlantic and Pacific Oceans, substantial amounts of water, and gravity to make the water flow. The first was no problem; the distance was less than 50 miles (80 kilometers) at Panama. The second was also no problem. As in most tropical areas, winter and summer in Panama are marked not by differences in temperature but by differences in precipitation. There is a plethora of precipitation. The third element was also readily available. In this activity students will use table 4.3 to prepare graphs of temperature and precipitation data for central Panama and compare those with data from some of the wettest places in the United States (as given in tables 4.4-4.7). Students will then draw conclusions about the advantages of Panama as a canal site.

Table 4.3. Temperature and Precipitation in Central Panama.

Month	Temperature (˚F)	Precipitation (mm)
Jan	76.8	9.04
Feb	79.5	3.86
Mar	79.7	3.94
Apr	80.9	11.23
May	78.0	31.17
Jun	78.9	34.19
Jul	77.3	42.98
Aug	78.4	39.45
Sep	76.4	32.44
Oct	77.7	36.07
Nov	77.3	52.22
Dec	78.1	31.72

Table 4.4. Temperature and Precipitation in Miami, Florida.

Month	Temperature (˚F)	Precipitation (mm)
Jan	67.0	5.33
Feb	68.0	5.33
Mar	72.0	4.83
Apr	75.0	7.87
May	79.0	16.51
Jun	81.0	23.37
Jul	83.0	15.24
Aug	83.0	17.78
Sep	82.0	20.57
Oct	78.0	18.03
Nov	73.0	6.86
Dec	69.0	4.83

Table 4.5. Temperature and Precipitation in Honolulu, Hawaii.

Month	Temperature (°F)	Precipitation (mm)
Jan	73.0	9.65
Feb	73.0	6.86
Mar	74.0	8.89
Apr	76.0	3.81
May	78.0	3.04
Jun	79.0	1.77
Jul	80.0	1.77
Aug	81.0	1.52
Sep	81.0	1.52
Oct	80.0	4.83
Nov	77.0	8.13
Dec	74.0	8.64

Table 4.6. Temperature and Precipitation in New Orleans, Louisiana.

Month	Temperature (°F)	Precipitation (mm)
Jan	52.0	12.70
Feb	55.0	13.21
Mar	61.0	11.94
Apr	69.0	11.43
May	75.0	12.95
Jun	80.0	11.68
Jul	82.0	17.02
Aug	82.0	15.24
Sep	79.0	14.99
Oct	69.0	6.86
Nov	60.0	10.41
Dec	55.0	13.46

Time

+ 1 class period

Materials

+ 2 sheets of graph paper for each student
+ copies of tables 4.3-4.7 for each student
+ colored pencils (optional)

Grouping

+ individuals

Directions

1. Make certain all students have two sheets of graph paper (if graph paper is all the same, e.g., set in ¼-inch squares, instructions to the class will be easier to give and to follow). Have the students hold the paper with the short side as the x-axis.

2. Have the students set up the axes on the graphs. On the first piece of graph paper ask the students to move in 3 or 4 lines from the edge of the paper and draw lines for the x- and y-axes. The x-axis will be the independent variable, month. Start at the origin, skip a line and label a month on every other line across the x-axis, starting with January and continuing through December. Abbreviations such as "Jan," "Feb," and "Mar" written vertically will save space and will not affect clarity. For the temperature graph the y-axis must accommodate a temperature range of 51° to 83° Fahrenheit. For the precipitation graph the y-axis needs to be able to accommodate a range of precipitation from 0 to 52.22 millimeters.

3. Have the students consider a title box for the graph, but do not place it on the graph yet. Add it to the graph after plotting so the box will not interfere with the graph. The box should include critical information such as student name, period, date, assignment number, and information about the graph itself such as title and legend of lines and symbols used.

4. Because the students will be plotting data for five sources on each graph they should consider a way of distinguishing those data on the graph. For instance, Panama can be plotted with a circle and a solid line, Miami with triangles and a dotted line, or students can select different colors. The colors or symbols need to be consistent on the temperature and precipitation graphs, and all ultimately shown in the legend in the title box.

5. Have the students plot the two graphs— temperature and precipitation— and place the title boxes where they won't interfere with the data.

6. Ask the students to compare the five sites. Based on precipitation only, which is most suitable for a canal? Why? [Panama, because it has the most precipitation.] If students have visited any of the locations, ask them to describe the weather to the class. Ask the students to discuss which site they would like to visit, when they would visit, and why.

Table 4.7. Temperature and Precipitation in Mobile, Alabama.

Month	Temperature (°F)	Precipitation (mm)
Jan	51.0	11.68
Feb	54.0	12.45
Mar	60.0	16.51
Apr	68.0	13.72
May	75.0	13.97
Jun	81.0	12.95
Jul	82.0	19.56
Aug	82.0	17.27
Sep	78.0	16.76
Oct	69.0	6.60
Nov	59.0	9.40
Dec	53.0	13.72

REFERENCES

Bascom, Willard. *Waves and Beaches*. Garden City, N.Y.: Anchor Books, 1980.

DuVal, Miles P. *And the Mountains Will Move*. Stanford, Calif.: Stanford University Press, 1947.

Hunter, Henry. "The American Isthmus and the Interoceanic Canal." *Engineering Magazine*, February/March, 1980.

Isthmian Canal Commission. *Report for 1899-1901*. Washington, D.C.: U.S. Government Printing Office, 1904.

Kimball, Lieutenant W. W. *Special Intelligence Report on the Progress of the Work on the Panama Canal During the Year 1885*. U.S. House of Representatives, Miscellaneous Document 395, 49th Congress, First Session. Washington, D.C.: U.S. Government Printing Office, 1886.

Latham, Jean Lee. *The Chagres; Power of the Panama Canal*. Champaign, Ill.: Garrard, 1964.

Legrand, Jacques. *Chronicle of America*. Mount Kisco, N.Y.: Chronicle Publications, 1989.

McCullough, David. *The Path Between the Seas*. New York: Touchstone Books, 1977.

Riegel, Robert Edgar. *The Story of the Western Railroads*. Lincoln: University of Nebraska Press, 1964.

Small, Charles S. *Rails to the Diggings*. Denver, Colo.: Railroad Monographs, 1981.

FIVE

Coal, Canals, and Black Bass: Johnstown, Pennsylvania

Much like living along coastal areas has both pluses and minuses, living along rivers has both virtues and vices. On the one hand, cities located along rivers have a convenient water supply, are close to the gold (when there is gold), have good bottom land for farming, and have a ready source of transportation. On the other hand, the natural system that created the floodplain is subjugated to allow for human development of that floodplain. In its own way and time the river gets even.

This chapter provides an opportunity to introduce the concepts of potential and kinetic energy as they apply to river systems and the hydrologic cycle. The energy of a river starts as precipitation falling from the sky. The kinetic energy of the falling precipitation is either continued as kinetic energy in running water or converted to potential energy when impounded behind a dam. If hydroelectric power is generated, the potential energy of the stored water is converted to kinetic energy of the water falling from the height of the dam through a generator, then to mechanical energy turning the generator, and ultimately electrical energy. In the case of the Johnstown floods of 1889, the kinetic energy of the water falling through the elevation difference between the South Fork Dam and the city of Johnstown was transferred to the objects (buildings, railroad equipment, debris, and bodies) lying in the water's path.

Johnstown, Pennsylvania was originally settled by Europeans on the site of a former Delaware Indian village. The fertile land of the floodplain of Stony Creek became a farm in 1771. Native Americans drove off the settlers, and in 1794 Joseph Johns was attracted to the floodplain, cleared 30 acres, and established the permanent settlement that was later to become Johnstown. Coal, iron, and timber drew increasing numbers of settlers to Johnstown. The Conemaugh Valley was a natural transportation conduit through the Allegheny Mountains, and in the 1830s a plan was put in place to build a canal from Johnstown west to Pittsburgh to compete with New York's Erie Canal. In 1836 money was appropriated by the state legislature to build a reservoir approximately 14 miles (23 kilometers) upstream from Johnstown to supply water for the new canal. It was to be one of the earliest high dams in the United States (Smith 1972, 176). Work began in 1838 and, after persevering through financial difficulties, the dam was completed in 1852. Unfortunately, so was the Pennsylvania Railroad to Pittsburgh. The railroad put the canal out of business and ultimately came to own the canal right-of-way, associated properties, and the South Fork Dam. Although the railroad owned the dam, it had no use for it, and it sat neglected from 1857 to 1879. In 1862, major storms in the area caused the dam to fail. Fortunately, the reservoir was only partially full, and the consequences were minor. However, it should have been considered a warning. In 1879 the dam and reservoir were sold to a business group for the establishment of a private vacation spot for Pittsburgh's elite, the Carnegies, Mellons, Fricks, and their cronies.

With absolute certainty the failure of the dam at the South Fork Fishing and Hunting Club was responsible for the horrific loss of life and property at Johnstown in 1889. With equal certainty, however, Johnstown was an accident waiting to happen. A natural drainage system is dependent on climate, lithology, structure, geologic history, and that great geologic intangible, time. A drainage system can be considered a water distribution system in reverse. A water distribution system would begin with a large quantity of water (a reservoir) and circulate that water through smaller and smaller pipes as it feeds the water to neighborhoods, then blocks, then individual homes, and finally to individual fixtures (e.g., a sink). A natural drainage system works in the opposite way, collecting water in first-order streams from small drainages, merging into larger second-order streams collecting water from multiple drainages, and continuing the process, merging into larger and larger streams, all flowing down toward the ultimate large body of water, the ocean. The precipitation falling around Johnstown ultimately finds its way to the Atlantic Ocean; on the way, however, all of it passes through the city of Johnstown. Johnstown acts as the narrow neck of a broad funnel concentrating all the water from the 700 square mile (1,813 square kilometers) drainage basins of Stony Creek and the Little Conemaugh River right through the middle of town. Figure 5.1 is a map of the streams that drain the watershed through Johnstown. The valley at Johnstown floods as a result of millions of years of geologic processes. It certainly was filling with water long before the Delaware Indians and Joseph Johns decided to settle on the floodplain of the river.

In his review of the geology of the area, W. C. Phalen observed, "The surface was shaped by stream erosion. . . . Water entering the streams in great quantity is carried off rapidly, with disastrous results to portions of towns lying along the flood plains" (1910, 2). He summarized the situation this way: "The Johnstown Quadrangle is a well-watered region" (1910, 15). None of this, of course, was news to the residents of Johnstown. Severe flooding was documented in 1808, 1820, 1847, 1875, 1885, 1887, and 1888. Much of that flooding was related to seasonal downpours; some was related to failures of small dams above town. The effects of the flooding were made even more severe by the residents themselves. Surrounding hills were stripped of trees for timber, allowing rainwater to enter the rivers quickly while simultaneously eroding the hillsides. As building within the town continued and bottomland became scarce, the river channels were narrowed. Because of the hard rock underlying the channels, high flows of water in the river system could only be accommodated by overflowing its banks. There was simply nowhere else for the water to go. "The rivers ran high every spring. . . . A few times the water had been level with the first floor windows along several streets. Floods had become part of the season, like the dogwood blooming on the mountain" (McCullough 1968, 33). In May of 1889 the population of Johnstown was about 30,000, most of whom lived or worked in the valley near the rivers.

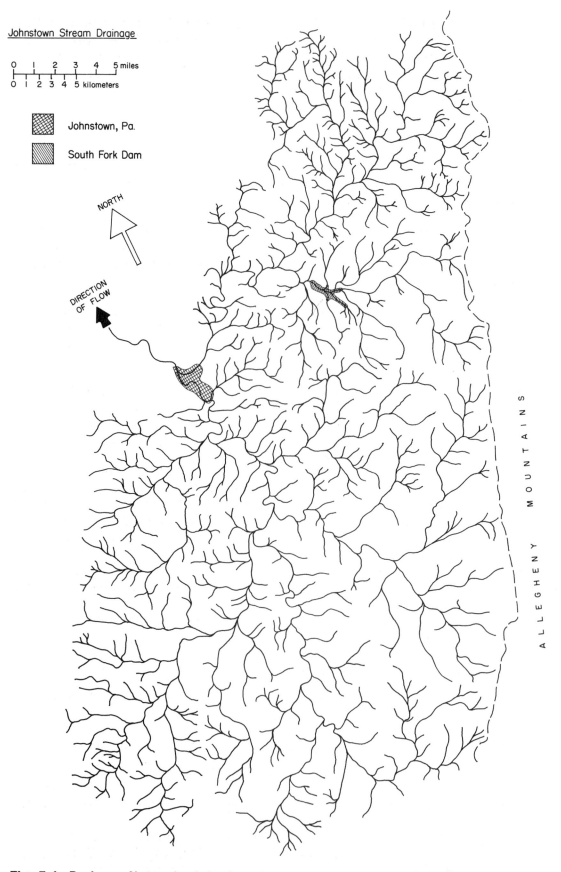

Fig. 5.1. Drainage Network of the Area South and East of Johnstown, Pennsylvania.

Flooding is as much a part of the natural process of rivers as is their flow downhill; neither should come as a surprise to even the casual observer. A clear understanding of the operation of a river system has been obtained by observation of present-day rivers as well as analysis of the material carried by rivers of the past. The following points are clear:

- Rivers move both laterally and vertically within a well-defined area called the floodplain.

- When it contains small amounts of water the river will occupy a narrow channel, within a small part of the floodplain, accompanied by natural levees.

- When the river system is required to carry large amounts of water it overflows the narrow channel, spreads out to cover portions of the floodplain, and breaches the natural levees along the banks of the original channel.

- When very high water levels are within the system the entire floodplain is inundated and the river is restricted only by the walls of the valley within which it flows. The extent of flooding can be predicted by the maximum height of the river and the topography.

- Besides water, rivers carry large amounts of material derived from the erosion of the land surface (including many organic materials that form rich soils).

Left alone, rivers can be considered almost intelligent. River systems respond to both positive and negative feedback about their flow. They constantly modify their own geometry to accommodate the volume of water they carry, becoming deeper, wider, or higher during times of maximum flow and staying within small channels when lower water volumes are carried. That modification process can take millions of years. As human populations, theoretically more intelligent and certainly less patient than rivers, encroach on a naturally developed river system, they modify that system to accommodate their own needs, narrowing and confining channels, removing natural levees, building on the floodplain, and blocking water flow with dams.

Anyone willing to look at the facts would have seen the ingredients for disaster at Johnstown in place:

river channels had been narrowed;

building and expansion of the population continued in the floodplain;

the hills were stripped of protective vegetation;

a major dam was built 14 miles (23 kilometers) upstream; and

the city had a history of flooding and dam failures.

There was no "if." The only questions were when the next flood would occur and how severe would it be.

The trigger for the disaster was created during the construction of "enhancements" for the dam of the South Fork Fishing and Hunting Club. Outlet pipes built at the base of the dam (as potential drains if the level of the reservoir needed to be lowered) were considered unnecessary and removed. The height of the dam, once considered one of the highest earthen dams in the world, was reduced so construction of a wider road across the top of the dam (allowing two horse-drawn carriages to pass at the same time) could proceed. During the construction the size of the overflow spillway was reduced. A screen was added so water exiting the spillway would not carry any of the stocked black bass with it. To make matters worse, the center of the dam had a sag, making the center the lowest point of the dam and the most likely point of exit for high water.

It started to rain. It rained all day and night of 30 May 1889. By the next morning rivers were rising rapidly and carrying large pieces of debris. By mid-morning much of the town was already flooding, workers were sent home to be with their families, and schools were closed. Late in the morning the rain renewed with a vengeance, and by noon the residents were in the throes of Johnstown's worst recorded flood (McCullough 1968, 82). As people began moving to higher ground or out of town, bridges were being destroyed by the torrents and the town recorded its first flood victim ever. Stony Creek rose 18 inches (46 centimeters) an hour. Train service was interrupted because of flooded and washed-out tracks. The good news for Johnstown was that the South Fork Dam seemed to be holding. The scene up at the dam, however, was bleak. By eleven in the morning the water was even with the top of the dam, and small leaks had appeared on the dam face. In a short few minutes the water level of the reservoir dropped over 60 feet (18 meters) (Smith 1972, 172) and by 3:15 in the afternoon 20 million tons of water, similar in volume to the water flow over Niagara Falls, was on its way to Johnstown. In less than an hour 2,209 people were dead.

After the flood, aid came from around the world, and the town was rebuilt. The dead were buried in Grandview Cemetery, safe from any flooding 450 feet (137 meters) above the town on a hill overlooking Johnstown. One would like to believe that 90 years after the disaster, with weather-monitoring satellites, virtually instantaneous radio and television communication, and computer-assisted weather forecasting, flood damage would be minimal and loss of life nil. However, on 19-20 July 1977, up to 20 inches (50 centimeters) of rain fell in the hills east of Johnstown. Swollen rivers generated flash floods that broke earthen dams, and another group of statistics was added to Johnstown's history of floods: Almost 2,700 people were injured, 413 dwellings were destroyed, 5,400 dwellings were damaged, and 76 more graves were added at Grandview Cemetery, safe from flooding. In a candid review of operations in the aftermath of the flood, the National Oceanic and Atmospheric Administration concluded, "On the disastrous night of 19-20 July 1977, neither the National Weather Service component of the Flash Flood Warning System nor that part of it involving local communities and Civil Defense did much good for anyone in the Johnstown, Pennsylvania, area" (NOAA 1977, 59). It is unlikely that forecasting technology is the remedy for Johnstown's problems. One of the great ironies of the 1977 Johnstown flood is that those homeowners responsible and aware enough to build up on the hillsides, out of the floodplain, were unable to file insurance claims for flood damage. The reason? They didn't build in the floodplain!

Unfortunately, Johnstown is not unique. Almanacs list many floods in the United States, some associated with dams breaking, some not. One such example is Cherry Creek. After several earlier attempts a town was built up around a gold discovery at the confluence of Cherry Creek and South Platte Rivers in the Kansas Territory in 1858. Native Americans of the Cheyenne and Arapaho tribes warned the settlers about the likelihood of floods.

The time: April 1864. The scene: Two Native Americans of the Cheyenne and Arapaho tribes approach a gold panner along the Platte River, near Cherry Creek, not far from the site of today's Elitch Gardens, in Denver, Colorado. The conversation may have gone something like this:

Cheyenne:
Having any luck?

Settler:
Yeah, all bad. Everybody's findin' gold but me!

Arapaho:
That's really a shame, but we wanted to let you know that you and the other settlers are in real danger here from floods.

Settler:
C'mon, we gotta stay here 'cause this is where the gold is.

Cheyenne:
We know that; we've been here for hundreds of years. We've seen the gold, but we've also seen what the floods can do.

Settler:
Well, we can't move 'cause this is where the gold is.

Arapaho:
This year the snowpack is thicker than ever. People are even tying thin boards to their feet and sliding down on the snow. Not only that but it's been raining for the last two weeks.

Settler:
Look. I hear what you're saying and thanks for lettin' us know, but this is where the gold is.

Cheyenne [*to Arapaho as the two ride to safety out of the floodplain to the west, up to what is now Federal Boulevard, near Mile High Stadium, Denver*]:
Well, no one can say we didn't warn them.

Arapaho:
It's a shame they have to learn the hard way.

In Denver, Cherry Creek flooded on 19 April 1864. On 19-20 May 1864, heavy rains caused another flood on Cherry Creek, killing several people and destroying many buildings, including the city hall. As the Corps of Engineers writes, "Major floods hit the area hard and often between 1864 and 1965" (Corps of Engineers, 1966). Despite the floods Denver continued to grow in the floodplains of the South Platte and Cherry Creek. Three rivers (the South Platte, Cherry Creek, and Bear Creek) drain through Denver. 22 May 1876 saw another Cherry Creek flood, and exactly two years later another Cherry Creek flood wiped out most of the city's bridges. In 1885 Cherry Creek did it again, this time threatening the newly rebuilt city hall. Other floods followed in 1912 and 1922. In August 1933 a privately built dam at Castlewood (30 miles [48 kilometers] south of Denver) failed, sending floodwaters down Cherry Creek once again. Denverites had had enough. Rather than move or build levees, the city residents complained loudly and often to the federal government to take action. In 1950 the $15 million Cherry Creek Dam was built. So far, so good. Unfortunately, the dam did nothing to alleviate flood danger from the South Platte or Bear Creek.

The South Platte flooded in 1844, 1864, 1867, 1894, and 1921; just one month after the Castlewood dam failure the Platte reached its highest level, flooding downtown Denver for the second time that summer. In June 1965 the Platte washed away many buildings, destroyed several bridges, and caused $300 million in damages. By 1976 the Chatfield Dam had been completed at a cost of $86 million. In 1982 the Bear Creek Dam was completed at a cost of $61 million and the Tri-Lakes Project (to dam all three rivers that drain through Denver) of the Corps of Engineers was finally in place to protect Denver from the streams that helped create it.

Another example of catastrophe is that which occurred in Corning, New York. Although hurricanes are often considered a coastal phenomenon, the damage they cause is not restricted to areas along the ocean (a lesson recently learned by residents of the Appalachian Mountains that endured flooding from Hurricane Fran in September, 1996). Corning, New York, is about 300 miles from the nearest ocean. Yet, in June 1972, heavy rains associated with Hurricane Agnes soaked the town for five days, caused the Chemung River in Corning to overflow its banks and protective dikes. Eighteen people drowned, and $230 million of damage occurred. Like Johnstown, Corning is located on the floodplain of a river in a high-walled valley. Johnstown is located at the confluence of two rivers forming a third; Corning is located at the confluence of *three* rivers forming the Chemung. When the town was settled in 1835 the river was 100 yards wide. As the town grew in the floodplain, the river was confined, and protective flood walls were built to protect the city. Corning is located only 150 miles northeast of Johnstown, has similar topography, and shares a comparable geologic history; the Corning flood shouldn't have come as a surprise to anyone.

What is often lost during the settlement of a river valley is the understanding that the river is not moving through the valley by happenstance; the river created the valley through which it travels as well as the sediments that cover the valley floor. Also, often lost is the fact that the river is not in a fixed position in the valley. Although within the context of human history it may appear to stay in one place, within the context of geologic history it does not. The river not only cuts down through rocks to create its channel, it most likely meanders from side to side to create its floodplain. For a river to flood out of its channel is not an aberration but a normal part of the operation of a river system. The river did not create the problem, people created the problem by placing structures where the river traveled for the previous millenia.

Activity: Why Was Johnstown So Bad?

In this activity students will construct three profiles; one from the South Fork Dam to Johnstown along the axis of the Little Conemaugh River and South Fork, the second upstream from Johnstown through a narrow part of the Little Conemaugh River valley, and the third across the floodplain and valley in which Johnstown sits. Much like a bobsled sliding down a track, the water from South Fork Dam gained energy as it moved down the valley toward Johnstown. The first profile will show how the flood was able to gain so much energy by the time it struck Johnstown, and the second and third profiles will show that once the flood reached Johnstown (because of the artificial channeling, valley shape, and the bedrock below the river) the water had nowhere to go but up and out. Figure 5.2 is a composite prepared from the Johnstown, Geistown, and Nanty Glo, Pennsylvania, 7½ minute topographic maps. Figures 5.7, 5.8, and 5.9 are completed profiles. In this activity it is assumed students have already been instructed in the preparation of profiles from topographic maps.

Time

+ 2-3 class periods

Materials

+ a copy of figure 5.2 (A-L), topographic map of the Johnstown, Pennsylvania area for Profile A, for each pair of students
+ a copy of figure 5.3, assembly guide (to be used as a transparency or handout)
+ a copy of figure 5.4, topographic map for Profile B, for each pair of students
+ a copy of figure 5.5, topographic map for Profile C, for each pair of students
+ a copy of figure 5.6, reduced topographic index map of profiles, for each pair of students
+ graph paper (portions of a roll work best, but sheets taped together can also be used)
+ pencils and erasers (I always insist that my students prepare graphs and profiles in pencil; too often they want to use markers, resulting in a sloppy job and mistakes that cannot be corrected easily or neatly.)
+ transparent tape
+ scissors

Grouping

+ pairs of students

Directions

1. Tell the students they will be preparing three profiles. Profile A will be down the axis of South Fork Creek and the Little Conemaugh River through Johnstown, showing the path the floodwaters took and the significant change in elevation of the water. Profile A will be prepared from figure 5.2. Distribute copies of figures 5.2 (A-L) to each pair of students. Figure 5.2 is a large topographic map and will need to be assembled from the twelve sections supplied. Figure 5.3 shows how the sections fit together edge to edge. Make certain students have their graph paper, pencils, and erasers once they have taped together the twelve sections of figure 5.2.

2. Profile B will be across the axis of the Little Conemaugh River showing the narrowness of the river canyon through which the floodwaters moved. (See fig. 5.4.) Profile C will be through Grandview Cemetery (where the flood victims were buried), Johnstown, and the opposite hill, showing the wide floor and steep walls of the valley in which Johnstown is located, through which the flood ultimately passed and because of which the victims had nowhere to run. (See fig. 5.5.)

3. Review the preparation of the profiles and scale with the class. Discuss the elevation differences they will have to represent and how to scale them. Also discuss the concepts of vertical exaggeration (which enhances elevation differences) and true scale (no exaggeration). Decide whether the profiles should be done at true scale or with vertical exaggeration. (You might want students to do both true scale and exaggerated scale profiles to better demonstrate the concept of exaggeration.)

4. Figure 5.6 is an overview of the completed mosaic of topographic maps, the lines of all three profiles and the locations of detailed maps used for Profiles B and C. (See figures 5.4 and 5.5, respectively.)

5. When the students have completed the profiles display them around the room and have the class act as a jury, either giving critical, constructive comments or allowing them to determine the grades. If you choose the latter option, discuss the grading criteria (e.g., neatness, appropriate scale, completeness, quality of artwork).

6. Figures 5.7, 5.8, and 5.9 (on pages 108, 109, and 110) are completed profiles. Discuss what the profiles indicate about the flood. The long, steep hill the flood traveled gave it tremendous energy by the time it reached Johnstown (Profile A). The narrow valley of the Little Conemaugh River allowed the water to reach high up the valley walls, destroying everything, like the railroads, that were built alongside the river (Profile B). At Johnstown, the energy, carried debris, and volume of water combined to devastate everything built on the flat valley floor (Profile C).

Activity: What About My Town?

Unfortunately, many cities are vulnerable to floods. In this activity students can evaluate the possible flood risk in their own town by examining how floods of different heights could affect essential services and evacuation routes.

Time

+ 3 class periods

Materials

+ topographic map of the area of your city (if a river flows nearby; if not, agree as a group on an appropriate city to study)
+ an overhead transparency of the critical portion of the map (or use an opaque projector)
+ photocopies of the topographic map for each pair of students
+ 3 colored pencils (red, yellow, blue) for each pair of students
+ the brochure "Topographic Map Symbols," available from the Map Sales Agency (see Introduction)

Grouping

+ pairs of students

Directions

1. Distribute materials to each pair of students.

2. Provide students the locations of critical services: police, fire, water and electrical supply, sewage treatment, schools, hospitals, and important stores. Have them locate the services on their copies of the topographic maps. If the map is for your own town, have students locate their homes as well.

Text continues on page 107.

Fig. 5.2A. Sections of the Topographic Map to Be Assembled as the Profile A Base Map (A-L).
From *American History Through Earth Science*. © 1997 Craig A. Munsart. Teacher Ideas Press. (800) 237-6124.

Fig. 5.2B.

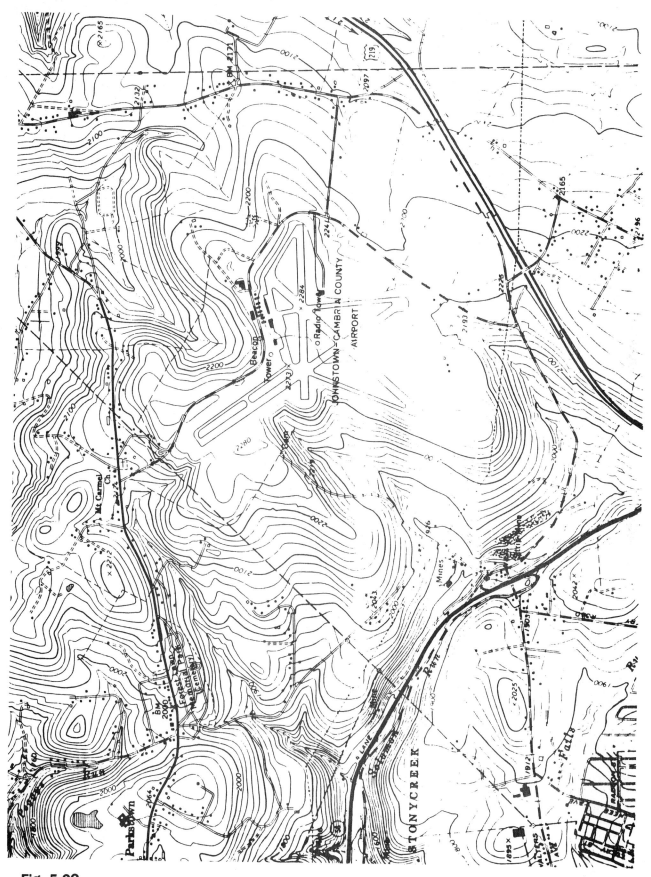

Fig. 5.2C.

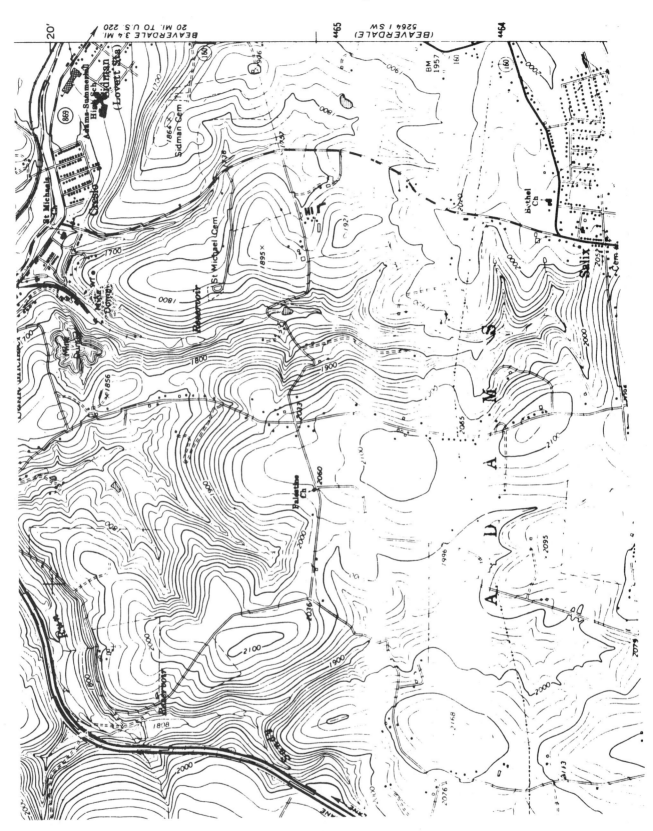

Fig. 5.2D.

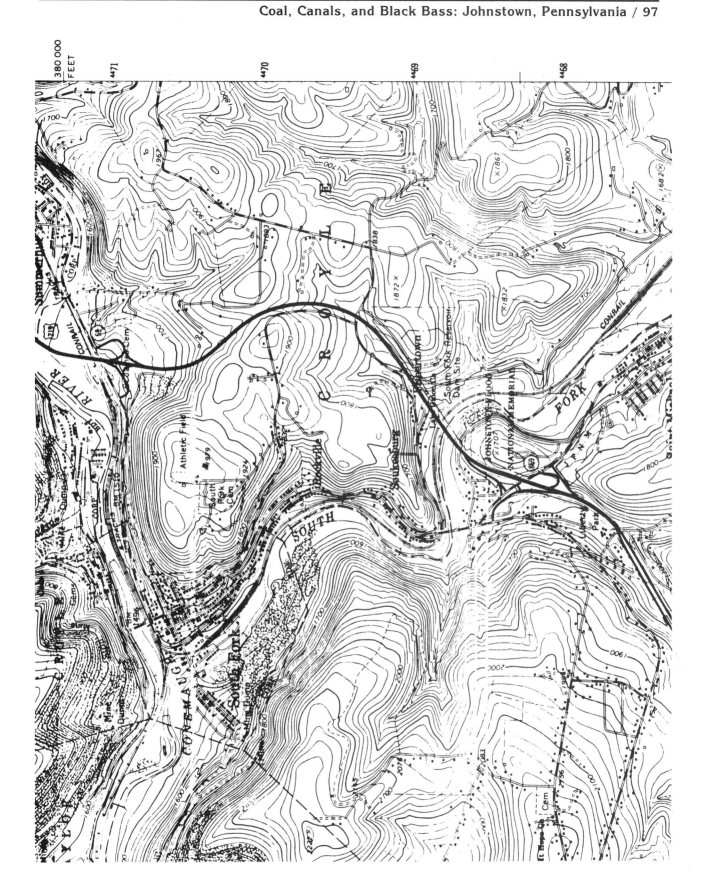

Fig. 5.2E.

Fig. 5.2F.

Fig. 5.2G.

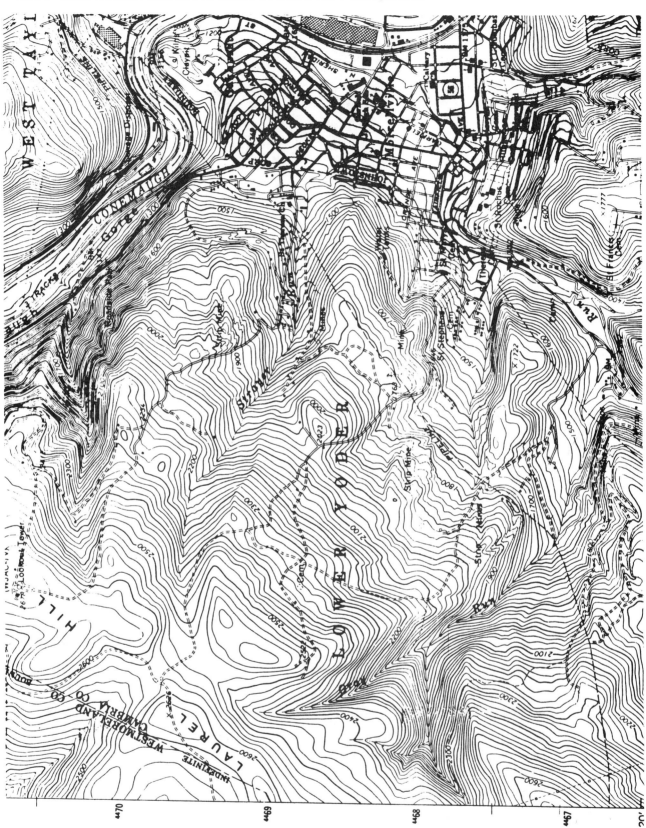

Fig. 5.2H.

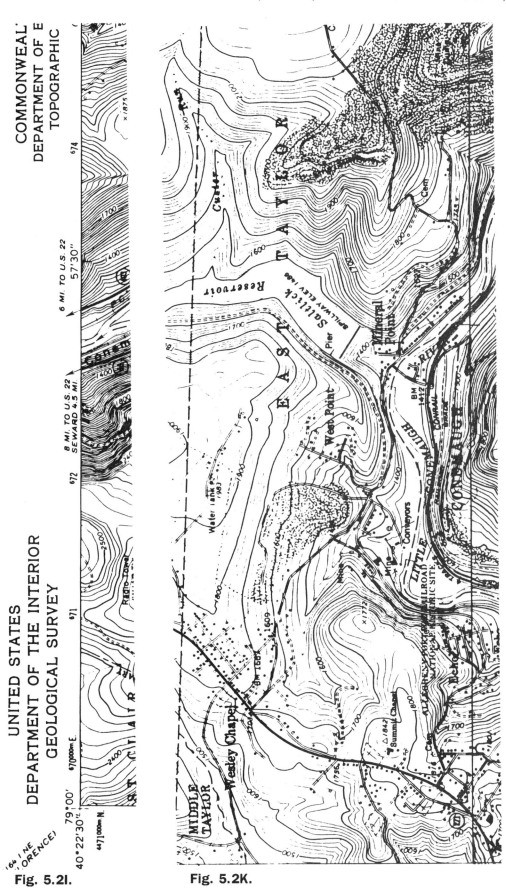

Fig. 5.2I.

Fig. 5.2K.

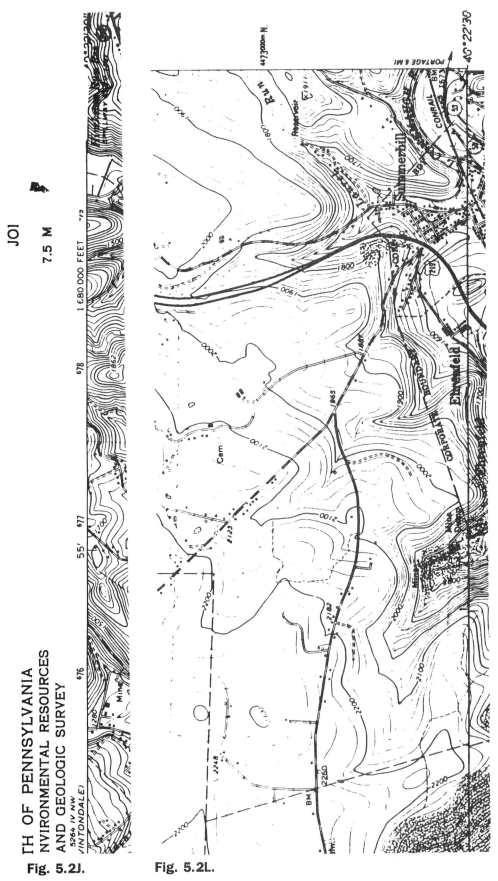

Fig. 5.2J.   **Fig. 5.2L.**

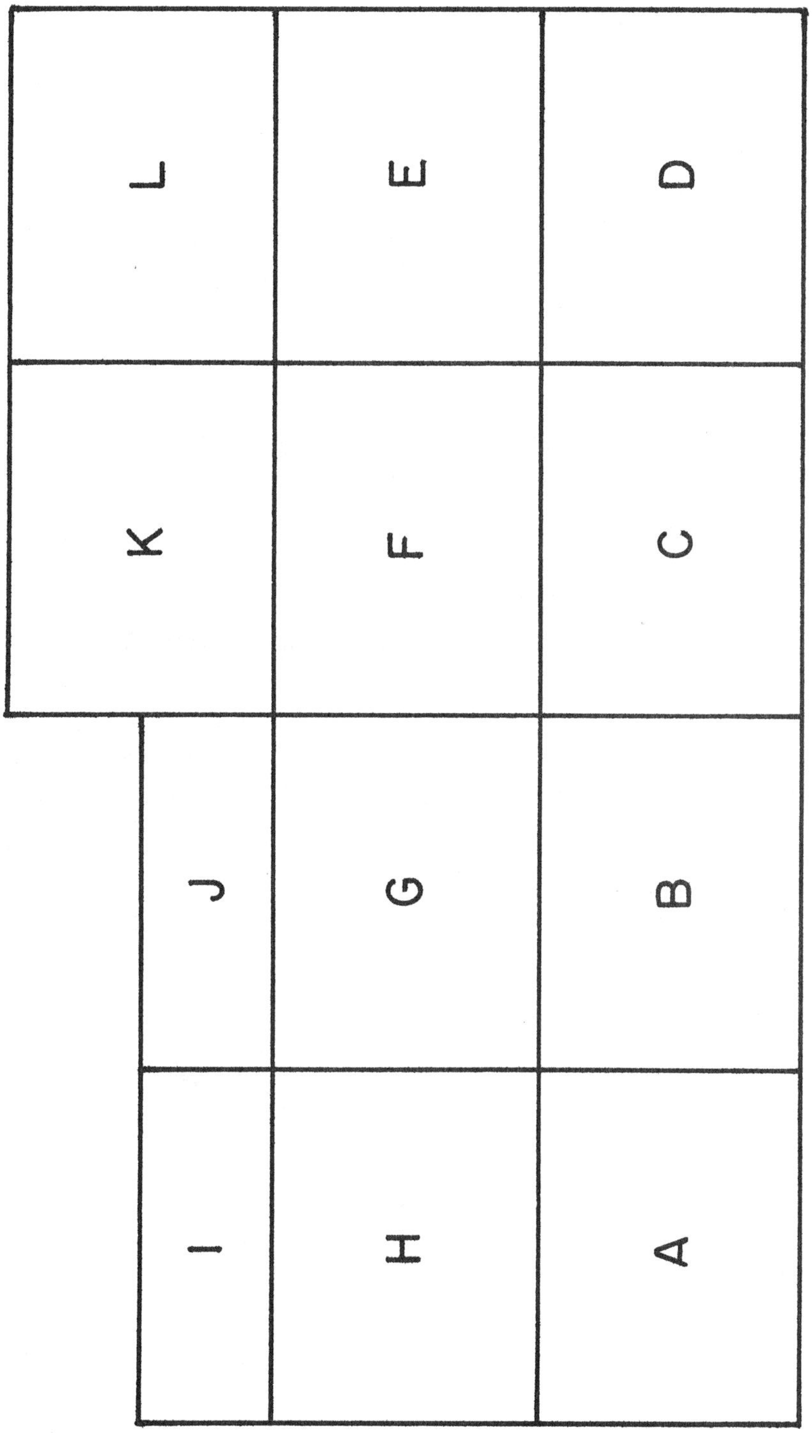

L	E	D
K	F	C
J	G	B
I	H	A

Fig. 5.3. Template for Assembly of Figure 5.2 (A-L).

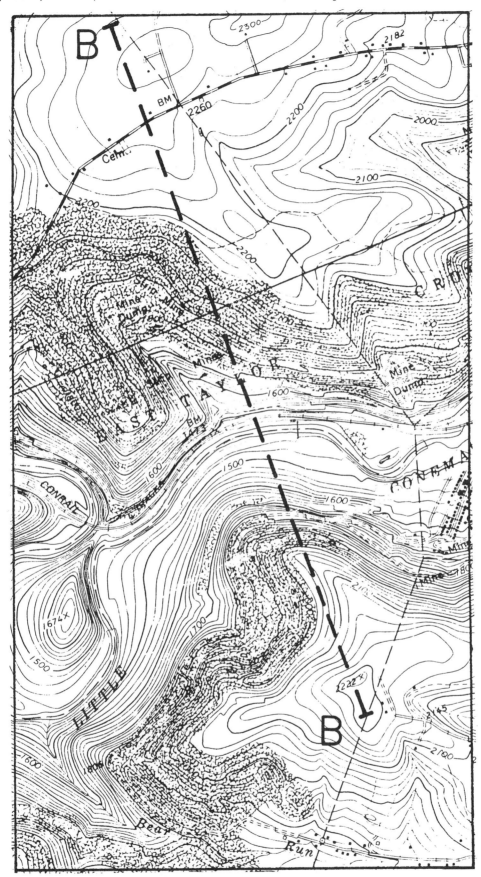

Fig. 5.4. Topographic Map Across the Little Conemaugh River (Profile B).

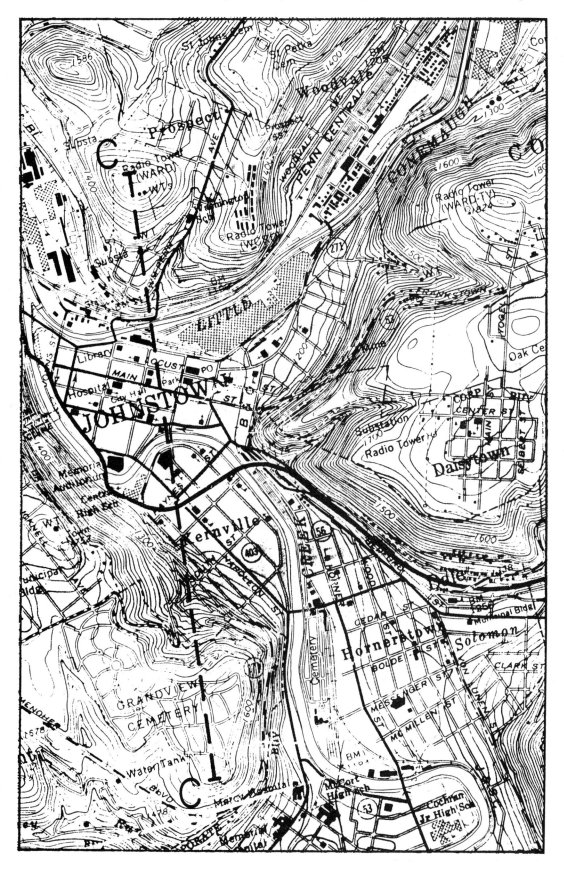

Fig. 5.5. Topographic Map Across the Valley of Johnstown (Profile C).

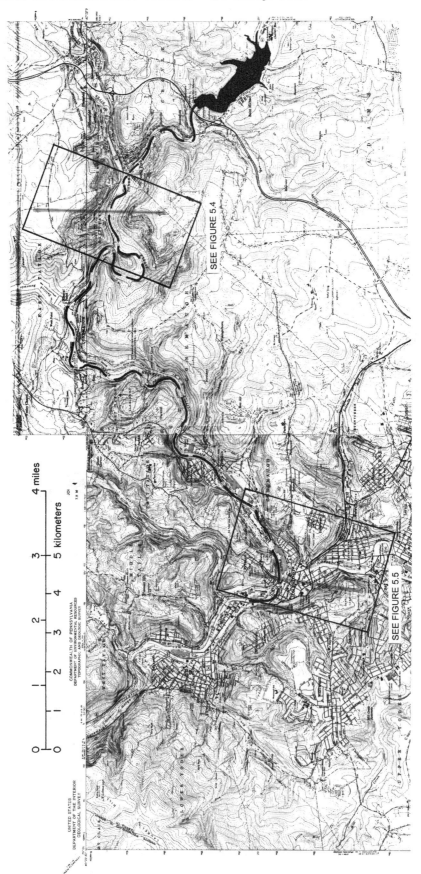

Fig. 5.6. Assembled Topographic Map of Figure 5.2, Showing the Locations of Figures 5.4 and 5.5.

3. Give the students three flood alerts: 10 feet above normal level, 20 feet above normal, and 30 feet above normal. For each alert, the students must
   a. color the affected area on the topographic map (use a different color for each alert);
   b. determine what, if any, areas of the city need to be evacuated;
   c. determine what evacuation routes will be used;
   d. determine what critical services will be affected; and
   e. determine how the missing critical services can be replaced.

Extensions

Using the topographic maps students can build models of the topography of a particular area and demonstrate the flood potential. Models can be made of waterproof materials such as styrofoam or wood, or built of cardboard and waterproofed with varnish. Important buildings can be located using library resources or by writing to chambers of commerce or newspapers. Stream tables can be used to demonstrate river flow patterns. Artificial channels can be duplicated using clay.

REFERENCES

Corning Glass Works. *The Flood and the Community.* Corning, N.Y.: Corning Glass Works, 1976.

Jones, William C., and Kenton Forrest. *Denver: A Pictorial History.* Boulder, Colo.: Pruett, 1985.

Levy, Matthys, and Mario Salvadori. *Why Buildings Fall Down.* New York: W. W. Norton, 1992.

McCullough, David. *The Johnstown Flood.* New York: Simon & Schuster, 1968.

National Oceanic and Atmospheric Administration. *Johnstown, Pennsylvania Flash Flood of July 19-20, 1977.* Natural Disaster Survey Report 77-1. Rockville, Md.: U.S. Department of Commerce, 1977.

National Park Service. *Johnstown Flood National Memorial.* Washington, D.C.: U.S. Government Printing Office, 1993.

Phalen, W. C. *Geologic Atlas of the United States, Johnstown Folio.* Folio Number 174. Washington, D.C.: U.S. Geological Survey, 1910.

Smith, Norman. *A History of Dams.* New York: The Citadel Press, 1972.

Trefil, James. *Meditations at Sunset.* New York: Charles Scribner's Sons, 1987.

U.S. Army Corps of Engineers. *The Tri-Lakes Project, Colorado.* Omaha District. Washington, D.C.: U.S. Government Printing Office, 1992.

World Almanac and Book of Facts. New York: Pharos Books, 1992.

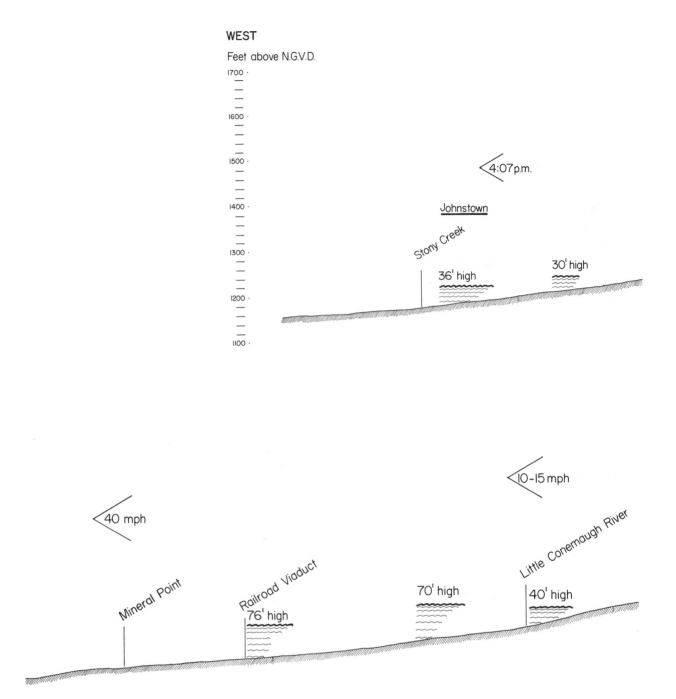

Fig. 5.7. Longitudinal Profile Along the Little Conemaugh River (Profile A).

From *American History Through Earth Science.* © 1997 Craig A. Munsart. Teacher Ideas Press. (800) 237-6124.

PROFILE A

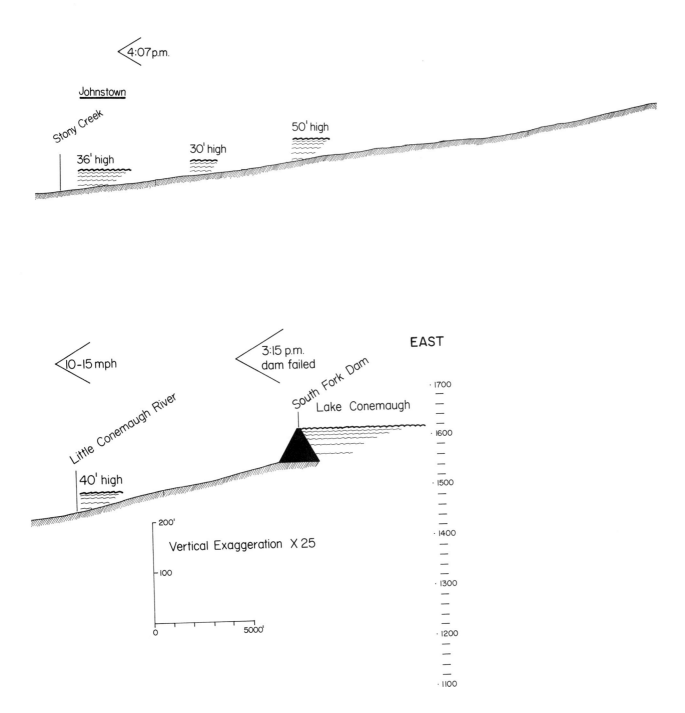

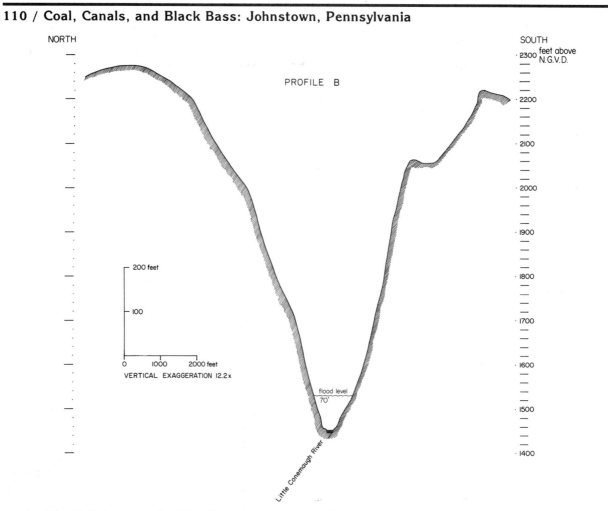

Fig. 5.8. Longitudinal Profile Along the Little Conemaugh River (Profile B).

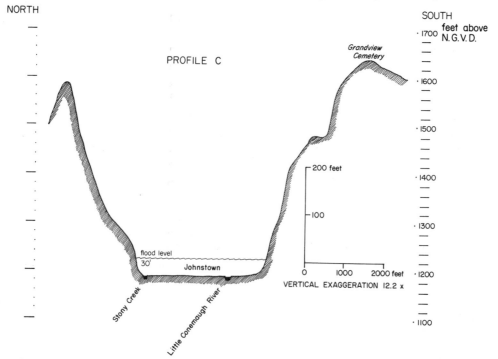

Fig. 5.9. Longitudinal Profile Through the Valley at the City of Johnstown (Profile C).

From *American History Through Earth Science.* © 1997 Craig A. Munsart. Teacher Ideas Press. (800) 237-6124.

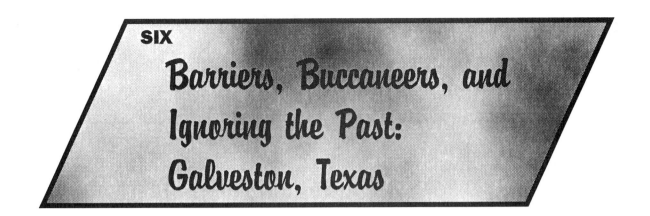

SIX

Barriers, Buccaneers, and Ignoring the Past: Galveston, Texas

In his book *Galveston: A History* David McComb offers a comprehensive history of the island and the city. The brief history provided here establishes a background for the natural events described in this chapter.

The native Karankawas called Galveston Island "Auia." The sixteenth-century Spaniards called it "Malhado," meaning the isle of doom (McComb 1986, 5). Four hundred years later nature would prove the clairvoyance of the Spaniards and create the greatest natural disaster the United States has experienced.

Fresh from his heroic exploits with Andrew Jackson at the Battle of New Orleans, and bearing a pardon from President Monroe absolving him and his men from former crimes of piracy, Jean Lafitte established a large settlement (with more than 200 buildings) on a sandy island off the southeastern Texas coast originally called Campechy (and later Galvez' Town, after Bernardo de Galvez, viceroy of Mexico and the former Spanish governor of Louisiana; McComb 1986, 5). The island was an ideal base from which Lafitte could continue his lucrative pirate activities, specializing in attacking ships and capturing slaves. In 1818, one of the earliest documented hurricanes in the area destroyed Lafitte's base and his influence in the Gulf of Mexico. Three years later Lafitte and his men disappeared.

Because of its natural port (the best along the Gulf Coast between Veracruz and New Orleans, McComb 1986, 8) Galveston became home to the Texas Navy during the war of independence with Mexico. It would have been Texas's last point of defense if the Mexican Army had won at the battle of San Jacinto. From the mid- to late-1800s the population of Galveston steadily increased. The port was a major export center for cotton, animal hides, sugar, molasses, cattle, pecans, and cottonseed to the East Coast cities of the United States and to Great Britain (McComb 1986, 47). By the end of the 1800s, however, Houston was establishing itself as a commercial center. It was on the mainland, closer to the newly developing oil fields, encouraging of the influx of manufacturing facilities, and far more capable of attracting investment capital than Galveston. Why? Potential investors were well aware of the vulnerability of Galveston and its history of floods and hurricanes. In 1876 a Galveston newcomer advised, "There are to-day untold millions of Northern capital looking southward for investment, of which Galveston would receive her legitimate proportion if we could offer a reasonable argument that the island will not one day be washed away" (McComb 1986, 48).

VULNERABLE BARRIERS

Galveston Island is one of the many barrier islands along the Atlantic and Gulf Coasts of the United States. Barrier islands are part of the natural evolution of coastal systems, where combinations of wind, tide, currents, sand supply, and water depth allow them to be formed. One reason they are called barriers is because they bear the brunt of the erosional energy of the oceans and consequently act as a barrier to mainland damage. The United States has hundreds of miles of barrier island systems protecting the heavily populated Atlantic and Gulf Coasts. By its very nature, the shape and existence of a barrier island is subject to the vagaries of the ocean and the weather; in short, it moves up and down, front to back, and side to side. That Galveston Island, Texas, is an unstable landmass that can be documented by comparisons of topographic maps representing more than 40 years of coastline changes. Figures 6.1 and 6.2 are a series of maps that show the eastern (The Jetties) and western (San Luis Pass) ends of Galveston Island. Morton (1974) also documents changes along the Galveston Island portion of the Texas shoreline.

Anyone with minimal technical background can see that locating large, permanent structures for people on an elongated pile of shifting sand and mud barely above sea level could be risky. Add the information that the unstable pile is sinking slowly into the sea and is located in an area that experiences storms generating very high winds and dramatic local increases in sea level, and the concept of locating permanent structures of residence there becomes absurd. Yet from the eastern end of Long Island, New York, to the southern end of Padre Island, Texas, the number of permanent structures on barrier islands has been increasing at an alarming rate. Coastal areas across the United States have population densities five times the national average (Williams, Dodd, and Gohn 1991, 2) with much of that population trying to squeeze onto a precarious, narrow strip of land surrounded by water. In 1995 half of the population of the United States lived in areas along the eastern coast prone to flooding by hurricanes (Catalano 1995, 66); a disaster waiting to happen.

The entire coastal area of the eastern United States is vulnerable to hurricanes, from Brownsville, Texas at the border with Mexico, to northern New England. In September 1938, with little warning, an intense, rapidly moving hurricane struck the coasts of Eastern Long Island, New York and southern New England. By the time the storm had passed northward through Quebec, Canada, 700 people had died and 63,000 were homeless. In 1972 Hurricane Agnes caused 117 deaths and millions of dollars in damage along the east coast and up into central New York and Pennsylvania (Arnold 1988, 33-40). Despite the fact that a hurricane caused the largest natural death toll in the United States we are comparatively "lucky." Similar storms in the Pacific (where they are called cyclones) have killed hundreds of thousands of people in southern Asia. For example, November 1970, 300,000 people died in Bangladesh when a cyclone struck.

Geologic Profile

For approximately one-half mile (0.8 km) below the surface Galveston Island is merely a stack of layers of waterlogged sand, shells, silt, and mud (as shown in fig. 6.3); older layers date back to when large sheets of ice covered much of North America. It is a pile of loose materials heaped up by previous storms, waves, and currents, and it is completely at their mercy.

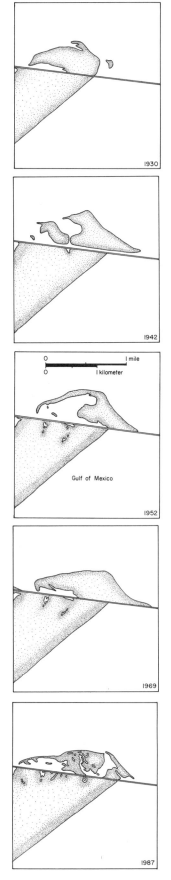

In addition to the inherent instability of such materials the Galveston area has been sinking into the sea at approximately 0.6 inches (1.5 centimeters) per year. Some of it is due to human activities, but much of it is due merely to the compression of mud, silt, and sand by the material above it. As the pile of materials that is Galveston Island gets thicker the water is squeezed out of the lower layers and the entire stack compresses even further. Even the seawall, built to protect the island from hurricanes, has been sinking ever since the earliest parts of it were built. Parts have sunk as much as 5 feet (1.5 meters), and the sinking continues today (U.S. Army Corps of Engineers 1981, 22). As sea level rises due to the effects of atmospheric warming the stability of the Texas coastal area becomes even more precarious.

The Houston and Galveston Bay areas are underlain by layers of rock filled with both hydrocarbons (oil and gas) and water. These fluids are contained within pores, or spaces in the rock, and help support the rock layers above them. As the fluids are removed from underground, the layers of rock compact, causing the level of the surface to subside. In the area of Baytown, Texas (on the north end of Galveston Bay), subsidence on the order of 6-8 feet (1.8-2.4 meters) has allowed inundation of homes (Canby 1980, 146-47). As the population of the southeastern Texas coast increases, so does the use of water. As the land surface becomes lower, the erosional effects of the surrounding bodies of water (such as wave and storm erosion) are exacerbated. To date, Galveston Island has been affected only little by subsurface fluid withdrawal from the area to the north, but as that subsidence continues it will likely extend toward Galveston (Morton 1974, 22). In addition, faults in the Galveston Bay area have been mobilized by subsidence. Such faults exists on Galveston Island (Kreitler 1978, 6) and may increase the effects of subsidence.

Astronomic Profile

Mean tidal range along the Gulf Coast is about 1.5-2.0 feet (45-60 centimeters). The range in the bays is much lower, approximately 0.5 feet (15 centimeters). On a daily basis tides move much coarse material between the bays and the Gulf of Mexico (Morton and McGowen 1980, 89), much of that material going to replenish sand in the barrier systems. Hurricanes often have a storm surge ten times higher than the tidal range and in several hours can move more material than a year's worth of tides.

Fig. 6.1. Changes in the Topography of the East End of Galveston Island: The Jetties.

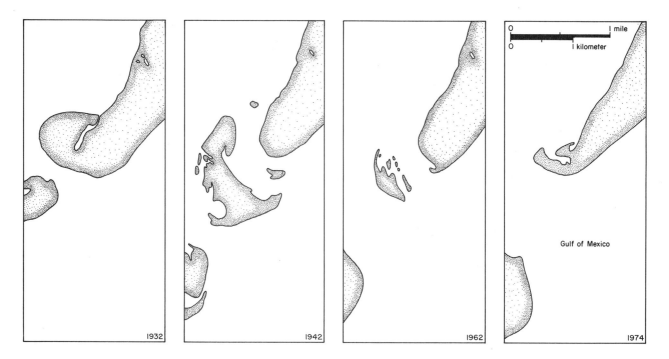

Fig. 6.2. Changes in the Topography of the West End of Galveston Island: San Luis Pass.

Meteorologic Profile

Hurricanes and tropical storms strike the Texas coast on an average of once every one and a half years (Hayes 1967, 7). Between 1900 and 1963 14 tropical storms (with maximum winds between 38 and 74 miles per hour [60-118 kph]) and 28 hurricanes (with maximum winds exceeding 74 miles per hour [118 kph]) struck the Texas coast. Figure 6.4 shows where and when such storms crossed the coastline. It is likely that similar frequencies, although largely undocumented, occurred during preceding centuries as well.

In August of 1900 a tropical depression formed in the Atlantic Ocean off the West African coast. As it moved westward, driven by prevailing winds, it gained energy from the warm tropical ocean waters and rapidly grew from a tropical storm and then a hurricane. It entered the Caribbean near the Island of Antiqua and continued west. After crossing Jamaica the storm turned north.

The Human Factor

As figure 6.3 shows the highest elevations on a barrier island are those of the sand dunes. As dynamic as dunes are they provide the best (and only protection) from the actions of wind and water which act to destroy the barrier island. In parts of eastern Long Island, New York, it is not only illegal to build on the dunes but to walk on the dunes. In the 1800s the U.S. Army Corps of Engineers removed 12-15 foot (3.5-5 meter) high dunes on Galveston to fill in low areas such as bayous (Morton and McGowen 1980, 131). The seawall that is now in place (also built by the Army Corps of Engineers) to protect Galveston is approximately the same height as the dunes that existed before humans built a city where they once stood.

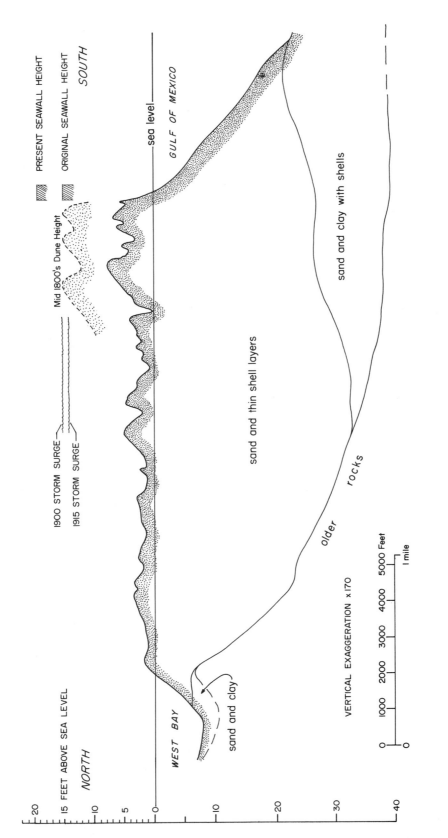

Fig. 6.3. A Cross Section of Galveston Island.

Note: Adapted from Robert A. Marten and J. H. McGowen, *Modern Depositional Environments of the Texas Gulf Coast*. Austin, Tex.: Bureau of Economic Geology, 1980, p. 131.

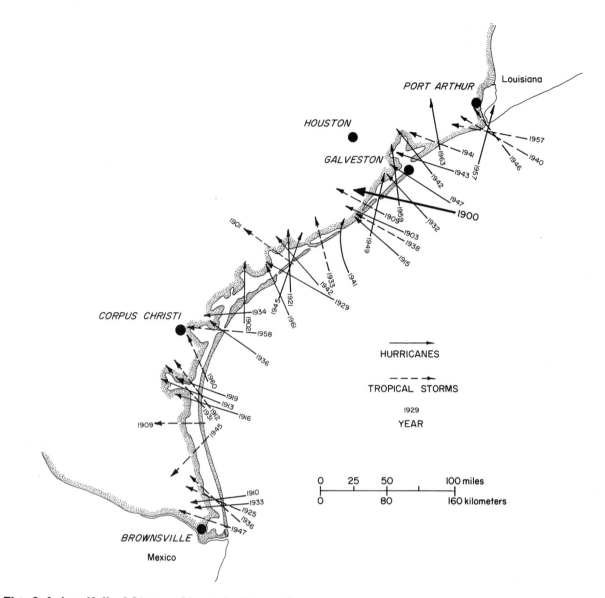

Fig. 6.4. Landfall of Storms Along the Texas Coast.

Note: Adapted from Miles O. Hayes, *Hurricanes As Geological Agents: Case Studies of Hurricanes Carla, 1961, and Cindy, 1963.* Report of Investigations Number 61. Austin, Tex.: Bureau of Economic Geology, 1967, p. 8.

Rivers bring erosional materials such as sand and silt to the sea, where actions of waves, winds, and currents can create barrier islands. Construction of dams along Texas rivers over the last 50 years has reduced dramatically the amount of island-building materials carried into Galveston Bay, from approximately 250 million cubic feet (7 million cubic meters) per year in 1936 to approximately 50 million cubic feet (1.4 million cubic meters) per year in 1975 (Morton and McGowen 1980, 92).

A subsiding and low-lying barrier bar system is simply a poor place to locate a permanent settlement. As W. J. McGee wrote of Galveston almost 100 years ago, "no worse coast-stretch for foundations exists in the world" (1900, 378).

Ignoring the historical record of human and property damage (in the virtually identical area of earlier storms) settlement and building construction was initiated at an unprecedented rate prior to the hurricane that hit Galveston in 1900. As McGee continues, "The makers of Galveston erred in building their houses on the sands, in planting their city within reach of the waves, in domiciling their helpless ones on a sinking coast . . ." (1900, 383).

Unfortunately, more than 6,000 Galvestonians died in the 1900 storm; McGee's description of the errors of the builders of Galveston applies today to barrier islands from New York to Texas; in ninety-five years we have apparently learned very little. McGee's final warning after the 1900 hurricane has been unheeded: "As they turn toward the future . . . their fellow-citizens have the right to be spared the shock of the inevitable disaster which would follow rebuilding on their devastated sand bank" (1900, 383).

HURRICANES

Hurricanes are intense, large-scale, low-pressure weather systems with a wide variety of associated phenomena capable of creating severe damage: high, counter-clockwise winds; low barometric pressure; heavy rains; tornadic activity; and thunderstorms with associated electrical activity. Low-lying coastal areas are particularly vulnerable to such processes. Those hurricanes that strike the U.S. Atlantic and Gulf Coasts form off the west coast of Africa and migrate west and north (Coch 1994, 41) in response to atmospheric circulation systems and the rotation of Earth.

Hurricanes incorporate two wind systems. The first consists of the high-velocity rotational winds associated with the low-pressure system (rotating counter-clockwise in the Northern Hemisphere). The second results from the interaction with other atmospheric winds and controls the direction the storm is moving (hence the name steering winds; Coch 1995, 117). As a hurricane moves landward the speed of forward movement of the storm combines with the velocity of the wind, making the forward, right quadrant of the system the most intense. High wind velocities create the flood (storm) surge that causes the most devastating damage to coastal cities. The flood surge is a doming of the water surface created by wind shear as the storm drives onshore. Low atmospheric pressure contributes only a small portion of the sea level rise, and is localized in the eye of the storm. Although the atmospheric contribution may be a local rise in sea level of 1-2 feet (0.3-0.6 meters) the flood surge may be more than 20 feet (6 meters). Contributing factors to the severity of the flood surge are: (a) wind speed, (b) central pressure, (c) slope and width of the continental shelf, (d) tidal stage, (e) shoreline configuration, (f) human coastal modification, and (g) impact angle (Coch 1994, 46; 1995, 120).

A second rise in sea level, the ebb surge, occurs as water impounded by the flood surge returns seaward, aided by the winds on the left side of the storm. The ebb surge causes only a fraction of the sea level rise of the storm surge but can affect structures damaged earlier in the storm and may follow low paths to the "backside" of an apparently protected area.

On September 8, 1900 a hurricane bore down on Galveston, Texas, where all the factors combined to create the highest death toll of any U.S. natural disaster.

For the residents of Galveston the hurricane could not have struck at a worse place or time:

a. The eye passed west of Galveston Island, placing the area of maximum winds near the city of Galveston.

b. The storm struck nearly perpendicular to the coast.

c. The shallow continental shelf off the coast added to an already high storm surge created by the winds.

d. The storm struck during high tide.

e. Removal of the dunes to provide fill eliminated natural protection.

f. The geometry of Galveston Bay and Galveston Island exacerbated the effects of the ebb surge.

g. Summer tourists increased the population.

h. Warning and evacuation procedures were ineffective.

THE STORMY PAST

Undoubtedly, hurricanes made their landfall near what was to become Galveston for hundreds of years before the island was home to permanent settlements. At least eleven hurricanes struck during the 1800s alone— 1810, 1815, 1818— and the town was rebuilt, in the same place, each time.

In October 1837 another major hurricane demolished the rebuilt settlement on Galveston: "Every house, camp, sod house, and inhabited structure was swept away, except the Old Mexican customhouse . . ." (Hughes 1990, 6) Twenty-nine of thirty boats were torn from their moorings and driven aground or washed out to sea. Eight days later the same storm demolished a new paddle-wheeled steamer near Cape Hatteras, North Carolina, drowning 90 of 130 passengers (only two life preservers were carried aboard; after that federal law required a life preserver be available for every passenger). After the 1837 storm one observer commented, "I take for granted that Galveston is done up. . . . The roads may be well enough for vessels to ride in, but the land will hereafter, be regarded as a dangerous place for a city or even a residence. . . . As sure as there is a God, the whole of Galveston will be swept away within ten years" (McComb 1980, 28). Six more hurricanes struck between 1842 and 1871.

In September 1875 high water from a hurricane almost covered Galveston. The city of Indianola, 113 miles (182 kilometers) to the southwest, was almost annihilated by that same storm; only 12 of 110 buildings survived. In August 1886 two other hurricanes struck the Galveston area, causing additional loss of property and life; Indianola again received substantial damage. This time the residents of Indianola had had enough: They abandoned the town (McComb 1980, 30). Finally, in 1878, the city of Galveston took action to minimize the disastrous damage from hurricanes; they planted salt cedar trees to help stabilize the sand dunes (McComb 1986, 30).

By the summer of 1900, Galveston was the fourth largest city in Texas, with a population of 37,789 (Hughes 1976, 1990), 44 steamship companies, train service to the mainland, 40 miles of electric streetcar lines, 2,028 telephones and 2 automobiles. As the low pressure system of the 1900 hurricane moved across Cuba it was blocked by a high pressure system in the eastern United States. Prevailing trade winds drove the storm westward. As it approached the Texas Gulf Coast a weaker low-pressure system was moving eastward through the central United States. The hurricane turned northward to join the second low pressure system; in doing so it crossed Galveston Island. On September 8, 1900, a hurricane with winds of 100 miles (160 kilometers) per hour created a storm surge of 20 feet (6 meters), 6-9 feet (2-3 meters) higher than any previously recorded flood. Water was pushed northward (storm surge) over the island from the Gulf of Mexico and southward (ebb surge) over the island from Galveston Bay. Horror stories abounded as people frantically (and often vainly) tried to save their lives as well as those of family members (Hughes 1976). Pieces of roofing slate, used to replace wood shingles for fire safety, became deadly projectiles as they were pushed along by the high winds. The railroad causeway and wagon bridge to the mainland were destroyed. Ships were moved tens of miles inland. Debris, created and swept inland by the storm, piled up like a retaining wall at the downtown area, fortuitously protecting it from total destruction. Water swept over the entire island, killing between 6,000 and 8,000 people and destroying 3,500 houses and property worth approximately $20 million. The death toll is uncertain because a physical count of bodies was impossible; the number was determined by the difference between an earlier census and a subsequent count of the survivors. To complicate matters the seasonal influx of tourists made prestorm numbers uncertain.

After devastating Galveston the storm continued north and east finally leaving North America through Newfoundland: from Antigua the storm traveled over 4,000 miles in approximately 14 days.

Other hurricanes followed the 1900 storm through Galveston.

- 1909, five dead $99,000 in damages.

- 1915, eight dead, $4-$5 million in damages.

- 1919, 1949, 1957.

- In 1961 Hurricane Carla, despite advance warnings, killed six people destroyed 120 buildings and caused damage between $15 -$18 million.

- In 1983 Hurricane Alicia caused property damage of approximately $300 million.

- 19??

- 20??

Activity: Where's It Going?

Even today, with satellites, radar, and airplanes flying into a hurricane itself, long-term predictions of the path of a hurricane are less accurate than one would like. In 1900 none of the above existed. Even radio communication was unavailable. It wasn't until 1905 that the U.S. Weather Bureau began receiving weather reports from ships at sea. On Galveston Island itself, communication had not advanced much beyond the "one if by land, two if by sea" signal given from Boston's Old North Church during the American Revolution. To a large degree, forecasting consisted of looking at a barometer and out the window. In the case of the 1900 Galveston hurricane, by the time the Weather Bureau in Washington telegraphed a definitive warning to the city, the streets were already flooding.

In the following activity students will plot the track of the 1900 storm at various times during its path and try to predict its landfall based on bearing and velocity. *Note: This activity will work only if students do not know in advance that the hurricane will hit Galveston, Texas. Do not share the history of the area with the class until after the conclusion of the activity.*

Much like forecasters do today students will determine landfall based on probability or likelihood. Students will use a 200 mile (320 kilometer) template (fig. 6.5) to determine landfall. The center 30 mile (48 kilometer) section is the lowest probability landfall (10 percent probability); the center 75 miles (120 kilometers) is a section that is more likely (25 percent probability); and the 150-mile center section (240 kilometers) is still more likely (50 percent probability). There is a 75 percent probability the storm will strike somewhere within the 200 mile template.

Time

+ several class periods

Materials

+ protractor or compass
+ scale (made from the scale on the map)
+ colored pencils
+ a copy of template figure 6.5 (presented at the same scale as the map, figure 6.6 for each student or pair)
+ a copy of figure 6.6 (base map) for each student or pair
+ a copy of table 6.1 for each student or pair
+ figure 6.7 prepared as transparency
+ calculator
+ blank paper to be turned in as part of the completed assignment

Grouping

+ individuals or pairs

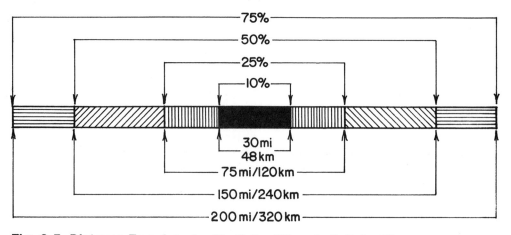

Fig. 6.5. Distance Template for "Activity: Where's It Going?"

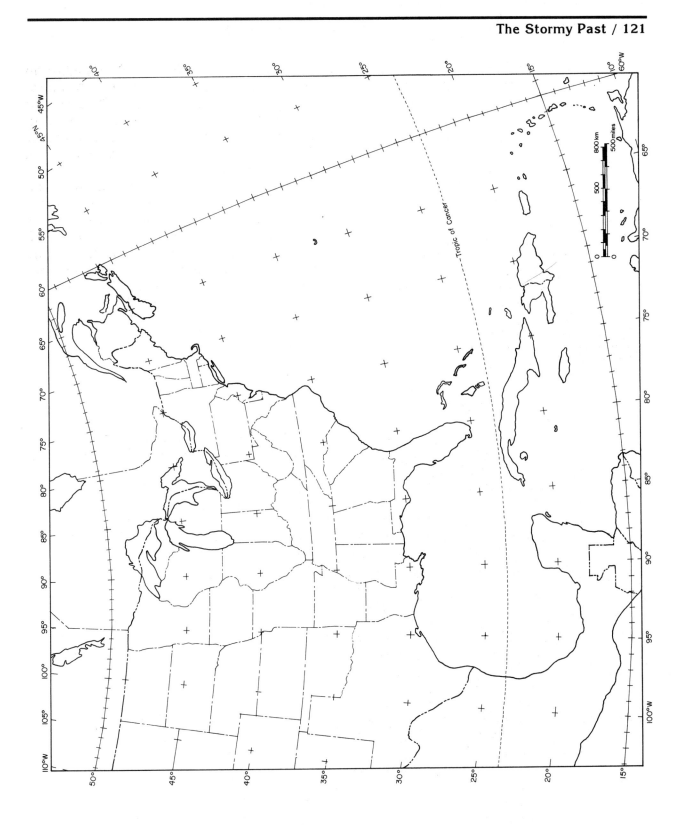

Fig. 6.6. Base Map for "Activity: Where's It Going?"

Directions

    1. Give each student (or pair of students) a copy of the base map (fig. 6.6). You might want to enlarge the map to fit on a larger piece of paper (e.g., 11" x 17"). A linear scale has been provided so that measurements using the scale will be valid independent of enlargement. Review the map with the class, discussing scales and what is shown (e.g., longitude, latitude, state boundaries). Discuss how, because of the map projection (Chamberlin Trimetric Projection), the parallels (lines of latitude) are evenly spaced, but the distance between meridians (lines of longitude) narrows as they converge toward the North Pole. As students plot longitude they must, therefore, be careful because the distances between meridians change. The overall longitude–latitude grid is shown by a small cross at 5-degree intervals. Individual degrees are also marked along the 15th and 50th parallel and the 60-degree meridian. For reference the Tropic of Cancer (23° 27' north) is also shown.

    2. Give each student (or pair of students) a copy of table 6.1. *Do not show students the completed version of the table.* Instruct them not to lose their copy of the table because they will be filling it in as the activity progresses. Review the column headings with the students:

        a. *Date.* The morning the position of the storm was taken.

        b. *Location description.* A location relative to a landmass or city.

        c. *West longitude.* Position relative to the Greenwich Meridian (degrees and minutes).

        d. *North latitude.* Position relative to the equator (degrees and minutes).

        e. *24-hour distance.* How far the storm traveled during the previous 24-hour period (kilometers/miles).

        f. *24-hour velocity.* How fast the storm moved during the previous 24-hour period (24-hour distance divided by 24; kilometers per hour/miles per hour).

        g. *True compass bearing.* The direction the storm was moving on the morning of the given date relative to true (not magnetic) north (degrees).

    3. The students' table 6.1 already lists Antigua, B.W.I. (British West Indies). Have the students determine its longitude and latitude and fill in the corresponding blanks on the table.

    4. Tell the students that the true compass heading of the storm is 240 degrees. Have them draw a light pencil line on their maps indicating the direction of the heading.

    5. Now tell them that the next morning, September 1, the storm was at longitude 69° 00' West and 15° 20' North Latitude. Have them plot the storm location. They should now be able to (a) determine the distance in miles and kilometers it traveled the previous 24 hours, and (b) calculate its velocity in miles per hour and kilometers per hour. They should also be able to fill in the location description.

    6. Distribute the prediction template, figure 6.5. *It is critical that the prediction template be reproduced at the same scale as the map* (fig. 6.6). As part of each prediction have the students name any cities that might be endangered by the storm two days later, for which evacuation should be ordered. Determine the probabilities using the template. After the next day's prediction review that evacuation order with the class to see if it was reasonable.

Table 6.1. Student Table for "Activity: Where's It Going?"

West Indian Hurricane

(Daily position, velocity, and bearing data of the storm from August 30th to September 15th, 1900.)

Student Name(s) _____   Date __ / __ / __   Period _____

Date	Location Description	West Longitude	North Latitude	24-Hour Distance km/miles	24-Hour Velocity kph/mph	True Compass Bearing
August 30	at Antigua, B.W.I.					
August 31						
September 1						
September 2						
September 3						
September 4						
September 5						
September 6						
September 7						
September 8						
September 9						
September 10						
September 11						
September 12						
September 13						
September 14						
September 15						

From *American History Through Earth Science.* © 1997 Craig A. Munsart. Teacher Ideas Press. (800) 237-6124.

7. Ask the students to predict the heading and distance the storm will travel over the next 24 hours. Record these on the chalkboard or an overhead projector. After they do so tell them the new heading and the longitude and latitude. See who was right. Again have them fill in the location description. Repeat predictions for each day as the storm progresses.

8. Repeat the process until the entire table is completed.

9. Figure 6.7 is a completed version of figure 6.5, showing the positions of the storm at 24-hour intervals. Have the students compare their completed map with that shown in figure 6.7. Table 6.2 is a completed version of table 6.1.

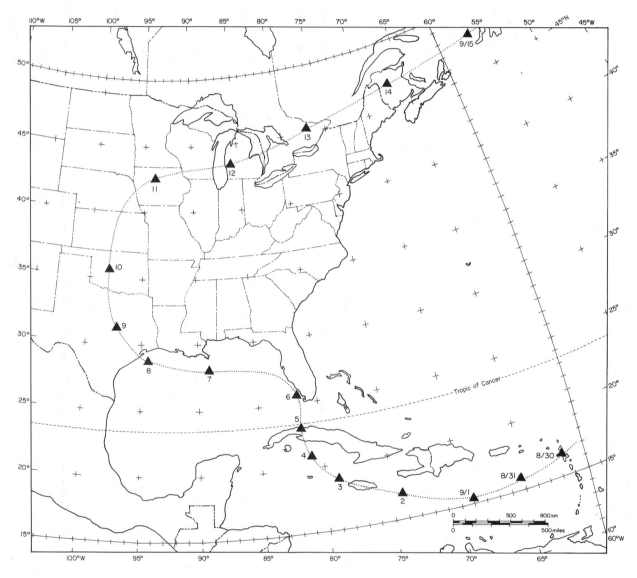

Fig. 6.7. Solution to Figure 6.6, Showing the Track of the Storm.

Table 6.2. Completed Student Table for "Activity: Where's It Going?"

West Indian Hurricane
(Daily position, velocity, and bearing data of the storm from August 30th to September 15th, 1900.)

Student Name(s) _____   Date ___/___/___   Period _____

Date	Location Description	West Longitude	North Latitude	24-Hour Distance km/miles	24-Hour Velocity kph/mph	True Compass Bearing
August 30	at Antigua, B.W.I.	61° 40'	17° 40'	—	—	240°
August 31	300 km (188 miles) SSE San Juan, Puerto Rico	65° 00'	16° 00'	408/255	17.0/10.6	255°
September 1	480 km (300 miles) SSW San Juan, Puerto Rico	69° 00'	15° 20'	425/266	17.7/11.1	288°
September 2	304 km (190 miles) ESE Kingston, Jamaica	74° 10'	17° 00'	610/381	25.4/15.9	288°
September 3	240 km (150 miles) WNW Kingston, Jamaica	78° 50'	19° 00'	560/350	23.3/14.6	306°
September 4	282 km (170 miles) SE Havana, Cuba	80° 50'	21° 00'	320/200	13.3/8.3	352°
September 5	112 km (70 miles) E Havana, Cuba	81° 20'	23° 00'	240/150	10.0/6.3	360°
September 6	128 km (80 miles) W of Miami, Florida	81° 40'	25° 40'	304/190	12.7/7.9	330°
September 7	240 km (150 miles) SE New Orleans, Louisiana	89° 00'	28° 00'	960/600	40.0/25.0	278°
September 8	80 km (50 miles) SE Galveston, Texas	94° 20'	28° 40'	528/330	22.0/13.8	315°
September 9	240 km (150 miles) NW Houston, Texas	97° 00'	31° 10'	400/250	16.7/10.4	350°
September 10	48 km (30 miles) NW Oklahoma City, Oklahoma	98° 10'	35° 40'	480/300	20.0/12.5	360°
September 11	112 km (70 miles) N Des Moines, Iowa	94° 00'	42° 30'	944/590	39.3/24.6	77°
September 12	48 km (30 miles) NNW Grand Rapids, Michigan	86° 00'	43° 20'	656/410	27.3/17.1	70°
September 13	96 km (60 miles) W Ottawa, Ontario, Canada	77° 10'	45° 20'	720/450	30.0/18.8	72°
September 14	208 km (130 miles) N St. John, New Brunswick	67° 00'	46° 50'	784/490	32.7/20.4	80°
September 15	640 km (400 miles) ENE Halifax, Nova Scotia	56° 30'	47° 50'	800/500	33.3/20.8	83°

Activity: What Now, Then?

Time

+ 3 class periods

Materials

+ a copy of figure 6.8 (A-B) (possibly enlarged) for each team of students
+ scissors
+ tape

Grouping

+ 2-4 students per team

In 1900 only a single road and a railroad linked Galveston Island with the city of Houston, approximately 50 miles (80 kilometers) to the northwest. Travel to the mainland is not improved significantly today. Limited rail, boat, and road links are still the only routes off Galveston Island. All such connections would be tenuous, at best, during a major hurricane.

Tell the student groups they are directors of emergency preparedness in 1899. Examining the history of the area, they have concluded that there is a strong possibility that a major hurricane will wreak havoc on the island. Their job is to prepare a plan designed to evacuate 30,000 people in the event of a hurricane. It is important to discuss with the students the following:

  a. *Communications.* There are no telephones, televisions, or radios in 1899.
  b. *Response time.* Officials may have little warning (perhaps a few hours) of an impending disaster.
  c. *Transportation.* Only a few people have personal transportation (such as horses or wagons). Railroad tracks and roads may be washed out.
  d. *Water and food supplies.* Officials must be able to not only obtain such supplies but distribute them efficiently where needed.
  e. *Emergency care.* How will emergency care workers reach, as well as attend to, the needs of hurricane victims? Where will they go? How will they get needed supplies?

Using figure 6.8 (A-B) as a base map students should prepare a plan showing where residents will go. Will they evacuate the island? How far inland do they need to go? How will they get there? What improvements can they recommend to make such population movements more efficient? What kind of plan do they have for communicating with all 30,000 residents in a timely manner? Hint: Transparent overlays used on top of figure 6.8 can show different aspects of the plan such as communications, transportation, and services needed to evacuate residents.

Have student teams present their plans to a community group (the class). They can incorporate the class comments into a revised plan to be part of a written report to be submitted to the teacher for a grade or a poster session to be reviewed by a panel of parents or other teachers.

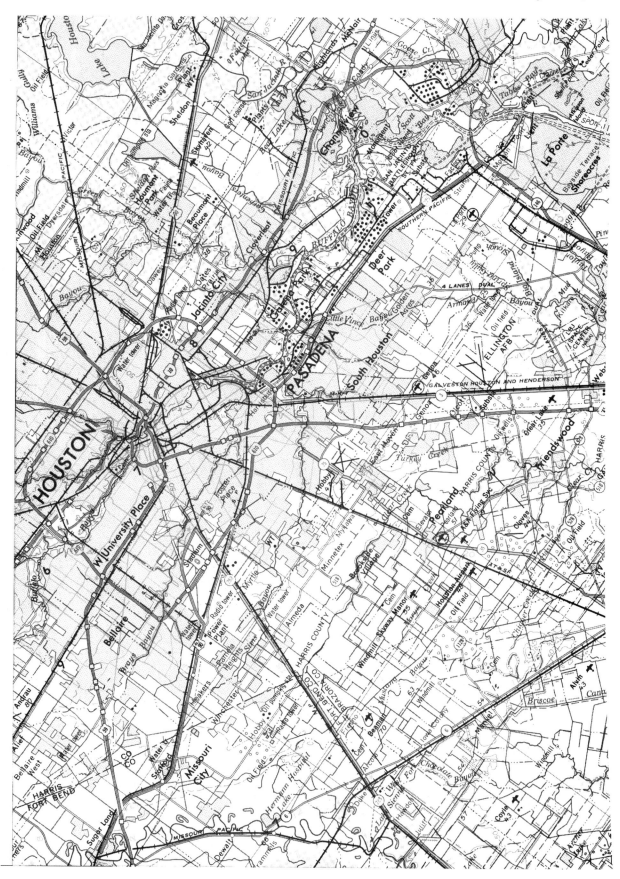

Fig. 6.8A. Topographic Map of Houston (A) and Galveston (B).
From *American History Through Earth Science.* © 1997 Craig A. Munsart. Teacher Ideas Press. (800) 237-6124.

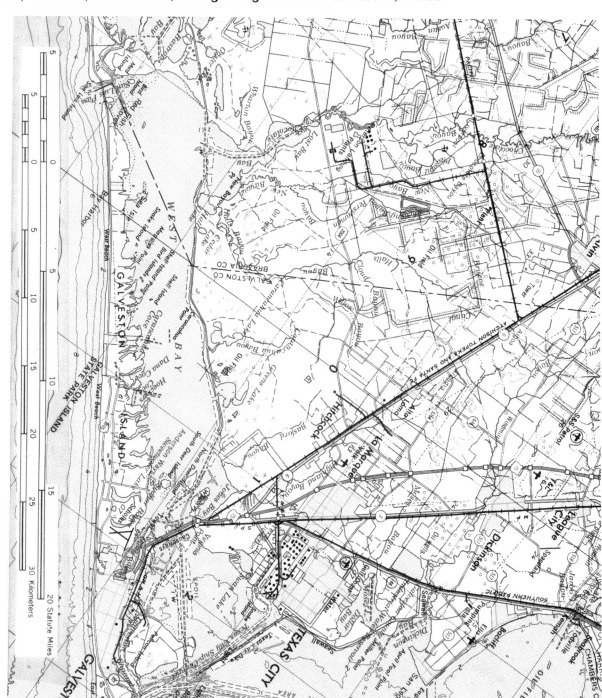

Fig. 6.8B.

From *American History Through Earth Science.* © 1997 Craig A. Munsart. Teacher Ideas Press. (800) 237-6124.

AFTERMATH

As the bodies of the victims of the 1900 hurricane were being cremated (the ground was too saturated for conventional burial and attempts at burial at sea were abandoned when the bodies washed ashore; McComb 1986, 130) a political upheaval took place in Galveston and the new politicos quickly acknowledged that hurricanes could no longer be ignored.

After some creative financing, construction of the first seawall began in 1903. It was built by a Denver company, was constructed of poured concrete 17 feet (5.2 meters) high, and 15 feet (4.6 meters) thick at the base, and weighed 20 tons per foot (21.8 kilograms per square centimeter) (McComb 1986, 139). Initial cost estimates were $3.5 million. The first 3.3 mile-long (5.3 kilometer-long) portion was completed in 1904.

Looking up to the top of the new construction residents soon realized the vulnerability of their homes, even with the new seawall. The seawall could protect them from waves approaching from the Gulf of Mexico, but if sea level were to rise (as it always does during a hurricane) they could still be flooded from Galveston Bay or around the west end of the wall, and water around the back side could seriously affect the structural integrity of the wall. The "obvious" solution? Raise the island and its structures. By 1911 2,156 structures (from outhouses to churches), all services (water pipes, sewer lines, and streetcar tracks), and even trees had been raised. The initial estimates were that 11 million cubic yards (8.4 million cubic meters) of sand would be required; final calculations determined more than 16.3 million cubic yards (12.5 million cubic meters) were needed. By 1911 500 city blocks were raised as much as 17 feet (5.2 meters) at a cost of more than $2 million (McComb 1986, 143-44; Hughes 1990, 198; Walden 1990, 14). More sand was added later.

Another mile-long seawall section was added to the southwest in 1905 to protect military facilities at Fort Crockett. In 1909 a small, but intense hurricane tested the newly built sections of wall. Water came over the wall, ran into the city, and eroded the back side of the wall. Shortly thereafter the wall was raised to 18 feet (5.5 meters) and extended back 200 feet (60 meters) from the Gulf. In 1913 it was recommended that the seawall be extended eastward by approximately 2 miles (3.2 kilometers) (this was not done until 1918).

On August 16, 1915, a 21 foot (6.4 meter) sea height (7 foot waves superimposed on a 14 foot storm surge) from a hurricane topped the new seawall, caused $4.5 million in damage, and killed eight people (U.S. Army Corps of Engineers 1981, 9; McComb 1986, 148).

As the population of Galveston increased, the city expanded west, beyond the seawall. In 1950 a 3-mile (4.8-kilometer) seawall extension was proposed. Shortly thereafter the seawall was raised to 19.2 feet (5.9 meters, figure 6.3). The sequence continued with alternating hurricanes and seawall extensions until 1962, when the seawall reached its current form: 10.4 miles (16.7 kilometers) long costing almost $14.5 million. Today, approximately one-third of the Gulf frontage of Galveston has a seawall.

In 1969, the U.S. Army Corps of Engineers determined that "the tremendous growth and development of the Texas Coast have necessitated that consideration be given to protection of [Galveston Bay] from inundation resulting from storm surges" (Brogdon, 1). Sixty-nine years after 6,000-8,000 people died, studies using a small-scale hydraulic model of Galveston Bay indicated the best way to protect the area would be a 74-mile (119-kilometer) long, 20-foot (6-meter) high storm wall extending from Freeport on the southwest, along the entire

Gulf shore of Galveston Island, and across the Bolivar peninsula to the northeast. To date, that storm wall has not been built. Galveston (as well as other barrier islands along the Texas and eastern U.S. coasts) contains a large city and is a playground for mainland residents with increasing construction of buildings near the water—some outside the seawall—and consequent destruction of protective dunes. Human attitudes about living in such areas have changed a little in the past 80 years; hurricanes have not changed at all.

Activity: What Now, Now?

The format of this activity is similar to that of the previous one. It is 98 years later. The same team is in charge of emergency preparedness in 1997. It has been a while since a "killer" hurricane hit Galveston. Neither hurricanes nor people's attitudes have changed. If anything, people feel more invincible in 1997. The issues surrounding the protection of civilians now have a two-part focus.

Short term. Almost 100 years later the problems are remarkably similar. There is still only a single road leaving Galveston for the mainland, a secondary road linking Galveston to Follets Island to the west, and a ferry to the Bolivar peninsula to the east. Using those routes during an evacuation would be like jumping from the frying pan into the fire; the physical evacuation problem still needs to be resolved. Although storm forecasting and communication are better now than they were 97 years ago, convincing people to leave their homes and businesses is still a problem. Your challenge will be to solve the problem without frightening the population. Will businessmen and politicians be willing to evacuate tourists (knowing it will cause economic losses) if the risk of a storm is anything but absolutely certain?

Long term. What can you do for the future? Increasing population growth, isolation from the mainland, subsurface water withdrawals, destruction of dunes, and construction of new buildings in areas susceptible to storm damage all continue. What type of plan can you develop? Do you restrict growth? Build more and higher seawalls? Build new roads to the mainland? Do you depend on the population to head for high ground, or do you need the National Guard to enforce the evacuation? Who pays for it all?

Contact the Galveston Chamber of Commerce or a local newspaper for information. Perhaps you could speak with a geologist or environmentalist from a local university. The Red Cross or a government agency (e.g., emergency preparedness, geological survey, water resources) could help you with your preparation and presentation. Insurance companies deal with such disasters all the time; they might be a good source of how claims might be handled or avoided.

Prepare a comprehensive report (including maps) to show how you would deal with both the short- and long-term solutions. Consider the class a citizens' group. Your team will be the experts presenting your plan using whatever visual aids might be appropriate (overheads, posters). Present your plan and be prepared to deal with questions and criticisms from people who might not be pleased with it. (No one wants to hear about a "solution" that will require him or her to make lifestyle changes, even if doing so would save his or her life.)

Extensions

Galveston is used here as the site of such a disaster. Unfortunately, Galveston is not unique. Similar evacuation exercises can be done for the following locales:

    a. Ocean City, Maryland. A storm in 1962 inundated much of Fenwick Island (on which Ocean City sits). Much of the new construction since then has occurred in the area flooded by that storm.

    b. South Carolina's Barrier Islands. These were severely damaged by Hurricane Hugo in 1989.

    c. North Carolina's Outer Banks that were damaged by Hurricane Fran in 1996.

    d. Miami Beach, Florida. An artificial barrier beach built to house vacationers is continually eroding. In the late 1970s $64 million was spent to add 17 million cubic yards (13 million cubic meters) of sand.

    e. Avalon, Catalina Island, California. Sand is moved from the mainland to replenish the town's popular beach after annual severe winter erosion problems, often created by the high Santa Ana winds generated on the mainland.

    f. Montauk Point, New York. The lighthouse, whose site was selected by surveyor George Washington, is now threatened by the sea. It was originally located 200 feet (60 meters) from the cliff edge. Washington estimated the rate of erosion would keep it safe for 200 years; he was remarkably close.

    g. Presque Isle, Pennsylvania. This heavily visited state park located on a sand spit in Lake Erie is in danger. Sand that once replenished the spit is being trapped by structures built along the shoreline. The Army Corps of Engineers is spending millions of dollars in an attempt to guarantee continued access to the park.

This list is just a sampling; others may exist in your area.

Ask students to research why hurricanes cause significantly more loss of life in southern Asia than they do in North America. Population densities, timeliness of warnings, mobility of the populations, topography, communication, and geometry of the coastline are all factors.

Beach replenishment (pumping sand from offshore onto an eroding beach) is a method commonly used to maintain shoreline communities. From the city of Avalon on Catalina Island, California, to Miami Beach, Florida, new sand is added to beaches to maintain the viability of the coastal communities. Does this method truly address the issue ecologically, or is it justified only from an economic standpoint? Is it a cure to the problem or merely a bandage for a terminal disease?

The hurricane that struck Galveston in 1900 was the *deadliest* natural disaster in United States history, but (with a word of caution) a hurricane can also be blamed for the *costliest* natural disaster in the United States. In August 1992 Hurricane Andrew generated a storm surge of 16.9 feet (5.2 meters) and more than 7 inches (17.5 centimeters) of rain across southern Florida, and a 7-foot (2.2-meter) storm surge and more than 11 inches (27.5 centimeters) of rain across parts of Louisiana. It killed 54 people and caused between $15 billion and $30 billion in damages. Dollar amounts make great headlines but are a poor means of comparing disasters of today to those of the past. Costs for recent disasters will generally be larger than those for past ones because of replacement costs. A destroyed house that may have cost $40,000 to replace in 1970 would cost more than $100,000 to replace today. In 1906, the damage resulting from the San Francisco earthquake was estimated at $524 million; that amount was equivalent to $2.5 billion in 1958 (American Institute of Architects Research Corporation 1975, xi).

Hurricanes will continue to strike the U.S. Atlantic coast. What is, perhaps, most frightening is that worse hurricane disasters may lie ahead. The frequency of hurricanes striking the U. S. Atlantic coast appears to correlate with "wet" and "dry" precipitation cycles in West Africa (Gray 1990). The year 1900 marked the end of a 21-year wet spell, when hurricanes appear most active. For the past century wet spells have been separated by dry cycles (with minimal hurricane activity) lasting 15-21 years. "Much of our coastal development has occurred in the 24 years since 1970 [the end of the last wet cycle] when few major hurricanes hit the Atlantic Coast of the United States (Coch 1994, 39). The early 1990s may have marked the beginning of the most recent wet cycle—and impending disaster. After a very active 1995 hurricane season, hurricane expert William Gray said, "We've gone 25 years with relatively little activity . . . inevitably, long stretches of destruction will return. Florida and the East Coast will see hurricane devastation such as they have never experienced before." In 1996 Hurricane Fran may have convinced some people that Gray was correct. Putting hurricane damage in perspective, Gray continued, "It's funny. People remember earthquakes a lot more than they do hurricanes. But in the United States, the number of people who have been killed this century by hurricanes is 10 times greater" (Catalano 1995, 70).

The story of Galveston is probably not over. Hurricanes will continue to strike the island, property damage will occur, and, unfortunately, people will probably die. People learn slowly; structures now exist in front of the seawall. Galveston perseveres today because of a willingness to spend prodigious sums of money for reconstruction, seawalls, raising of the town, and victims assistance.

Morton concludes, "It seems evident that eventually nature will have its way. This should be given utmost consideration when development plans are formulated. While beach-front property may demand the highest prices, it may also carry with it the greatest risks" (1974, 27).

RESOURCES

Public Affairs Officer
U.S. Army Corps of Engineers
P.O. Box 1229
444 Barracuda Avenue
Galveston, TX 77553-1229
(409) 766-3004

REFERENCES

American Institute of Architects Research Corporation. *Architects and Earthquakes.* Washington, D.C.: American Institute of Architects Research Corporation, 1975.

Arnold, Caroline. *Coping with Natural Disasters.* New York: Walker, 1988.

Brogdon, N. J. *Galveston Bay Hurricane Surge Study, Report 1, Effects of Proposed Barriers on Hurricane Surge Heights. Technical Report H-69-12.* Galveston, Tex.: U.S. Army Corps of Engineers, 1969.

Brown, Billye Walker, and Walter R. Brown. *Historical Catastrophes: Hurricanes and Tornadoes.* Reading, Mass.: Addison-Wesley, 1972.

Canby, Thomas Y. "Water: Our Most Precious Resource." *National Geographic* 158 (1980): 144-79.

Catalano, Peter. "Hurricane Alert." *Popular Science* 247 (1995): 3.

Coch, Nicholas K. "Geologic Effects of Hurricanes." *Geomorphology* 10 (1994): 37-63.

———. "Hurricane Hazards Along the Northeastern Atlantic Coast of the United States." *Journal of Coastal Research* Special Issue No. 12 (1995): 115-47.

Davis, Lee. *Natural Disasters.* New York: Facts on File, 1992.

Funk, Ben. "Hurricane." *National Geographic* 158 (1980): 346-79.

Garriott, E. B. "The West Indian Hurricane of September 1-12, 1900." *National Geographic* 11 (1900): 384-92.

Gray, W. M. "Strong Association Between West African Rainfall and U.S. Landfall of Intense Hurricanes." *Science* 249 (1990): 1251-56.

Hayes, Miles O. *Hurricanes As Geological Agents: Case Studies of Hurricanes Carla, 1961, and Cindy, 1963.* Report of Investigations Number 61. Austin, Tex.: Bureau of Economic Geology, 1967.

Hughes, Patrick. *American Weather Stories.* Washington, D.C.: National Oceanic and Atmospheric Administration, 1976.

———. "The Great Galveston Hurricane." *Weatherwise* 43 (1990): 190-98.

Kreitler, Charles W. *Faulting and Land Subsidence from Ground-Water and Hydrocarbon Production, Houston-Galveston, Texas.* Research Note 8. Austin, Tex.: Bureau of Economic Geology, 1978.

McComb, David G. *Galveston: A History.* Austin, Tex.: University of Texas Press, 1986.

McGee, W. J. "The Lessons of Galveston." *National Geographic* 11 (1900): 377-83.

Morton, Robert A. *Shoreline Changes on Galveston Island (Bolivar Roads to San Luis Pass): An Analysis of Historical Changes of the Texas Gulf Shoreline.* Geological Circular 74-2. Austin, Tex.: Bureau of Economic Geology, 1974.

Morton, Robert A., and J. H. McGowen. *Modern Depositional Environments of the Texas Gulf Coast.* Austin, Tex.: Bureau of Economic Geology, 1980.

Rappaport, Ed. "Hurricane Andrew— A First Look." *Mariner's Weather Log. National Oceanographic Data Center* 36 (1992): 16-25.

Tannehill, Ivan Ray. *The Hurricane Hunters.* New York: Dodd, Mead, 1961.

U.S. Army Corps of Engineers. *Galveston's Bulwark Against the Sea: History of the Galveston Seawall.* Galveston, Tex.: U.S. Army Corps of Engineers, 1981.

U.S. Army Corps of Engineers. *The Galveston Seawall.* Galveston, Tex.: U.S. Army Corps of Engineers.

Walden, Don. "Raising Galveston." *American Heritage of Invention and Technology* 5 (1990): 8-18.

Williams, S. Jeffress; Kurt Dodd; and Kathleen Kraft Gohn. *Coasts in Crisis.* U.S. Geological Survey Circular 1075. Washington, D.C.: U.S. Government Printing Office, 1991.

SEVEN
Growlers, Greenland, and Lifesavers Candies

The explorations of the northeastern part of North America by the Norwegians, English, French, and Dutch occurred largely because of prevailing ocean currents and winds favoring vessels sailing westward from Northern Europe. Following favorable winds and ocean currents Irish monks discovered Iceland in the eighth century. In the latter part of the ninth and tenth centuries Viking longboats traveled westward from Scandinavia. Well-known sailors such as Eric the Red and his son Leif Ericson followed the Irminger and East Greenland Currents in the North Atlantic to reach Iceland and Greenland, where they established settlements in 874 and 985, respectively. (Viking ships were remarkable in their design and construction. On its way to Chicago for the 1893 World's Fair, and taking advantage of ocean currents and prevailing winds, a replica of a Viking longboat sailed from Norway to St. John's, Newfoundland in just 27 days [Villiers 1973, 63].) In 986, Bjarni Herjulfsson sailed westward from Iceland, missed Greenland, but possibly sailed along the coast of North America as far south as New England. Shortly after 1000 Thorfinn Karlsefni settled in North America, and his wife bore him the first child of European descent in North America.

Strong interest in North America by European countries began inadvertently in the late 1400s as the Europeans searched in vain for a westward passage to China. John Cabot (really an Italian whose name was changed from Giovanni Cabota in Genoa, Italy; Hale 1966, 99) sailed from England in the late 1490s. Assisted by the Greenland and Labrador Currents, Cabot sailed along southern Greenland, eastern Canada, and eastern New England. Gaspar Corte Real sailed from Portugal in 1501, west to the Azores, turned northward, and followed the Irminger Current to southern Greenland. He then followed the Greenland and Labrador Currents westward past the coast of Newfoundland. In the 1530s Jacques Cartier sailed westward from France to eastern Canada. Other voyages searching for a northern route to China were made by Martin Frobisher in 1577 and 1578, and by John Davis in 1585, 1586, and 1587; all were unsuccessful. In 1609 Henry Hudson sailed north from the Netherlands, and followed the Irminger, Labrador, and coastal currents to New York to reach his namesake river. A year later, at first thinking it was the Pacific Ocean, he sailed into (what is now) Hudson Bay, where his crew set him adrift in a small boat. He was never seen again.

135

Ice was a hazard on the early voyages across the North Atlantic; icebergs were very capable of crushing the vulnerable wooden ships. To prevent a damaging impact by ice, ship captains often ordered the sides of the hull to be padded with ropes and bedding. The crew used pikes to help push the ice away from the ship. Such efforts were not always successful. In a 1619 expedition looking for a northern passage to China, Danish explorer Jens Munck lost 61 of a crew of 64 when his ship was damaged, presumably by ice.

A year later the *Mayflower* sailed from Plymouth, England, and following the wind and ocean currents of its predecessors arrived in Massachusetts 67 days later. Figure 7.1 shows the routes of these early northern voyages. By 1824 competition among shipping companies had shortened the sailing time from "Old" England to New England to just over 15 days, and by 1838 steam propulsion was powering the ships crossing the North Atlantic. Burning 30 tons of coal a day the giant side-wheeler *Great Western* crossed the ocean in the same amount of time as a sailing ship did 14 years earlier. The Blue Riband (represented by the garish Hales trophy), awarded to the fastest ship crossing the North Atlantic, was held by British-built ships for 100 years after 1852, the year when the liner *Baltic* crossed from England in approximately 10 days. Such ships allowed Irish immigrants escaping the potato famine a rapid westward transit to the United States. In January 1856 one of the *Baltic*'s sister ships, *Pacific*, disappeared en route from Liverpool to New York, presumably the victim of ice. The contest for fastest ship across the Atlantic became tempered by the reality of safety. In the early 1900s the competition was intense; Germany, France, and England did whatever they could to attract the most passengers with the fastest, most glamorous, or biggest liners afloat. For all intents and purposes the competition ended in 1952, when the *United States*, a state-of-the-art liner designed by William Francis Gibbs and built in secrecy, wrested the Blue Riband from the British with a time across the Atlantic of 3 days, 10 hours, and 40 minutes: a 990-foot ship moving as fast as a water ski towboat. It was an empty victory. Long-range passenger aircraft soon shortened the Atlantic crossing time from days to hours, and the grand transatlantic liner competition faded into history. The legacy of the *United States*'s speed record is kept alive by two of her propellers near what was once the pier of United States Lines on New York's Hudson River in the shadow of the aircraft carrier *Intrepid*.

In 1902 American businessman J. P. Morgan assembled a shipping conglomerate that included British-owned and -operated White Star Line. Within 10 years the American funds allowed the shipping line to launch the first of three superliners, the *Olympic*, shortly followed by a sister ship with a third following later (Fenster 1996, 102). The three White Star superliners were planned to wrest British passengers from the rival Cunard Line, whose ships *Mauretania* and *Lusitania* were the best the British had to offer since 1907. In 1912 the sister ship of *Olympic* sank. (Coincidentally, in that same year, Lifesavers candies were introduced.) Sinkings happened many times before and since, sending only a minor ripple through the annals of what was to become history. This time, however, the sinking was more memorable. Why? Because the ship was the biggest in the world at the time, on its maiden voyage, transporting a virtual "who's who" of American society, and, most noteworthy of all, was designed and built to be *unsinkable!* It represented the leader among the three international rivals for prestige across the North Atlantic. *Olympic*'s sister ship was the Royal Mail Steamer *Titanic*.

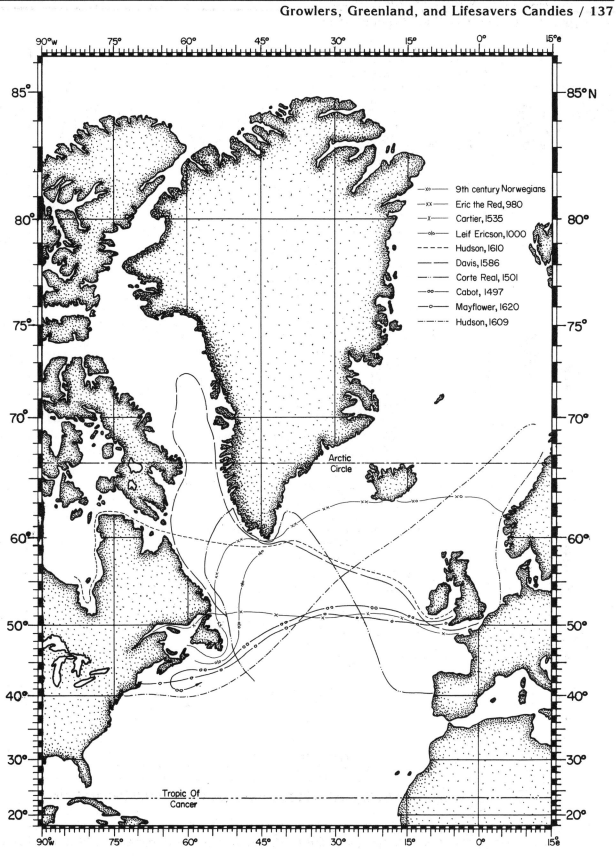

Fig. 7.1. Early North Atlantic Exploration Routes.

It seems almost incredible that a large, natural object being moved by the vagaries of ocean currents for almost two years and the largest moving human-made object (at the time) speeding across the North Atlantic should, by pure misfortune, collide in the almost infinite spaces of the open ocean on a cold, calm, clear, starry spring evening. But it happened, and more than 1,500 people died as a result. As John Maxtone-Graham (1972) writes, "The *Titanic* sank because of reckless seamanship and a scheme of design inadequate for the particular accident that befell her" (62). The British Court of Inquiry laid the blame for the collision with the iceberg on "the excessive speed at which the ship was being navigated."

After the *Titanic* disaster procedural changes were made for all vessels sailing the North Atlantic:

a. Navigators took reports of ice floes seriously, steering clear of them or proceeding at a slower speed.

b. Shipping lanes for the winter were moved farther south.

c. The International Ice Patrol was established to monitor potentially dangerous icebergs.

d. Radios aboard ships were required to be operated 24 hours a day.

e. Enough lifeboats were to be provided to accommodate every passenger.

It would be easy to feel complacent about the safety of sea travel in the North Atlantic today, what with computers; airplane, satellite, and radar surveillance; and an eighty-year history of dealing with ice in this area. It would be easy—but also unwise. The International Ice Patrol information booklet (1993) indicates that

"this [iceberg] menace is a natural hazard which we, in all our ingenuity and resourcefulness, have not been able control, regulate, or entirely avoid."

". . . it is not feasible to hold back, destroy or significantly alter the course of these icebergs."

" . . . the potential for catastrophe still exists" (3).

The problem is the nature of the area and icebergs themselves. Because of their shape and material, icebergs are not seen as readily by radar as sailors would like.

a. Much like a stealth fighter, ice reflects radar waves approximately 60 times less effectively than a similar-sized ship.

b. Under good conditions an iceberg can be detected 4-15 miles (6.4-24 kilometers) away. When fog and ice crystals are present in the air, however, this distance diminishes significantly.

c. High waves and rough sea conditions can hide completely a 17-foot (5.2 meter) high ice mass.

Activity: Fancy Meeting You Here!

Greenland is ideally suited to generating icebergs. It is a large, bowl-shaped island filled with ice, which covers 670,000 square miles (1,735,000 square kilometers) and is 10,824 feet (3,300 meters) thick at the center. Extreme pressures at the base of the ice move the ice outward from the center. The coastal area (the rim of the bowl) contains narrow slits through which the outward moving ice passes to the sea as tidewater glaciers. Icebergs form when the vertical motions of the sea (tides) break off pieces from the glacier's forward edge.

Of the approximately 100 tidewater glaciers in western Greenland twenty major glaciers are responsible for producing between 10,000 and 15,000 icebergs that are calved each year. A smaller number of icebergs are generated by glaciers along Greenland's eastern coast and from Ellsemere Island, northwest of Greenland. The fateful *Titanic* iceberg, having calved from a glacier in southwestern Greenland, was first moved northward by a spur of the West Greenland Current and then southward by the Labrador Current. (See fig. 7.2.) Warm weather the previous two years created an unusually high number of large icebergs. According to Maxtone-Graham (1972), "there was not only more ice but more ice further south" (62). In the eighty-four-year history of the International Ice Patrol only nine seasons have been recorded as having more than the 1,000 icebergs noted during the spring and summer of 1912. After its two-and-one-half-year voyage, and undaunted by its collision with the *Titanic*, the iceberg continued southward to melt ignominiously in the North Atlantic.

Using a Mercator Projection base map with a longitude, latitude grid, as shown in figure 7.3, students will plot (a) the path of a typical iceberg (similar to the one that made contact with the *Titanic*) and (b) the *Titanic*'s path from its construction in Belfast. The path of the iceberg will allow students to understand the motions of the ocean currents responsible for bringing the iceberg and the *Titanic* together. Because of the greater mass of ice below the water compared with that above, iceberg movements can be related more strongly to ocean currents well below the surface rather than surface currents and wind. Figure 7.4 shows the completed map.

Time

+ 1 class period and possible library time

Materials

+ a large world map or one displayed on an overhead screen
+ copies of tables 7.1 and 7.2 for each student
+ figure 7.2, presented as an overhead
+ a copy of figure 7.3 for each student (enlarged to 11" x 17")
+ figure 7.4 as a transparency
+ a straightedge for each student, long enough to reach across figure 7.3
+ atlases (or a library visit)
+ colored pens or pencils

Grouping

+ individuals

Text continues on page 143.

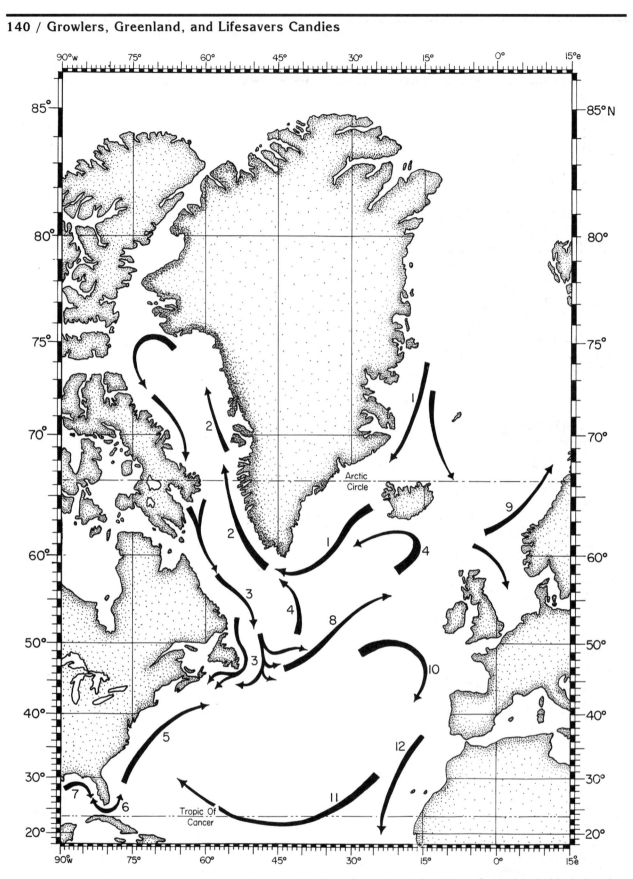

Fig. 7.2. Ocean Currents of the North Atlantic: (1) East Greenland; (2) West Greenland; (3) Labrador; (4) Irminger; (5) Gulf Stream; (6) Florida; (7) Loop; (8) North Atlantic Drift; (9) Norway; (10) Azores Anticyclone; (11) North Equatorial; and (12) Canary.

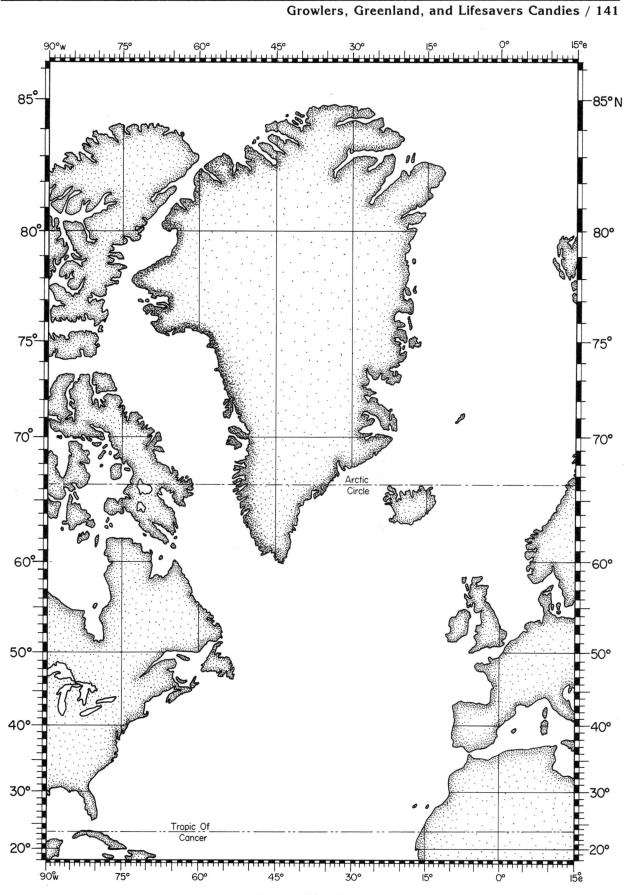

Fig. 7.3. Base Map for "Activity: Fancy Meeting You Here!"

From *American History Through Earth Science.* © 1997 Craig A. Munsart. Teacher Ideas Press. (800) 237-6124.

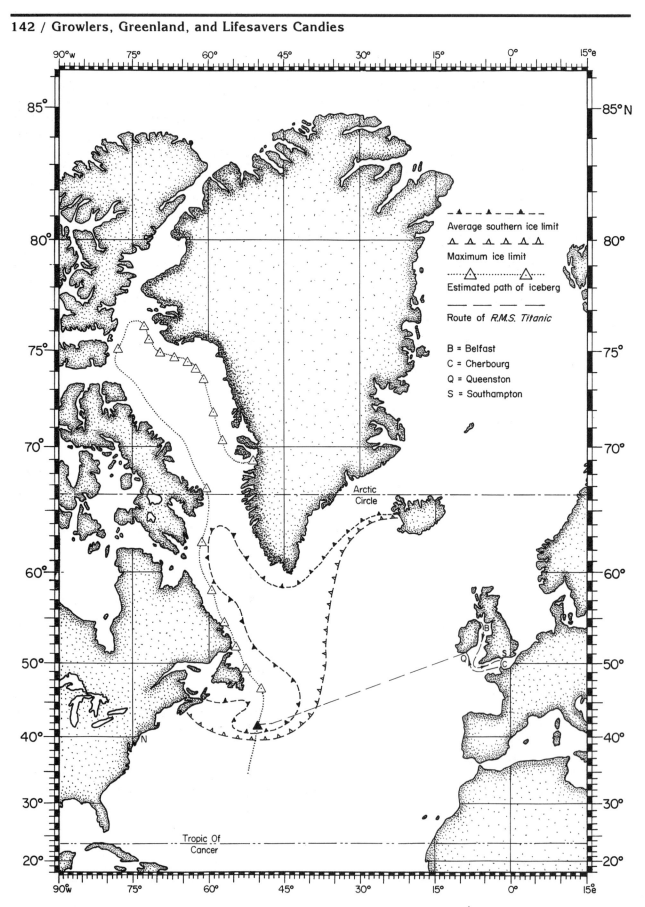

Fig. 7.4. Completed Base Map for "Activity: Fancy Meeting You Here!" (▲ identifies collision site.)

Directions

1. Discuss with the students the general pattern for iceberg and current movements in the North Atlantic: the Gulf Stream moving north, rotating eastward as the North Atlantic Drift, the West Greenland Current, moving northward along the west coast of Greenland, moving icebergs that calved off glaciers on Greenland's west side northward, and those same icebergs then moving southward due to the Labrador Current into the busy shipping lanes of the North Atlantic. This pattern was well known before the *Titanic* began its maiden voyage. Keep this circulation pattern on the overhead (as shown in figure 7.2) or draw it on the chalkboard so that the students can keep the overall circulation in mind as they proceed.

2. Give each student a copy of figure 7.3. This is a Mercator Projection of the North Atlantic. Greenland appears overly large on a Mercator Projection because of the way northern latitudes are artificially stretched. (This might be a good time to introduce map projections.) Tell the students what they will be doing on this map:

locating the cities important to the short history of the *Titanic*;

naming the important landmasses on the map;

plotting the course of the *Titanic*;

plotting the path of the iceberg the *Titanic* hit; and

locating important ocean currents in the area.

3. Allow students access to the library or provide atlases in class so that students can locate cities important to the history of the *Titanic* and indicate them on figure 7.3 as follows:

Belfast, Northern Ireland (indicate with a *B*), where the *Titanic* was built;

Southampton, England (*S*), location of the home offices of the White Star Line, where the *Titanic* first embarked passengers;

Cherbourg, France (*C*), the *Titanic*'s second stop for passengers;

Queenstown, now Cobh, Ireland (*Q*), the last land the *Titanic* touched and from where final passengers boarded; and

New York City, United States (*N*), the *Titanic*'s unreached destination.

As part of the same exercise students should also be asked to label some of the important landmasses: Greenland, Newfoundland, Iceland, and the Ellsemere and Baffin Islands as well as the countries of England, Ireland, Canada, and the United States.

4. Give each student a copy of table 7.1, on which the *Titanic*'s positions are listed for the first and final voyage. Have the students plot each of the points during the voyage, then, using a colored pen or pencil, draw the route of the *Titanic* from where it was launched to where it sank.

Table 7.1. The Positions of the *Titanic*.

Date and Time	Location
May 31, 1911	Belfast, Northern Ireland (launched)
April 10, 1912, Noon	Southampton, England (pick up passengers)
April 10, 1912, 7 P.M.	Cherbourg, France (pick up passengers)
April 11, 1912, 12:30 P.M.	Queenstown (Cobh), Ireland (pick up passengers)
April 12, 1912, Noon	At sea, approximately 47°00'N, 18°30'W
April 13, 1912, Noon	At sea, approximately 45°00'N, 30°30'W; traveled 519 miles the previous 24 hours
April 14, 1912, Noon	At sea, approximately 43°10'N, 41°00'W; traveled 546 miles the previous 24 hours
April 14, 1912	At sea, "Turning Point," 42°00'N, 47°00'W; course change for New York
April 14, 1912, 11:40 P.M.	At sea, hit iceberg, 41°46'N, 50°14'W
April 15, 1912, 2:20 A.M.	*Titanic* sinks; position on bottom (of bow section) 41°44'N, 56°49'W

5. From the data given in table 7.1 students can also calculate the speed for two full days at sea (in miles per hour). To convert from miles per hour to knots (one nautical mile [6,076 feet] per hour) divide miles per hour by 1.15. (The answer should be approximately 22 miles per hour, or 19 knots.)

6. This activity would be meaningless without the other protagonist, the iceberg. Table 7.2 indicates hypothetical positions of the iceberg. Only one of the actual positions is known; the other positions are based on estimates made by Richard Brown in *Voyage of the Iceberg* (1983) as inferred from ocean currents and present-day ice movements. Students can plot the position of the iceberg during its speculated 30-month voyage to the crash site. The monthly distances traveled by the iceberg are erratic because of seasonal ice, current variation, and groundings. Also, because the iceberg extended far below the sea surface, it often dragged along the bottom. It may have taken the iceberg three times as long to arrive at the crash site as did the *Titanic* from the time of its launch.

7. Have the students locate the following ocean currents that are critical to the events surrounding the sinking of the *Titanic*: Gulf Stream, Labrador Current, East and West Greenland Currents, and the North Atlantic Drift.

Table 7.2. The Positions of the Iceberg that Hit the *Titanic*.

Month/Year	North Latitude	West Longitude
10/1910	68° 55'	51° 00'
11	70° 20'	57° 20'
12	71° 45'	59° 00'
1/1911	73° 40'	61° 00'
2	74° 10'	62° 30'
3	74° 30'	64° 00'
4	74° 40'	66° 45'
5	74° 50'	69° 30'
6	75° 30'	71° 45'
7	76° 15'	72° 30'
8	75° 05'	78° 00'
9	66° 45'	60° 30'
10	62° 30'	61° 20'
11	58° 00'	59° 30'
12	54° 30'	57° 00'
1/1912	51° 45'	54° 30'
2	49° 20'	52° 30'
3	47° 00'	49° 30'
4	41° 46'	50° 14'

Activity: What Would You Have Done?

The *Titanic* traveled along the regular shipping lanes from Ireland to New York and received warnings of ice from many vessels. Ships at sea may encounter several different types of ice:

a. Sea ice, which forms entirely from the sea. The ice fields formed can be dense enough to stop or damage a vessel. The ice contains some salt, retained during the freezing process.

b. Growlers—masses of ice less than 17 feet (5 meters) high. These often are ice blocks that have calved from larger masses. They can damage ships. The ice formed on land from compacted snow and is salt free.

c. Icebergs, large masses of ice more than 17 feet (5 meters) high; like the growlers, they are salt free and originate on land from glaciers.

In the following activity students will note the position of the ice from the radio warnings, locate the *Titanic* at the time of the warning, and determine if the ice indicated in the warning would have caused a problem for the ship. One of the problems with travel at sea is that there are no landmarks to help you know where you are. Today, ships are equipped with locators that use a Global Positioning (satellite) System (GPS) to locate their position to within a few tens of feet. At the time of the sailing of the *Titanic* the only navigational instruments available were hand-held tools such as a sextant and were only accurate to within a couple of miles. Ballard (1988, 197-98) discusses possible discrepancies between the reported and actual collision positions of the *Titanic*, suggesting that the *Titanic* was actually 10 nautical miles east of her reported crash position. Students should assume the ice from the warnings was drifting South 10° West at 3 miles per hour (approximately 2.5 knots) due to the Labrador Current. (See fig. 7.2.) Figures 7.5 to 7.8 have an upper and lower map grid. The lower grid is an answer key and, using an open circle with a dot, shows the position of the *Titanic* at the time it received the radio warning from the ship indicated. The time and date of that position are also shown (0900 is 9 A.M., 2140 is 9:40 P.M.). The *Titanic*'s course is shown as a solid line for the part of the trip completed and a dashed line for the part of the trip yet to come. Also shown on the map (with a diamond) is "the turning point," a routine mid-ocean course correction keeping the *Titanic* in the shipping lanes inbound to New York. Ice conditions at the time of the radio message are shown with filled-in symbols as follows; triangle = iceberg, double triangle = growler, rectangle = field ice. Open symbols show the ice position at the time *Titanic* reached the crash site. Using the data in table 7.3 the students will need to (a) draw the path of the *Titanic*, (b) note the elapsed time between the time of the radio report and the time of the *Titanic*'s crash, (c) determine how far the radioed ice position would have changed during the elapsed time, (d) draw the course of the *Titanic* to the crash site, and (e) determine if the new ice position could have caused the crash of the *Titanic*.

Text continues on page 151.

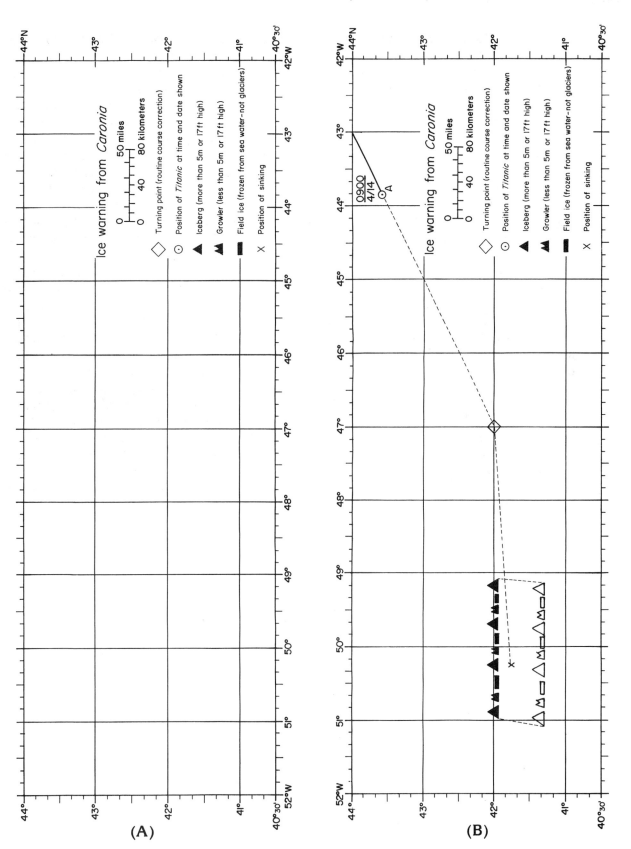

Fig. 7.5. Blank Grid for Ice Warning from the *Caronia* (A) and Completed Grid with Ice Position and the *Titanic*'s Course Plotted (B).

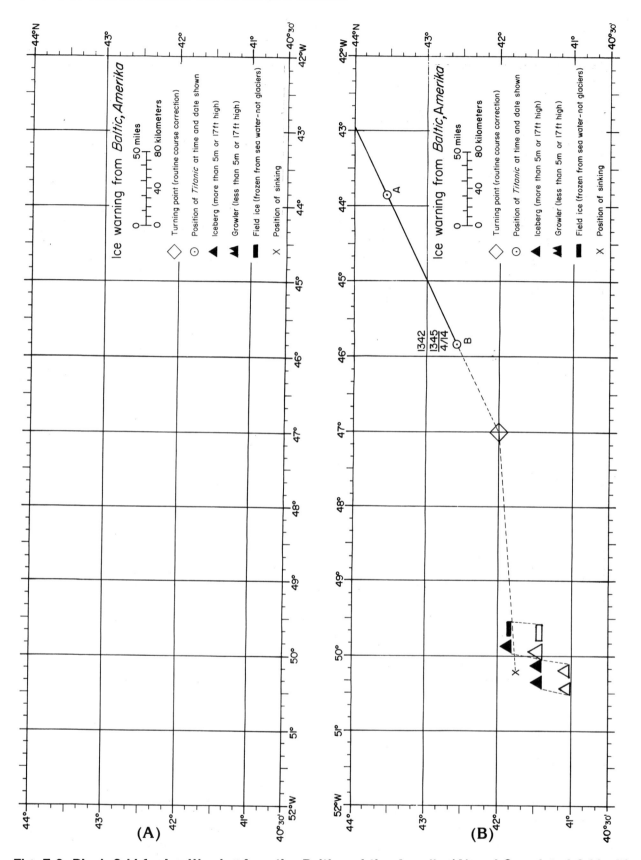

Fig. 7.6. Blank Grid for Ice Warning from the *Baltic* and the *Amerika* (A) and Completed Grid with Ice Position and the *Titanic*'s Course Plotted (B).

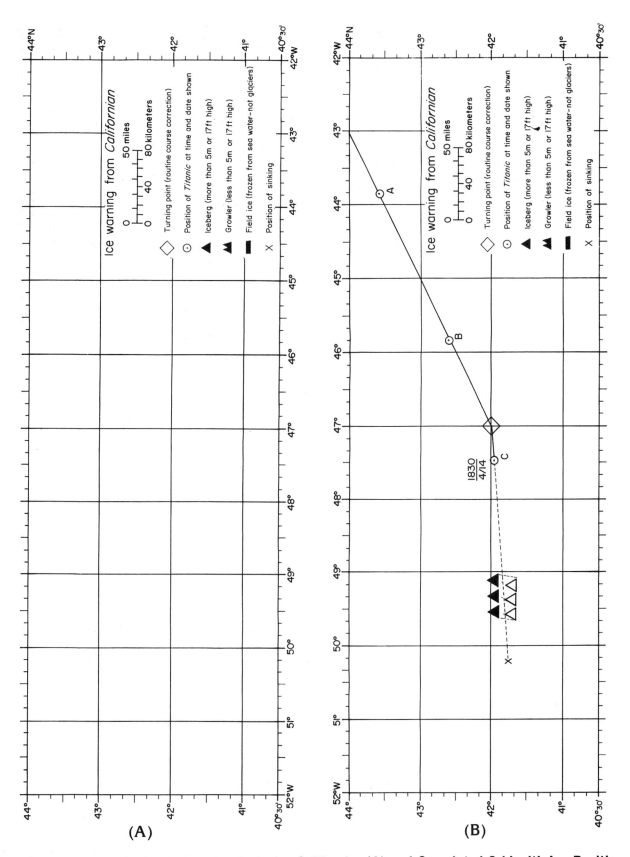

Fig. 7.7. Blank Grid for Ice Warning from the *Californian* (A) and Completed Grid with Ice Position and the *Titanic*'s Course Plotted (B).

From *American History Through Earth Science.* © 1997 Craig A. Munsart. Teacher Ideas Press. (800) 237-6124.

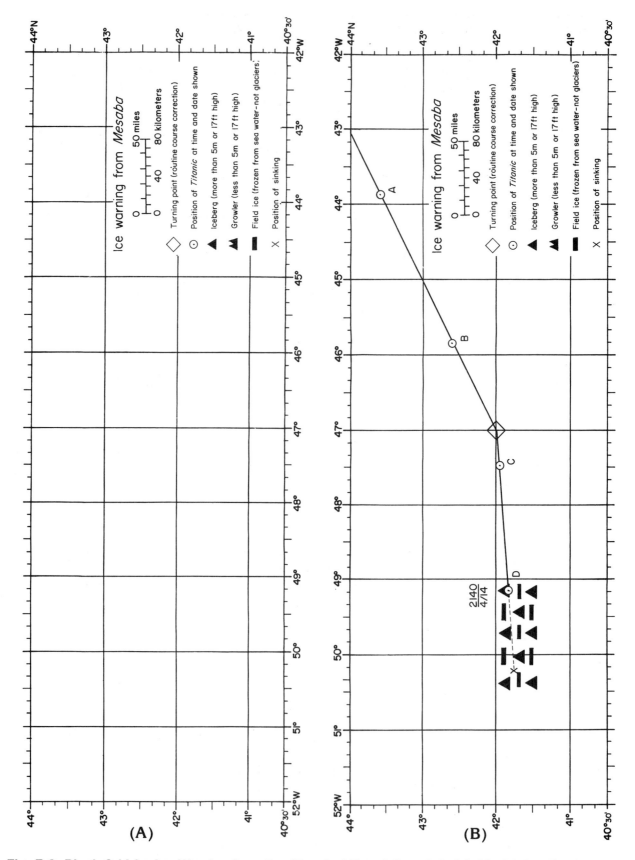

Fig. 7.8. Blank Grid for Ice Warning from the *Mesaba* (A) and Completed Grid with Ice Position and the *Titanic*'s Course Plotted (B).

From *American History Through Earth Science.* © 1997 Craig A. Munsart. Teacher Ideas Press. (800) 237-6124.

Table 7.3. Ice and *Titanic* Positions at Times of Radio Warnings.

**(*Titanic* position when it entered the map area: 44°North, 43°West;
turning point: 42°North, 47°West; crash site: 41°46'N, 50°14'W;
time: 2340, April 14, 1912)**

Ship Issuing Warning	Date and Time	*Titanic* Position When Ice Was Sighted (N Long/W Lat)
Caronia	4/14—0900	43°35'N/43°50'W

Message: "Captain, 'Titanic'—Westbound steamers report bergs, growlers, and field ice in 42 degrees N. from 49 degrees to 51 degrees W., 12th April. Compliments. —Barr."

Baltic	4/14—1342	42°35'N/45°50'W

Message: "Captain Smith, 'Titanic.'— Have had moderate, variable winds and clear, fine weather since leaving. Greek steamer 'Athenai' reports passing icebergs and large quantities of field ice to-day in lat. 41 degrees 51'N., long. 49 degrees 52'W."

Amerika	4/14—1345	42°35'N/45°50'W

Message: relayed from the Hydrographic Office in Washington, " 'Amerika' passed two large icebergs in 41 degrees 27' N., 50 degrees 8' W., on the 14th April."

Californian	4/14—1830	41°58'N/47°30'W

Message: sent to the *Antillean* but picked up by the *Titanic*, "To Captain, 'Antillean,' 6:30 P.M. apparent ship's time; latitude 42 degrees 3' N., long 49 degrees 9' W. Three large bergs five miles to southward of us. Regards. —Lord"

Mesaba	4/14—2140	41°50'N/49°08'W

Message: "From 'Mesaba' to 'Titanic' and all eastbound ships. Ice report in lat. 42 degrees N. to 41 degrees 25' N., long. 49 degrees to 50 degrees 30' W. Saw much heavy pack ice and great number large icebergs. Also field ice. Weather good, clear."

Time
+ 1 class period

Materials
+ a copy of figures 7.5 (A), 7.6 (A), 7.7 (A), and 7.8 (A) for each student or pair
+ a copy of table 7.3 for each student or pair
+ a straightedge or ruler for locating positions
+ a protractor

Grouping
+ individuals or pairs at first, then small groups

Directions

1. Explain to the students that during the *Titanic*'s trip to New York it received five radio warnings about ice. Have the students locate the position of the *Titanic* and the ice at the time of each warning. The Labrador Current caused the iceberg to drift south-southwest in the time between receipt of the radio message and the time the *Titanic* reached the crash site. Have the students then locate the position of the *Titanic* and the ice at the time of the sinking and determine if the sinking was caused by the ice reported in the radio message. The students can then locate the *Titanic*'s course on the map and the position of the ice.

2. Distribute table 7.3 and figures 7.5 (A), 7.6 (A), 7.7 (A), and 7.8 (A) to the students. Review the information shown on table 7.3.

3. Using the symbols shown on each map legend the students will plot the original ice position reported on the radio message from the captioned ship. For instance, on figure 7.5 (A) students will plot the ice reported from the *Caronia*. The ice reported on the radio message will be plotted with filled-in symbols and the later ice position at the crash site with open (not filled-in) symbols. Protractors are necessary to project the course at South 10° West. *Remember, the velocity of the current is 3 mph (2.5 knots).*

4. Students will then plot the *Titanic*'s course across the map using the information in table 7.3; position when it entered the map area, position at the time of the radio message, turning point, and crash site position are all given in table 7.3.

5. Students will then draw the position of the ice at the time of the crash. Knowing the time of the crash and the time of the radio message, students can determine the elapsed time between the message and the crash. Knowing the number of hours, and a projected ice drift of 3 miles per hour (2.5 knots) in the direction of South 10° West students can draw the new ice position at the time of the crash (using open symbols for the ice).

6. Students should then be able to answer the following question: Did the ice indicated in that radio message cause the sinking of the *Titanic*?

7. As an evaluation students can present their conclusions to the class and the class can discuss the results. Does the entire class agree with the conclusion? Why or why not? It might be useful to make a smaller version of one of the student maps to use as an overhead during the discussions. Rather than prepare individual presentations, students can combine all four maps as part of a comprehensive report including all the activities related to the *Titanic* disaster.

[The question might be asked, "If the message from the *Mesaba* (see fig. 7.8 (B)) was received only two hours before the crash and clearly showed ice in the path of *Titanic*, why did the ship not slow down?" The sad truth is that the radio message apparently was never received by the captain of the *Titanic*. At the time, the radio room personnel were very busy with passenger messages and never forwarded the warning to the captain or any other officer.]

Extensions

The story of the *Titanic* is filled with "what-ifs." Walter Lord speculates about these "what if's" in his classic history of the last few hours of the *Titanic*, *A Night to Remember*: "if ice conditions had been normal . . . if the night had been rough or moonlit . . . if she had seen the berg 15 seconds sooner—or 15 seconds later . . . if she had hit the ice any other way . . . if her watertight bulkheads had been one deck higher . . ." (1955, 100). If any of these "what-ifs" had happened the history of the *Titanic* might have been like its less notorious sister ship *Olympic*, quietly retired and scrapped after 24 years of successful, relatively uneventful service. Ironically, if it had survived the iceberg the *Titanic* could also have met the fate of its other sister, *Gigantic* (renamed *Brittanic*). Converted to a hospital ship in World War I, the *Brittanic* sank in the Mediterranean in 1916 after hitting a mine (Maxtone-Graham 1972, 132). In addition to the "what-ifs" given below students might be able to compare the differences between ship travel in 1912 and today: how the voyage might have been different with radar and satellites or how safety requirements changed between 1912 and today (e.g., the International Ice Patrol began in 1913 as a result of the *Titanic* disaster). If possible, invite a Coast Guard spokesperson to discuss ship travel and ship safety with the class. The capabilities to mollify the subsequent death toll existed prior to sailing. Watertight compartments could have been built higher and sealed at the top, and the ship could have carried additional lifeboats. Of course, such speculation is like Monday morning quarterbacking. At the time, the watertight compartments were considered absolutely safe, and the lifeboat capacity (1,178 capacity for 2,207 passengers) exceeded that required by British law (Lord 1955, 61).

1. The hull damage on the starboard side of the *Titanic* allowed water to fill five watertight compartments, causing the vessel to sink. **What if** the *Titanic* never attempted to turn and rammed the iceberg dead ahead? It can be argued that only the first three compartments would have been flooded. Certainly the ship would have been damaged, but it would have survived; other vessels prior to the *Titanic* (in 1879, 1907, 1911) had collided with icebergs in this way and survived as had one vessel sixteen years after the *Titanic* disaster (Maxtone-Graham 1972, 64; Gardner 1986, 34).

2. Forty minutes prior to striking the iceberg the *Titanic* began receiving a radio message from the *Californian*, located approximately 10 miles from the *Titanic*. Busy with personal messages from the *Titanic*'s passengers, radio operator Jack Phillips told the *Californian*'s radio operator to, "Shut up!" Consequently, the *Californian*'s message about being blocked by ice and icebergs was never received by the *Titanic*. Later, when the *Titanic* was broadcasting "CQD" and "SOS," the *Californian*'s radio operator was asleep. **What if** either message had been received? Would Captain Smith have slowed down or increased lookouts? Would the *Californian* have been able to save more passengers?

3. Beginning at about 12:30 P.M., eight white rockets signalling distress were fired from the *Titanic* and observed by the *Californian*, approximately 5-8 miles away. Crew members aboard the *Californian* saw the rockets and the *Titanic*'s lights, but the *Californian*'s radio operator was asleep, and efforts to contact the stricken ship using Morse light signal were in vain. The *Titanic* disappeared two hours after the rockets were fired. **What if** the *Californian* had responded immediately?

4. There are many stories and personal visions foretelling the *Titanic* disaster. **What if** those warnings were heeded? How would a passenger go about convincing a cruise line of impending doom? Davie (1986, 30) examines the long string of coincidences between the *Titanic* disaster in 1912 and a short story written by a merchant navy officer in 1898 about a ship called the *Titan*.

5. Recent evidence (Ballard 1987; Gannon 1995) suggests that the steel used in the construction of the *Titanic*'s hull was much more brittle than that used today. The kind of steel and the riveted construction used at the time could have made the ship considerably more vulnerable to impact damage (Gannon 1995). **What if** the *Titanic* was built using today's standards, hull construction materials, and methods? Would it have stayed afloat?

Activity: So, How Big Was It Really?

During the United States's inquiry into the *Titanic* disaster, Senator William Alden Smith asked the *Titanic*'s Fifth Officer what the iceberg was made of. Officer Lowe replied, "Ice." Officer Lowe was greatly mistaken; there's ice . . . and then there's *ice!* Most think of ice as a former liquid that a short time earlier was put into a freezer; something full of bubbles that can be chewed on. However, iceberg ice is different. It starts on land as compacted snow and is transformed ultimately to a metamorphic rock, compressed under the weight of thousands of feet of glacier possibly hundreds of thousands of years old. It is pure water, is salt free, and makes a unique additive to cold drinks. As Davie writes, hitting an iceberg like the *Titanic* did "would have been like hitting a small island" (1986, 34).

As ice floats, more is below the water than above the water. The relative volumes of ice exposed and submerged are a function of the density of the ice itself and the liquid within which it floats. The formula for calculating the volume of ice floating above water is:

$$\frac{\text{density of water—density of ice}}{\text{density of water}} \times 100 = \% \text{ volume of ice above water}$$

Equation 7.1. (Barhydt and Morgan 1993, 363)

By using the above formula, observations made by lookouts of the height of the iceberg, and some educated guesses about density, students can determine the amount of the iceberg below water and draw a cross section of what the iceberg might have looked like relative to the *Titanic*.

As icebergs go, the one the *Titanic* struck was not particularly large. Sailing charts in 1909 listed icebergs in the North Atlantic that were more than 200 feet high. *Titanic*'s lookouts estimated the top of the iceberg to be 100 feet above the water. The crow's nest from which they made their observation was approximately 100 feet above the water, so their estimate was probably fairly close. *The following calculation is for teacher reference only; the students should be allowed to discuss estimates about density and make the calculations.* For reference, the standard density of pure water at 3.98° Celsius is 1.000 grams/cc (Weast 1986, F-10). Seawater of 35 parts per thousand (ppt; 3.5% salt) freezes at -2°C. The density of seawater surrounding the *Titanic* is unknown but can be approximated. At -1°C, and a salinity of 33 ppt, the density is 1.0266 gms/cc (Donald L. Murphy, personal communication). The International Ice Patrol (1993, 18) gives a value for the density of glacial ice between 0.82 and 0.87 grams/cc; Weast (1986, F-3) gives a value of 0.917 grams/cc. A sample calculation can be made as follows:

$$\frac{1.0266-0.87}{1.0266} \times 100 = 15.25\% \text{ of the ice volume was above water}$$

Time

+ 1 class period (or allow library time to obtain density data)

Materials

+ a copy of figure 7.9 for each student
+ the density formula displayed on an overhead projector or written on the chalkboard
+ ice cubes (tall and thin, with dark food coloring added, would be better) and clear containers of liquids of different densities (glycerin, fresh water, saturated saltwater, milk, corn syrup)
+ plastic metric ruler

Grouping

+ individuals or pairs

Directions

1. Start a class discussion based on the following types of questions: Why does ice float? (The density of ice is less than that of water.) What happens differently when freshwater and saltwater freeze? ((a) Frozen freshwater ice is salt free, frozen seawater has much less salt than the original water did; (b) in both cases the ice will float; and (c) the ice will float higher in the saltwater because the ice has a lower density than the saltwater.) What amount of ice is above water relative to that below water? (Normally, the ice below the water cannot be seen.) If the students were steering a ship, how far away would they need to be to feel safe from contact with the ice?

2. Gather the class around a convenient location. Use ice cubes and liquids of different densities to demonstrate variations in the position of the ice relative to liquids of different densities. Provide the class with the densities of the ice and the various liquids (see Weast 1986, F-1, F-3). Ask the class to generalize about the position of the ice and the liquid density (the greater the liquid density, the more ice is exposed). Have some students measure the height of the ice above water and the depth below. Have each student sketch the relative positions of the ice in each liquid.

3. Put the density equation (equation 7.1) on the chalkboard or show it to the class on an overhead. Explain the terms of the equation. Calculate the ratios for the liquids examined in step 2.

4. Discuss the relative densities of the water and ice. Using the densities you arrive at during this discussion and equation 7.1, have each student or pair determine the volumes of ice above and below the water. Although the numbers will be different, they should all be fairly close. Navigation charts in 1909 used a rule of thumb of 1:7 (1 volume above water, 7 volumes below). The International Ice Patrol also uses a rule of thumb of 1:7. Any large discrepancies should be discussed with the class.

5. Distribute figure 7.9 to each student. Explain that it is a cross section of the area around the *Titanic* at the time of the collision with the iceberg. The lookouts estimated the height of the iceberg at 100 feet (30.49 meters). Figure 7.9 shows a front view of the *Titanic* to scale along with an iceberg above water. This drawing of the profile of the iceberg above water was

made from a photograph taken of what was thought to be *the* iceberg that the *Titanic* struck from the German ship *Prinz Adalbert.* What helped make this iceberg a likely suspect was a scar of red paint found along its waterline (Ballard 1988, 197).

6. The results of the calculations from step 3 give *volume* of ice, not feet of ice. If the results were 15.25% of the ice volume above water, then the remainder, or 84.75% of the ice volume was below the water. Because the lookouts gave their estimates in feet, the volumes must be converted to feet. To do this, a significant assumption must be made: that the ratios of volumes are proportional to the ratios of feet; that is, if 15.25% of the *volume* is above the water, 15.25% of the *height* will also be above the water. Because many factors affect these numbers (e.g., air temperature, radiant energy from the sun, and the overall geometric shape of the iceberg) some error is being introduced. The simple volume/height relationship is only valid for regular, blocky, or spherical shapes. Unique features, such as spires, can affect this assumption dramatically. The assumption of a 1:1 volume/height relationship, therefore, must be considered only a guess. The conversion from volume percentage to feet can be made using the following ratio:

$$\frac{\text{feet of ice above water}}{\text{calculated \% volume above water}} = \frac{\text{feet of ice below water}}{\text{calculated \% volume below water}}$$

The following are all known: feet of ice above water (100) and the two calculated volumes (determined from equation 7.1). Thus it is possible to solve for the feet of ice below water. We know that the International Ice Patrol uses a 1:7 ratio for volumes. So, if 100 feet stick out above the water, approximately 700 feet will be below the water. Compare that ratio with the numbers obtained by the students from the formula.

For the example iceberg this becomes

$$\frac{100}{15.25} = \frac{x}{84.75}$$

In this example the answer is 556 feet are below the water or a ratio of 1:5.6, compared with the International Ice Patrol ratio of 1:7. Possible explanations for this difference in ratio are poor assumptions about the densities of ice and water or an invalid correlation between volume and height. Discuss these differences with your students.

7. Once the students have determined the number of feet below the water, have them draw the iceberg below the water on figure 7.9. Students should now be in awe of the relatively puny mass of the *Titanic* compared to that of the iceberg. Although the vertical height and depth have been determined, the geometry of the iceberg is still not known. Based on geometry the International Ice Patrol uses five descriptors for the general shape of icebergs, from *pinnacle* (relatively thin and vertical) to *tabular* (wide and flat) with *dome-shaped, sloping,* and *blocky* in between. Students can make their guesses about the geometry of the iceberg as they make their drawings. They will also become aware that it is impossible to determine where the ice may be below the water merely by observing its height—the same problem the *Titanic*'s First Officer Murdoch faced when first notified by the *Titanic*'s Lookout Fleet of the iceberg.

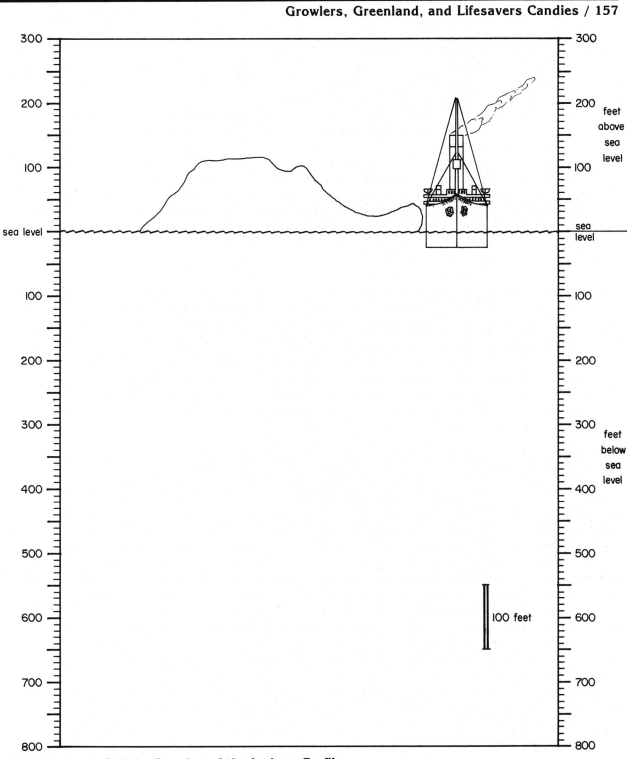

Fig. 7.9. Graph Grid for Drawing of the Iceberg Profile.

RESOURCES

International Ice Patrol
1082 Shennecossett Road
Groton, CT 06340-6095
(203) 441-2626
(203) 441-2773 (fax)

Other information about operations of the International Ice Patrol can be found in the article by Dane, cited in the "References" section of this chapter.

REFERENCES

Ballard, Robert D. *The Discovery of the Titanic.* Toronto: Madison, 1987.

——. *Exploring the Titanic.* Toronto: Madison, 1988.

Barhydt, Frances Bartlett, and Paul W. Morgan. *The Science Teacher's Book of Lists.* Englewood Cliffs, N.J.: Prentice-Hall, 1993.

Bascom, Willard. *Waves and Beaches.* Garden City, N.Y.: Anchor Books, 1980.

Brown, Richard. *Voyage of the Iceberg.* New York: Beaufort Books, 1983.

Dane, Michael. "Icehunters." *Popular Mechanics* 170 (10): 76-131 (1993).

Davie, Michael. *Titanic: The Death and Life of a Legend.* New York: Alfred A. Knopf, 1986.

Fenster, J. M. "A World in the Middle of the Ocean." *American Heritage* 47 (2): 96-116 (1996).

Gannon, Robert. "What Really Sank the Titanic?" *Popular Science* 246 (2): 49-83 (1995).

Gardner, Martin. *The Wreck of the Titanic Foretold?* Buffalo, N.Y.: Prometheus Books, 1986.

Hale, John R. *Great Ages of Man: Age of Exploration.* New York: Time, 1966.

Hammond's Historical Atlas. Maplewood, N.J.: Hammond, 1960.

International Ice Patrol. Washington, D.C.: U.S. Government Printing Office, 1993.

Kent, Deborah. *The Titanic.* Chicago: Childrens Press, 1993.

Lord, Walter. *A Night to Remember.* New York: Bantam Books, 1955.

MacLeish, William H. *The Gulf Stream.* London: Hamish Hamilton, 1989.

Maddocks, Melvin. *The Great Liners.* Alexandria, Va.: Time-Life Books, 1982.

Maxtone-Graham, John. *The Only Way to Cross.* New York: Collier, 1972.

Mersey, Lord. Shipping Casualties (Loss of Steamship "Titanic"). *1912, The Final Report of the British Investigation into the Sinking of the Titanic.* Published by His Majesty's Stationery Office, London.

Murphy, Donald J. Chief Scientist, International Ice Patrol, personal communication. February 29, 1996.

National Geographic Society. *The Making of America; Northern Approaches,* map supplement to *National Geographic*, February 167 (2): 208a (1985).

"On Thin Ice." *Denver Post*, March 16, 1995, p. 2.

Stewart, R. W. "The Atmosphere and the Ocean." *Scientific American* 221 (3): 76-86 (1969).

Villiers, Captain Alan. *Men, Ships and the Sea.* Washington, D.C.: National Geographic Society, 1973.

Weast, Robert D., ed. *Handbook of Chemistry and Physics.* 67th ed. Boca Raton, Fla.: CRC Press, 1986.

U.S. Senate. *"Titanic" Disaster; Report of the Committee on Commerce.* Report 806, 62-2. Washington, D.C.: U.S. Government Printing Office, 1912.

EIGHT

Hilo, _Hekla_, and the U.S. Virgin Islands

There are waves, and then there are WAVES! Tsunamis are the latter. As D. M. Souza writes, "The power of a tsunami is like that of no other wave in the ocean" (1992, 45). What are erroneously considered by many to be tidal waves are waves generally created by near-surface disturbances, most frequently seismic events, volcanic activity, landslides, or other land failures. They have nothing to do with tides. In an attempt to correct that misconception the name _tsunami_ is often used. _Tsunami_ comes from the Japanese _tsu_, meaning harbor, and _nami_, meaning long wave. A literal translation then is a long wave in a harbor or port. It sounds better, but as Bascom writes, "tsunami merely means tidal wave in Japanese" (1980, 112).

In the United States and its territories such waves have been responsible for at least 470 fatalities and hundreds of millions of dollars in property damage (Lander and Lockridge 1989, 1). Tsunamis have also created political havoc. Only twenty days after a destructive hurricane struck St. Thomas, on November 18, 1867 an earthquake between St. Thomas and St. Croix in the U.S. Virgin Islands created the most damaging tsunami ever to affect the Virgin Islands. Prior to this tsunami the United States had been interested in purchasing St. John and St. Thomas from Denmark for use as a naval base.

Although the sale was overwhelmingly approved by the islanders on January 9, 1868, it was not ratified by the U.S. Senate (Lander and Lockridge 1989, 211). As you might have guessed, the back-to-back disasters of hurricane and tsunami raised questions about the suitability of the islands for a naval facility. The submarine threat after World War I finally encouraged the Senate to overcome its trepidations, and it approved the purchase of the Virgin Islands from Denmark in 1917.

Approximately 80 percent of tsunamis occur in the Pacific Ocean, which averages one per year. It is not mere coincidence that the Pacific Ocean is associated with both the Ring of Fire and the high incidence of tsunamis. Such linkages helped lead to the theory of plate tectonics. Because the center of seafloor spreading in the Pacific is so close to the west coast of the United States, most of the Pacific Rim is an area of plate destruction. Zones of subduction, transform faulting, and volcanism associated with hot spots all can generate seismic disturbances that, in turn, can create tsunamis. Crescent City, California, was struck by 10-foot and 28-foot (3-meter and 9-meter) high tsunamis associated with a Chilean earthquake in 1960 and the Alaskan earthquake in 1964. Even local earthquakes (creating submarine landslides) can generate tsunamis in California similar to those that occurred after an 1812

160

earthquake in Santa Barbara and a 1927 earthquake at Point Arguello. A tsunami reportedly 90-100 feet (27-30 meters) high destroyed a lighthouse and its five inhabitants after a 1946 earthquake in the Aleutian Islands. The same tsunami washed away a radio tower 105 feet (32 meters) above sea level. Despite warnings issued by the Pacific Tsunami Warning Center (originally the Seismic Sea Wave Warning System) tsunamis associated with the March 1964 Alaskan earthquake caused 119 deaths (most in Alaska) and more than $102 million in damage along Pacific Coast cities of the United States.

Most tsunamis cause damage in areas near the original disturbance. Reviewing tsunamis over the past 100 years Lockridge (1988, 173) determined that only 9 of 104 damaging tsunamis created damage beyond the local area of generation. Earthquakes of magnitude 7.5 and larger along the west coast of South America have the greatest potential for creating damaging tsunamis in the Pacific (Lockridge 1988, 175).

Approximately 5-10 percent of reported tsunamis occur in the Atlantic Ocean. A destructive earthquake in Lisbon, Portugal, in 1755 created 23-foot (7-meter) high waves in the Caribbean and probably generated some waves along the eastern seaboard (the absence of tide gauges makes documentation difficult; James Lander, personal communication 3/6/96). In addition, the broad continental shelf along the eastern seaboard tends to moderate the effects of a tsunami (Lander and Lockridge 1989, 202). The islands of St. Thomas and Puerto Rico suffered tsunami damage immediately after earthquakes in 1867 and 1918, respectively. No tsunamis were reported for the U.S. Gulf coast from any of the Caribbean earthquakes. Although the effects on the United States have been significant, they pale by comparison to worldwide tsunami statistics. In 1737 a 210-foot (64-meter) high wave covered the Kamchatka Peninsula in Russia; in 1896 a tsunami striking the northeast coast of Japan killed more than 27,000 people, and in 1883 a wave associated with the eruption of Krakatoa killed 35,000 in the southwestern Pacific (Steinbrugge 1982, 233).

In general, tsunamis are initiated by a seismic (or other physical disruption such as a volcanic eruption or landslide) disturbance that creates a rapid change in the shape of the ocean basin, in turn causing a disturbance in the adjacent water column. That disturbance moves outward as a large ripple would after a rock lands in a pool of water. As tsunamis travel across the open ocean, at speeds of several hundred miles per hour, they go unnoticed by ships at sea. Even a 50-foot (15-meter) high wave crashing ashore would be a relatively insignificant wave, perhaps 3 feet (1 meter) high, at sea, where the crests may be hundreds of miles apart. The size of the typical wave at the ocean surface depends on the wind velocity and the fetch (distance across the water surface on which the wind blows). What makes a routine, wind-driven (meteorologic) wave crash at the shore is the circular water motion of the wave "feeling" or being interrupted by the sea bottom; that only happens close to shore. As the wave motion touches bottom, the lower part of the wave slows down, the top part continues forward and the wave just falls over, creating the surf that is so popular on Hawaii's north coast during the winter. The same process occurs with tsunamis, only more dramatically. A 50-foot (15-meter) high wave moving rapidly across the ocean unnoticed by ships can become deadly when it crashes ashore, exerting a pressure of 5.4 tons per square foot (5.9 kilograms per square centimeter) (Arnold 1988, 64) and smashing everything in its path.

Deaths from tsunamis occur for two main reasons.

1. *People ignore or are unaware of the warnings, or warnings have not been given.* A survey taken of residents after a tsunami flooded an area in Hawaii indicated that more than half of the respondents heard the warnings but waited at home for the wave to strike rather than evacuate.

2. *People are unaware of wave motions.* A wave consists of a high portion (the crest) and a low portion (the trough). As a wave approaches the shore the water level rises as the crest arrives and falls when the trough arrives. The former is usually seen as the surf running up onto the shore; the latter is usually seen as the water receding. With most common shoreline waves the differences between the arrival of crest and trough are noticeable but not threatening. When a group of tsunamis approach the effects are noticeable and deadly. The crest of the first wave may raise the water level only a few feet above normal, not unlike what the wake of a large ship might do as it passes nearby. Souza (1992, 36) describes witnesses who reported a hissing noise associated with the first wave. The succeeding trough, following the crest by minutes, is significantly deeper than normal, revealing parts of the ocean bottom not normally seen. This is the most dangerous point in the wave progression and the first manifestation of the tsunami. People, unaware of rapidly approaching, larger waves, are often overcome with the desire to grab a vulnerable fish, examine an interesting shell, or explore this newly exposed land. Technical observers of a tsunami that struck Hilo, Hawaii, as a result of an earthquake in Chile in 1960 described what happened (the lowest point of the trough occurred at 1:00 A.M. and dropped the water level 7 feet below the prewave level):

> For a short while a strange calm prevailed as ground water cascaded from among rocks that are rarely exposed to view along the shore. At first there was only the sound, a dull rumble like a distant train that came from the darkness far out toward the mouth of the bay. By 1:02 A.M. all could hear the loudening roar as it came closer through the night. As our eyes searched for the source of the ominous noise, a pale wall of tumbling water, the broken crest of the . . . wave, was caught in the dim light. . . . At 1:04 A.M. the 20-foot high nearly vertical front of the in-rushing bore churned past our lookout, and we ran a few hundred feet toward safer ground. (Eaton, Richter, and Ault 1961, 139)

Four minutes had elapsed between the trough and the arrival of this devastating crest, not nearly enough time for the escape of those unfortunate enough to have been exploring the sea bottom.

Activity: Reassemble the City

Kodiak Island is approximately 280 miles (450 kilometers) from the epicenter of the 1964 Good Friday Alaska earthquake. Damage to the U.S. Naval Station on Kodiak Island resulted from two factors. Large-scale motions from the earthquake itself caused the land surface of the U.S. Naval Station and the town of Kodiak to subside 5.6 feet (1.7 meters) and move many feet. At Seward, Alaska, the horizontal motion was 40 feet (12 meters) and in some places was as much as 70 feet (21 meters; Lander, personal communication 3/6/96). A series of at least ten tsunamis then flooded the vulnerable land areas. Maximum rise of the water level resulting from the waves was 25 feet (7.6 meters). An eyewitness described the first wave arrival as follows:

> The water began to recede rapidly leaving an 85-foot King Crab, Inc. vessel sitting on bottom . . . even though there is ample water even during low tide . . . the first tsunami hit at about 6:15 P.M. It raised the 85-foot boat from the bottom and hurled it at least 50 feet in a southwest direction. The water level rose at least 15 feet in 5 seconds. (Kachadoorian and Plafker 1967, F22)

When the waves struck the city of Kodiak many boats and buildings in their path were moved inland. Others were completely destroyed. In this activity students will study the damage at Kodiak by analyzing the damage to both boats and buildings.

Time

+ 2 class periods

Materials

+ copies of figures 8.1 and 8.2 for each student or pair (enlarged if possible)
+ student-prepared tables (using guidelines below)

Grouping

+ individuals or pairs

Directions

1. Discuss tsunamis with students and read the passage from the eyewitness at Kodiak (see above). Ask the students to speculate about the kind of damage a large wave, or series of large waves, might cause to a coastal city.

2. Tell the students that they are part of a government team that must assess the damage at Kodiak Island after the 1964 tsunamis. They will assess boat and building damage using figures 8.1 and 8.2, respectively. To assess boat damage they will prepare a table (from figure 8.1) that indicates the following:

name of boat

length of boat (feet and meters)

condition of boat when found

    a. moderate damage, can be saved or salvable or

    b. severe damage, unsalvable

approximate distance the boat was moved by the wave

Text continues on page 166.

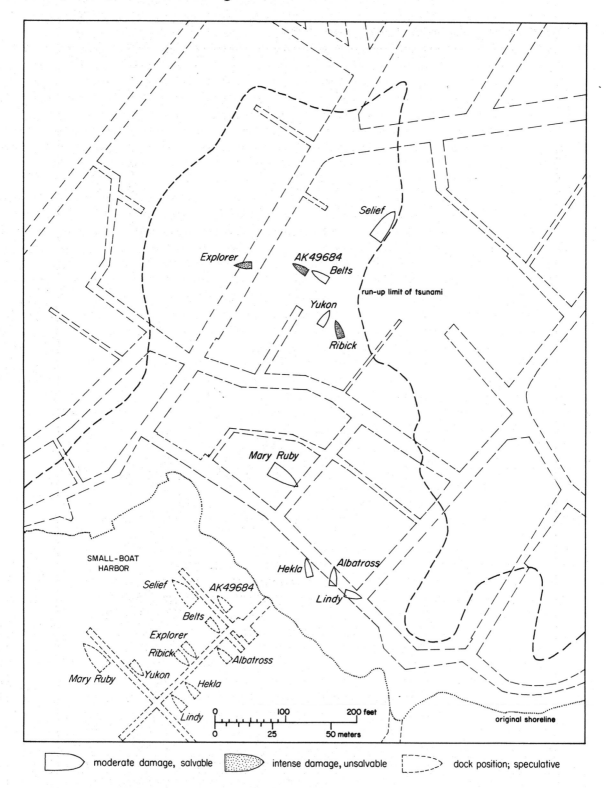

Fig. 8.1. Tsunami Effects on Boats in Kodiak, Alaska.

Note: Adapted from Kachadoorian, Reuben, and George Plafker. *Effects of the Earthquake of March 27, 1964 on the Communities of Kodiak and Nearby Islands*. U.S.G.S. Professional Paper 542-F. Washington, D.C.: U.S. Government Printing Office, 1967.

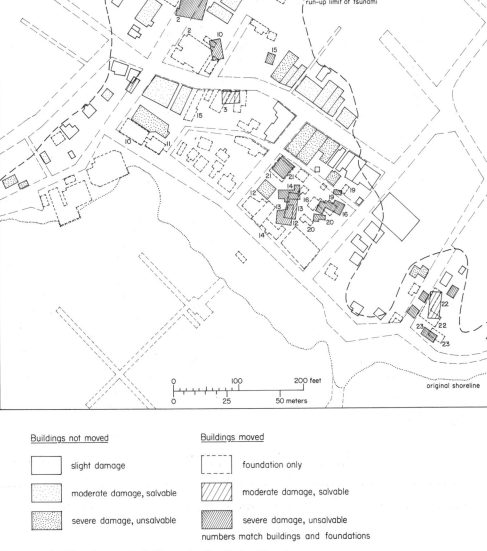

run-up limit of tsunami

original shoreline

0   100   200 feet

0   25   50 meters

Buildings not moved

☐ slight damage

▨ moderate damage, salvable

▨ severe damage, unsalvable

Buildings moved

⌐⌐ foundation only

▨ moderate damage, salvable

▨ severe damage, unsalvable

numbers match buildings and foundations

Fig. 8.2. Tsunami Effects on Buildings in Kodiak, Alaska.

Note: Adapted from Kachadoorian, Reuben, and George Plafker. *Effects of the Earthquake of March 27, 1964 on the Communities of Kodiak and Nearby Islands.* U.S.G.S. Professional Paper 542-F. Washington, D.C.: U.S. Government Printing Office, 1967.

3. To assess building damage within the area affected by the tsunami the students will prepare a similar table from figure 8.2 indicating the following:

For buildings not moved:

    a. how many sustained only slight damage and can be saved

    b. how many sustained moderate damage and are salvageable

    c. how many sustained severe damage and are unsalvageable

For buildings moved:

    a. how many were completely destroyed with only foundations remaining

    b. how many were moved with only slight damage and were salvable

    c. how many were moved with severe damage and were unsalvable

4. List all of the moved buildings by number. Match the moved building with the foundation and determine (in feet and meters) how far the building moved.

5. Ask the students to write a short essay describing what precautions they might take to avoid the financial catastrophe resulting from the destruction of their fishing boat or business in a coastal area susceptible to tsunamis. Answers might include, "buy lots of insurance," "see how the buildings that survived were built and rebuild mine that way," "build protective walls," or "build only in high areas of the city." With enough warning boats could be evacuated. After the 1964 Alaska earthquake Kodiak residents had only 20 minutes to move their boats before the first wave arrived—not nearly enough time. Hawaii generally receives a warning of several hours; evacuation to deeper water is the most effective way to save a boat.

Extension

Students can build scale models of the buildings and boats of Kodiak. By placing them on a stream table they can try to duplicate the damage created by the tsunami.

Activity: How Fast Was It Moving?

The typical ocean wave observed by someone aboard a ship has been generated by the wind and is moving across the sea at an average speed of about 35 miles (56 kilometers) per hour; the range is between 7 and 70 miles (11 and 112 kilometers) per hour (Souza 1992, 11). By contrast, a tsunami generated by a subsea disturbance often travels at the speed of a commercial jet aircraft (i.e., several hundred miles per hour). The determination of the average velocity of a tsunami is a fairly simple matter. The time of the initial disturbance is known and the time the wave arrives at a tide gauge can also be determined; from those two pieces of data the wave travel time can be determined by subtraction. The distance between the point of initial disturbance and the point at which the tsunami arrives can be measured from a globe or determined by satellite. With the time and distance known the wave velocity can be determined as follows:

$$\text{average velocity} = \frac{\text{distance}}{\text{time}}$$

Equation 8.1.

The Good Friday Alaska earthquake of March 28, 1964, occurred at 03:36:12.7 GMT (Greenwich Mean Time 5:36 P.M. Alaska time) at 61°6' North latitude and 147°36' West longitude. Greenwich Mean Time is the official time kept by the National Observatory at Greenwich, just south of London, England; it is a worldwide time reference that is known as Coordinated Universal Time or sometimes referred to as Zulu Time. For this activity the only critical time is the elapsed time between the initiation of the wave and the recording of the wave at some distant station. Whether the wave arrives at 2:15 P.M. or 11:29 A.M. is of no significance in this activity; the only concern is that a wave took 4 hours and 31 minutes to travel from the seismic event to the tidal recording station. Students will use 0 hours and 0 minutes as the time of the seismic event and read the elapsed time directly from the charts of the tidal records (marigraphs; see fig. 8.3 [A-G]). They will then use longitude and latitude to locate the earthquake epicenter and recording stations on a map showing the Pacific Rim countries and islands. (See fig. 8.4). Students will be given copies of the marigraphs from thirty stations around the Pacific Ocean affected by the tsunami. On each of these records a black arrow indicates the arrival of the tsunami. Although the students will only be using the left side of the marigraphs, almost a full day's record is shown to illustrate (a) the range of tidal fluctuation in a given site, (b) the twice-daily fluctuation of the tides, and (c) the arrival of the tsunami relative to the tidal cycle. What may appear as a 5-foot tsunami may only be a 1-foot tsunami superimposed on a 4-foot-high tide. Students will need to read the scale on the bottom of the record to obtain the arrival time (or, in this case, "elapsed" time). The Great Circle Distance is given in miles in table 8.1 (students will need to convert it to kilometers). Students will then calculate the wave velocities in both miles per hour and kilometers per hour. They will then use those calculated velocities in the next activity.

Time

+ 3 class periods

Materials

+ a copy of table 8.1 for each student
+ a copy of figure 8.3 (A-G) for each student (enlarged to 11" x 17" if possible); once duplicated, the marigraphs can be placed back to back and laminated for a permanent classroom set)
+ a copy of figure 8.4 for each student (enlarged to 11" x 17")
+ straightedge (ruler or triangle)
+ pencil
+ calculator (recommended)
+ transparent tape
+ scissors

Text continues on page 178.

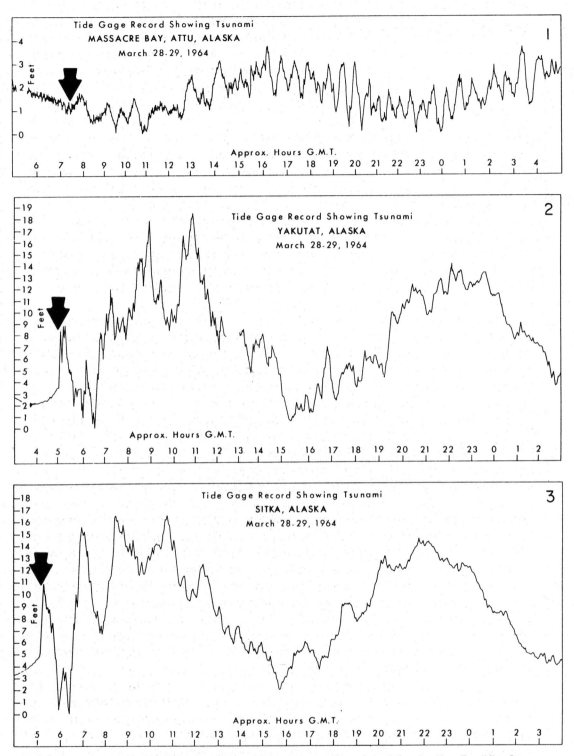

Fig. 8.3A. (A-G) Marigraphs for Thrifty Tidal Recording Stations in the Pacific Ocean.

Note: Modified from Spaeth, M. G., and S. C. Beckman. *The Tsunami of March 28, 1964 as Recorded at Tide Stations*. Rockville, Md.: U.S. Department of Commerce, 1965, pp. 29-50.

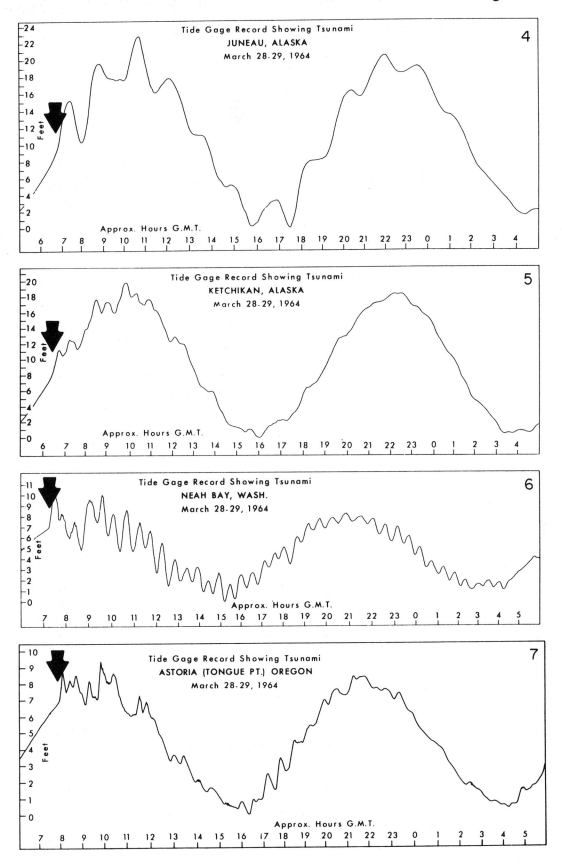

Fig. 8.3B.

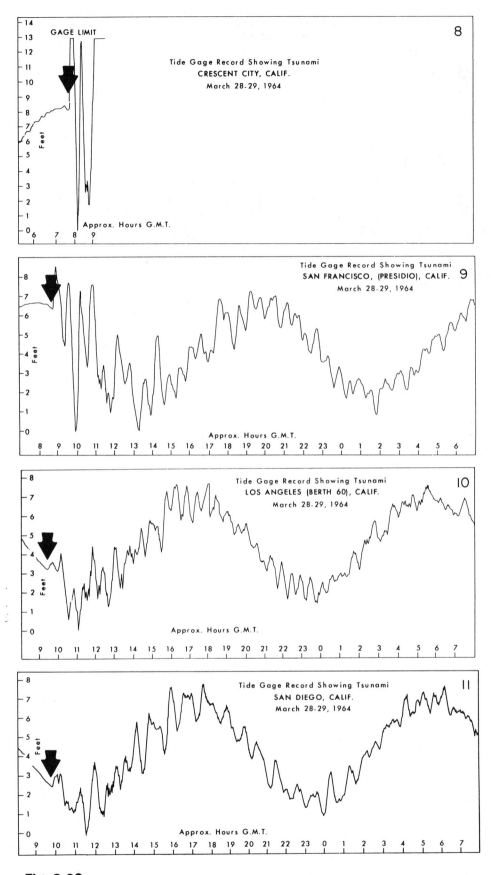

Fig. 8.3C.

From *American History Through Earth Science*. © 1997 Craig A. Munsart. Teacher Ideas Press. (800) 237-6124.

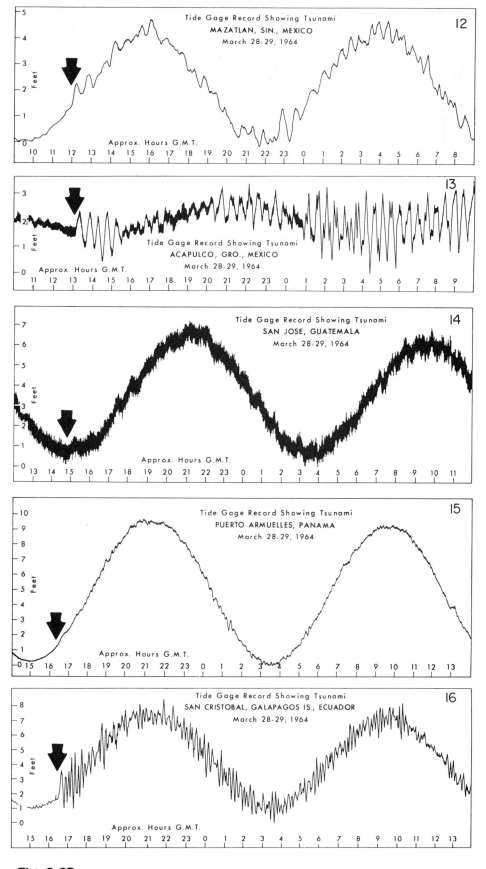

Fig. 8.3D.

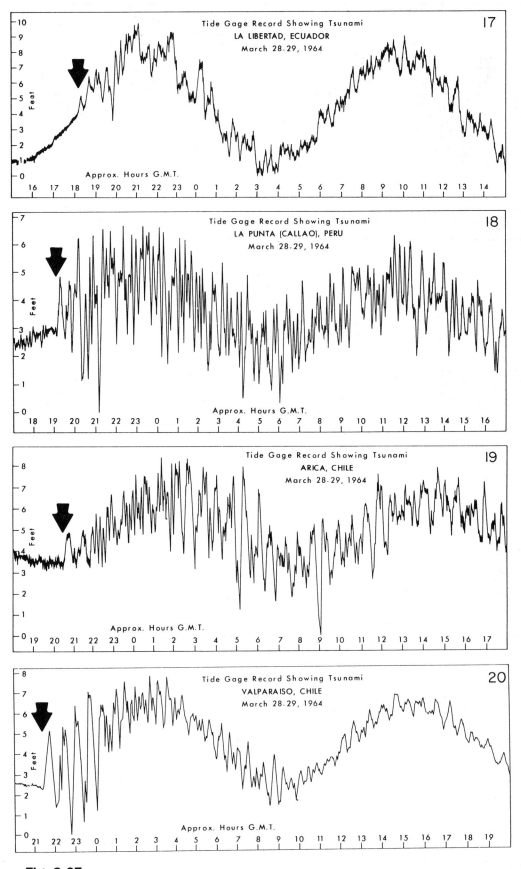

Fig. 8.3E.

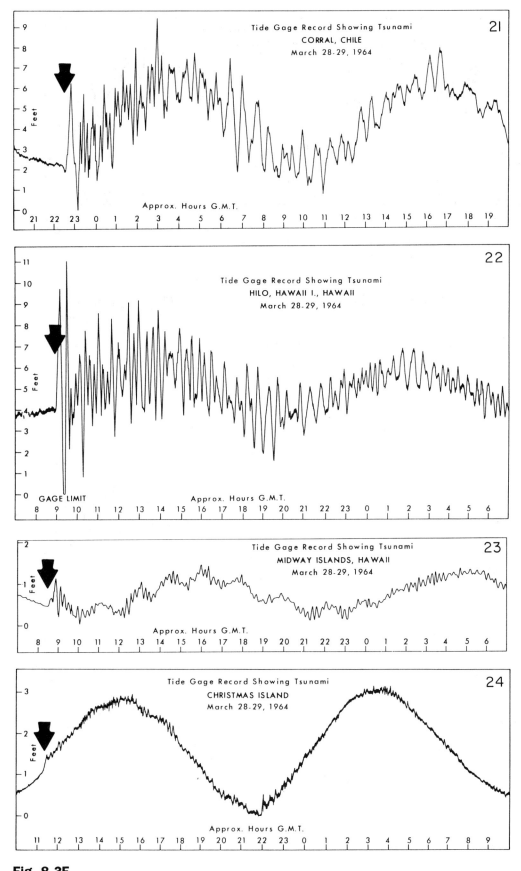

Fig. 8.3F.

From *American History Through Earth Science*. © 1997 Craig A. Munsart. Teacher Ideas Press. (800) 237-6124.

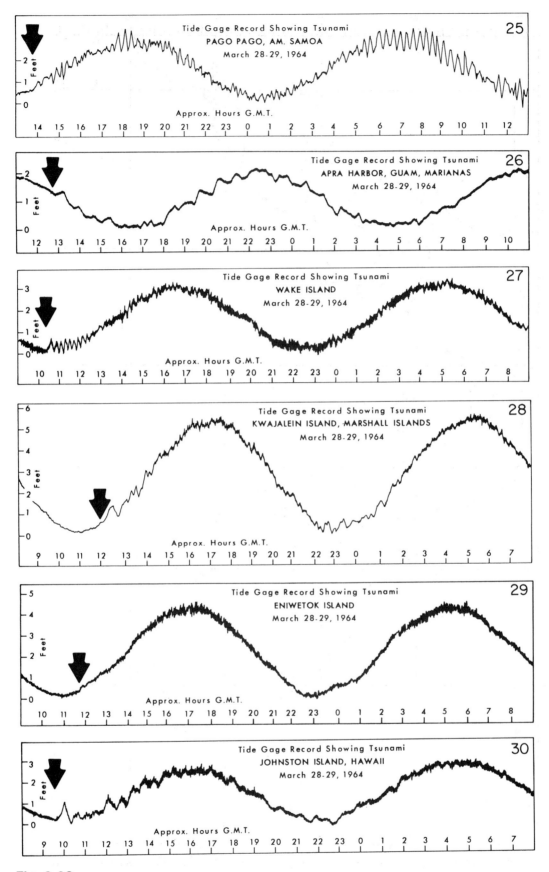

Fig. 8.3G.

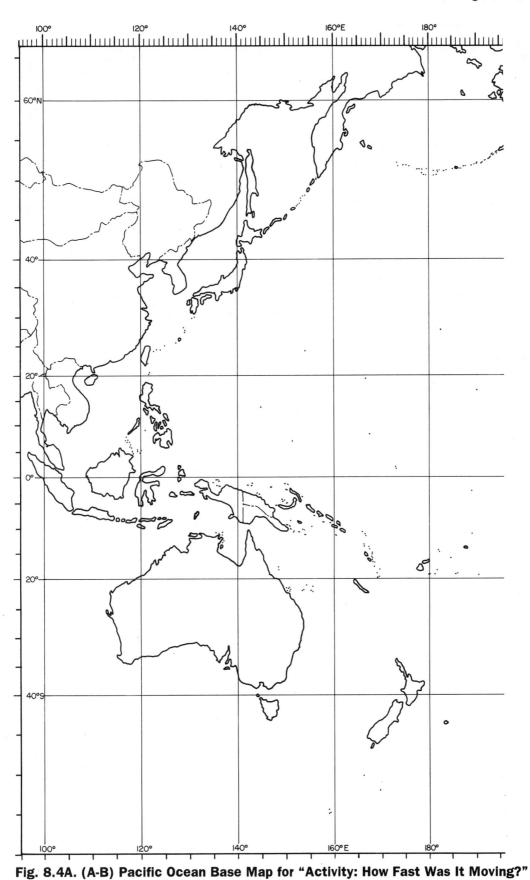

Fig. 8.4A. (A-B) Pacific Ocean Base Map for "Activity: How Fast Was It Moving?"

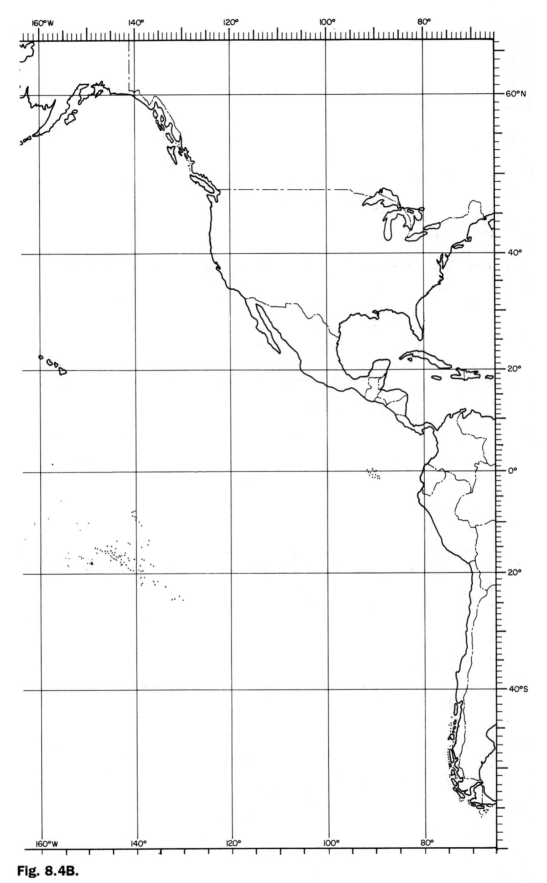

Fig. 8.4B.

Table 8.1. Locations of Tidal Recording Stations.

Station #	Name	Dgrs Min Longitude	Dgr Min Latitude	Miles From Epicenter	Time of 1st Wave Arrival	Velocity mph/kph	Water Depth feet/meters
1	Attu, Aleutian Isl., Alaska	52° 50'N	186° 48'W	1571			
2	Yakutat, Alaska	59° 33'N	139° 44'W	256			
3	Sitka, Alaska	57° 03'N	135° 20'W	466			
4	Juneau, Alaska	58° 18'N	134° 25'W	483			
5	Ketchikan, Alaska	55° 21'N	131° 39'W	649			
6	Neah Bay, Washington	48° 22'N	124° 37'W	1199			
7	Astoria, Oregon	46° 13'N	123° 46'W	1341			
8	Crescent City, California	41° 45'N	124° 12'W	1588			
9	San Francisco, California	37° 48'N	122° 28'W	1872			
10	Los Angeles, California	33° 43'N	118° 16'W	2229			
11	San Diego, California	32° 43'N	117° 10'W	2319			
12	Mazatlan, Mexico	23° 11'N	106° 26'W	3202			
13	Acapulco, Mexico	16° 51'N	99° 55'W	3782			
14	San Jose, Guatemala	13° 55'N	90° 50'W	4241			
15	Pacific End, Panama Canal	08° 55'N	79° 32'W	4949			
16	Galapagos Islands, Ecuador	00° 54'S	89° 37'W	5191			
17	La Libertad, Ecuador	02° 13'S	80° 55'W	5543			
18	Callao, Peru	12° 03'N	77° 09'W	6264			
19	Arica, Chile	18° 28'N	70° 20'W	6871			
20	Valparaiso, Chile	33° 02'N	71° 38'W	7699			
21	Corral, Chile	39° 52'N	73° 26'W	7809			
22	Hilo, Hawaii	19° 44'N	155° 03'W	2810			
23	Midway Islands, Hawaii	28° 13'N	177° 22'W	2614			
24	Christmas Island	01° 59'N	157° 29'W	4046			
25	Pago Pago, Amer. Samoa	14° 17'S	170° 41'W	5297			
26	Guam, Marianas	13° 26'N	144° 39'E	4671			
27	Wake Island	19° 17'N	166° 37'E	3612			
28	Kwajalein, Marshall Islands	08° 44'N	167° 44'E	4238			
29	Eniwetok Island	11° 22'N	162° 21'E	4228			
30	Johnston Island, Hawaii	16° 45'N	169° 31'W	3192			

From *American History Through Earth Science*. © 1997 Craig A. Munsart. Teacher Ideas Press. (800) 237-6124.

Grouping

+ individuals

Directions

1. Distribute figure 8.3 to the students and explain briefly its purpose.

2. The epicenter of the Alaskan earthquake was 61°6' North latitude and 147°36' West longitude. Distribute figure 8.4 and have the students locate the epicenter on the figure.

3. Distribute table 8.1. Table 8.1 gives the location (using longitude and latitude) of the tidal recording stations. Using those locations students should find and neatly label the recording stations on figure 8.4.

4. Remind students of the mathematical relationship

$$\text{velocity} \times \text{time} = \text{distance}$$

Have them rearrange the terms to determine the velocity. They should find that

$$\text{velocity} = \frac{\text{distance}}{\text{time}}$$

Be certain they understand this mathematical relationship before proceeding.

5. Ask the students what information they will need to determine the velocity of a tsunami. [Their answers should be distance and time.]

6. Refer the students back to figure 8.3 (A-G). Explain to the students that it presents the tidal records from each of the stations they located on figure 8.4. On each tidal record is an arrow indicating the arrival of the tsunami. Using the scale along the bottom of the record students can determine the elapsed time (the time between the seismic event and wave arrival at the recording station). Reminder: The time of the earthquake was 3:36:12.7 Greenwich Mean Time.

7. Using the tide records they should determine the elapsed time of the waves to each recording station and enter these times in the appropriate column in table 8.1.

8. Using the distances provided on table 8.1 and the elapsed times determined in step 5 the students should be able to calculate the wave velocities in miles per hour. To determine the velocities in kilometers per hour, they need to multiply the miles per hour by 1.609.

9. Discuss what factors might influence the velocity. Student responses might include earthquake intensity, water density, tides, and distance. Don't tell them which answer is correct. Let them brainstorm and list the ideas on the chalkboard or overhead. As they will learn in the following activity, the wave velocity is a function of water depth.

Extension

After the first wave arrivals are plotted on the map, students should be able to show the progress of the wave across the Pacific by contouring the position of the wave front. For instance, where is the wave after one hour, four hours, or ten hours?

To gain a perspective of how fast tsunamis travel students could be encouraged to visit the library to find velocities of other moving objects and plot them on a graph with the tsunami speeds. Keep a master graph in the class to which additional items can be added as they are found; make a contest among the different classes for the most objects plotted. Students might use human-made objects such as cars, aircraft, spacecrafts, or ships. Add velocities of natural systems as well: hurricanes, water and wind currents, turbidity currents, avalanches, and P- and S- and Raleigh seismic wave propogation velocities.

Activity: How Deep Was the Water?

Like other waves, tsunamis slow down as they approach land because of friction with the sea bottom. In open ocean, where the waves cannot touch the bottom, they travel quickly. The equation that relates the velocity of the wave to the depth of the sea is as follows (Bascom 1980, 115):

$$C = \text{square root } (gd)$$

where *C* is the velocity of the wave, *g* is the gravitational constant (32 feet per second per second or 9.8 meters per second per second), and *d* is the water depth (in feet or meters, as needed). If the wave velocity and gravitational constant are known, the equation can be solved for the depth as follows:

$$\text{depth} = \frac{C^2}{g}$$

Equation 8.2.

Once students have determined the velocity of the tsunami as it traveled across the Pacific they can then calculate the average water depth between the origin of the wave and the tidal recording station. To calculate successfully the water depth, all data must use the same unit of measure. (The velocity calculations students added to table 8.1 are in miles per hour and kilometers per hour.)

Time

+ 1 class period or homework

Materials

+ the completed table 8.1 from "Activity: How Fast Was It Moving?"
+ calculator (helpful)
+ equations 1 and 2, presented on an overhead projector or chalkboard

Grouping

+ individuals or pairs (the same arrangement as in "Activity: How Fast Was It Moving?")

Directions

1. Be certain students have *completed and corrected* table 8.1 and have it with them. They will need the velocity numbers from the table for this activity and will be adding the results of this activity to the table.

2. Discuss the general wave relationship with the students (that, on the open ocean, tsunamis move quickly as table 8.1 should now indicate, and that once they approach land, and shallower water, they move more slowly and can cause considerable damage because they crash).

3. Explain that there is an equation that relates the depth of the water to the velocity of the wave: $C = \text{square root } (gd)$. Explain the terms. Discuss the knowns (velocity and gravitational constant) and the unknown

(water depth). Have the students transpose the equation and solve for the water depth, using the equation

$$\text{depth} = \frac{c^2}{g}$$

4. Using the average velocities students determined from the epicenter to the various stations as part of "Activity: How Fast Was It Moving?", and the appropriate gravitational constant, they should now be able to calculate the average water depths for those same stations. It is critical to use the same units for both the velocity and gravitational constant, that is, all feet or all meters (miles per hour x 1.467 equals feet per second; use g = 32 feet per second per second). Kilometers per hour x 0.278 equals meters per second; use g = 9.8 meters per second per second).

Perhaps what is most depressing about the study of tsunamis is that people seem to learn almost nothing from previous catastrophes. The major part of the energy of tsunamis is generated at right angles to the disturbance; a disturbance along the coast will generate a tsunami moving perpendicular to the coast (Lander and Lockridge 1989, 3). Because of their location in the central Pacific the Hawaiian Islands are vulnerable to tsunamis generated anywhere along the Pacific Rim. Hilo, on the northeast coast of the Island of Hawaii, is a city in a particularly precarious position. When not threatened from land by lava spewing from one of the most active volcanoes in the world, residents must be aware of tsunamis generated anywhere in the Pacific. One of Hilo's greatest natural assets, the harbor, is also its greatest liability; the geometry of the harbor funnels tsunamis ashore, dramatically increasing their energy and damage potential (Eaton, Richter, and Ault 1961, 147).

A disastrous 1946 tsunami that struck Hilo prompted three observers to offer several commonsense suggestions: avoid building in dangerous areas, develop a warning system, and educate the public about the need to evacuate susceptible areas (Eaton, Richter, and Ault 1961, 155). Fourteen years later the warning system was in place but not much else. Businesses in the most susceptible areas relocated—but many to other low areas. In addition, flimsy, crowded housing was built in areas swept clean by the 1946 waves. Public education did not prevent sightseers or encourage evacuation during subsequent tsunamis in 1952 and 1957. The tsunami following the 1960 earthquake in Chile demonstrated that warnings and public education were not enough: In Hilo, Hawaii, 61 people were killed and 282 injured. People not only failed to heed the warnings but many went to the harbor to observe the arrival of the wave (Lander and Lockridge 1989, 5).

The Pacific Tsunami Warning System effectively predicts the time of arrival of a tsunami, but not its height. Because most tsunamis are small a tendency develops among those living in susceptible areas to ignore the warnings. A survey, taken after the tsunami in 1960, indicates the problems. Of 329 adults surveyed in Hilo, almost all received (what turned out to be) an accurate warning of the oncoming waves. Yet 49 of them went about their normal routine and made no plans to evacuate, 105 evacuated shortly after receiving the warning, and the remaining 175 waited at home until the wave struck. Somewhere in this system exists what Eaton, Richter, and Ault call "a fatal flaw" (1961, 156).

REFERENCES

Arnold, Caroline. *Coping with Natural Disasters*. New York: Walker, 1988.

Bascom, Willard. *Waves and Beaches*. Garden City, N.Y.: Anchor Book, 1980.

Eaton, J. P., D. H. Richter, and W. U. Ault. "The Tsunami of May 23, 1960, on the Island of Hawaii." *Bulletin of the Seismological Society of America* 51 (2): 135-57 (1961).

Kachadoorian, Reuben, and George Plafker. *Effects of the Earthquake of March 27, 1964 on the Communities of Kodiak and Nearby Islands*. U.S.G.S. Professional Paper 542-F. Washington, D.C.: U.S. Government Printing Office, 1967.

Lander, James F. *Cooperative Institute for Research in the Environmental Sciences*. Boulder, Colo.: personal communication, March 6, 1996.

Lander, James F., and Patricia A. Lockridge. *United States Tsunamis 1690-1988*. Publication 41-2. Boulder, Colo.: National Geophysical Data Center, 1989.

Lockridge, Patricia A. "Historical Tsunamis in the Pacific Basin." In *Natural and Man-Made Hazards*, edited by M. I. El-Sabh, and T. S. Murty, 171-81. D. Reidel, 1988.

Souza, D. M. *Powerful Waves*. Minneapolis, Minn.: Carolrhoda Books, 1992.

Spaeth, M. G., and S. C. Beckman. *The Tsunami of March 28, 1964 As Recorded at Tide Stations*. Rockville, Md.: U.S. Department of Commerce, 1965.

Steinbrugge, Karl V. *Earthquakes, Volcanoes, and Tsunamis*. New York: Skandia America Group, 1982.

GLOSSARY

Barrier Island	A long, narrow body of sand separated from the mainland by water.
Bathymetry	The measurement of the depth of large bodies of water.
Beringia	The former landmass connecting Asia to North America.
B.P.E.	Before Present Era; before the birth of Christ.
Coriolis Effect	A motion created by the earth's rotation such that moving wind or water in the Northern Hemisphere is deflected toward the right; the opposite occurs in the Southern Hemisphere.
Derelicts	Abandoned vessels or hulks adrift at sea.
Drainage Basin	The area from which water is carried away by a network of streams.
Ebb Surge	A rise in water level on the "back side" of a hurricane as impounded water fills low topographic areas, exacerbating earlier damage.
El Niño	An oceanic and weather phenomenon involving changes in ocean temperatures, current flow, and weather patterns; named after the Christ child.
Eustatic Sea Level Change	Change in the level of the ocean surface created by variation in the amount of water in the ocean basins.
Flood Surge	Doming of the water surface by wind shear as a hurricane drives onshore; worst in the right, front quadrant of a hurricane.
Floodplain	The area bordering a stream channel that is periodically covered by water from that stream.
Growler	A floating mass of formerly glacial ice projecting less than 5 meters (17 feet) above the water.
Gyre	An ocean current or series of currents moving in a circular or spiral form.
Hot Spots	A fixed source of heat in the mantle above which crustal plates move to create linear chains of islands.
Iceberg	A floating mass of formerly glacial ice projecting at least 5 meters (17 feet) above the water.
Isostasy	The balancing of low-density materials as they are supported by high-density materials.
Kinetic Energy	The ability of a moving object to create activity; the energy of motion.
Knot	A rate of speed equal to 1 nautical mile per hour or 1.15 statute miles per hour.
Levee	A bank of sand and silt built by a river during floods along both sides of the active channel.
Long Ton	A weight equal to 1016.06 kilograms or 2,240 pounds.

Mantle	The middle layer of the earth, below the crust and above the core.
Mantle Plumes	Drifting outpourings of heat from the mantle up to the crust of the earth.
Marigraph	The graphic recording of a tide gauge.
Metric Ton	A measure of weight equal to 1,000 kilograms or 2,204.59 pounds.
Nautical Mile	The length of one degree of arc of a great circle used in navigation; equal to 1,852 meters or approximately 6,076 feet.
N.G.V.D.	National Geodetic Vertical Datum. The standard reference for sea level.
Nueé Ardente	A hot cloud of particles and gases issued from a volcano that moves rapidly downslope. (French, "glowing cloud.")
Pores	Spaces between particles of granular materials.
Potential Energy	The ability of an object whose position has been changed to create activity.
Seamount	An isolated peak rising above the ocean floor but submerged below the ocean surface.
Sedimentary Differentiation	A process in which material is sorted by size, shape, or composition by the medium through which it travels.
Short Ton	A weight equal to 907.20 kilograms or 2,000 pounds.
Statute Mile	A distance equal to 5,280 feet or 1,609 meters.
Tectonic Sea Level Change	Apparent change in the level of the water in the oceans due to vertical movement of the land.
Tsunami	A water wave generated by an impulsive vertical displacement of the surface of the ocean or other body of water.
Vertical Exaggeration	The stretching of the vertical axis on a profile to enhance features of relief and slope; not true scale.

CHRONOLOGY OF EVENTS IN TEXT

(B.C.E. = Before Common Era; C.E. = Common Era)

Date	Event
4.5 billion B.C.E.	Earth forms.
43 million	Bend in Hawaiian Island/Emperor Seamount Chain develops toward the east.
50,000	Sea level drop creates the Bering Land Bridge. Human migrations from Asia to North America and related migrations from southeast Asia to Australia occur.
27,000	Paintings made in cave in France now underwater.
19,600	Age of skull found in Los Angeles, California.
17,000	Stone tools used in Pennsylvania.
12,000	Human and wildlife migration across the Bering Land Bridge occurs.
9500	Clovis society kills off mammoths.
5000	Mount Mazama erupts, creating Crater Lake, Oregon.
3200	First Dynasty of pharaohs begins in Egypt.
3113	Mayan calendar begins.
1500	Human migrations from Asia arrive on Fiji.
1000 B.C.E.	Human migrations arrive on Tonga.
1 C.E.	Human migrations arrive on Samoa.
500	Human migrations arrive on Marquesas.
874	Eric the Red settles Greenland.
987	Leif Ericson settles Greenland.
1000	Viking child (first European) born in North America. Human migrations to Hawaii from western Pacific occur.
1200	First North Americans travel to Hawaii.
1345	Canals built in Tenochtitlan, Mexico.
1497	Amerigo Vespucci sails to North America.
1498	John Cabot lands in Newfoundland.
1502	Columbus establishes city of Porto Bello, Panama.
1515	Balboa reaches the Pacific Ocean.
1524	Giovanni Verrazano discovers New York Harbor.
1536	Jacques Cartier discovers Canada.
1578	Martin Frobisher explores islands of northern Canada.

1606	Jamestown Colony is founded in Virginia.
1609	Henry Hudson trades with Indians on Manhattan.
1619	Danish explorer Jens Munck loses sixty-one of a crew of sixty-four to ice while searching for a northwest passage to China.
1620	The *Mayflower* lands in Massachusetts.
1737	210-foot (64-meter) high tsunami strikes Kamchatka, Russia.
1755	Earthquake in Lisbon, Portugal, causes tsunami in Caribbean.
1770	Postmaster Benjamin Franklin charts the Gulf Stream.
1786	Pearl Harbor visited by British Navy.
1794	Joseph Johns settles along the Little Conemaugh River in western Pennsylvania.
1818	Jean Lafitte's settlement on Galveston Island, Texas, destroyed by hurricane.
1835	Corning, New York is settled along the Chemung River.
1836	Money approved to build reservoir for canal in western Pennsylvania.
1838	Steamship *Great Western* crosses the North Atlantic in fifteen days.
1849	California Gold Rush starts.
1851	Clipper ship *Flying Cloud* sails from New York to San Francisco in a record-setting ninety days.
1852	The Pennsylvania Railroad reaches Pittsburgh, Pennsylvania; the liner *Baltic* crosses the Atlantic in ten days.
1855	First transcontinental railroad built across Panama.
1856	Liner *Pacific* disappears in North Atlantic, presumed victim of ice.
1858	Denver, Colorado, founded between Cherry Creek and the South Platte River.
1864	Floods damage new city of Denver, Colorado.
1867	Earthquake occurs in the U.S. Virgin Islands.
1869	Final segments of second transcontinental railroad joined in Promontory, Utah.
1879	South Fork Fishing and Hunting Club buys Pennsylvania reservoir.
1883	Krakatoa eruption generates tsunami that kills 35,000 people in the South Pacific.
1887	U.S. Navy receives coaling rights to Pearl Harbor, Hawaii.
1889	Compagnie Universelle du Canal Interoceanique abandons the Panama project; Johnstown flood of historical proportions occurs.
1893	418 derelicts reported in North Atlantic.
1896	27,000 people killed by tsunamis in Japan.

1898	The battleship *Maine* explodes in Havana, Cuba. The battleship *Oregon* travels from San Francisco to the East Coast. Short story published about the steamship *Titan*, sunk by ice in the North Atlantic.
1899	Average sailing time from west coast to east coast is 140 days by sailing ship.
1900	Hurricane destroys Galveston, Texas.
1903	Construction of Galveston seawall begins.
1911	Galveston Island and structures are raised by pumping in sand; Pearl Harbor Naval Base is put into service.
1912	The *Titanic* hits an iceberg and sinks.
1913	The International Ice Patrol is founded.
1917	U.S. gains possession of the Virgin Islands from Denmark.
1936	The maiden voyage of the *Queen Mary*, from England to New York, takes place.
1938	Hurricane strikes U.S. East Coast all the way to Canada.
1941	Japanese attack U.S. naval facilities at Pearl Harbor, Hawaii.
1946	Earthquake in Aleutian Islands generates a tsunami that strikes Hilo, Hawaii.
1950	Cherry Creek Dam is built to protect Denver.
1952	The *United States* crosses the North Atlantic in a record 3 days, 10 hours, and 40 minutes; maximum speed 43 knots (49.5 mph).
1960	Earthquake in Chile generates tsunami that affects Hilo, Hawaii; the U.S. Atlantic Coast is rising 2 feet (60 centimeters) per year.
1962	Galveston seawall is completed.
1964	Good Friday Earthquake, Alaska, generates tsunamis across the Pacific.
1969	Study of bridge between Siberia and Alaska, begins.
1970	Cyclone in Bangladesh kills 300,000; Thor Heyerdahl crosses the Atlantic in a papyrus boat.
1972	Hurricane Agnes causes floods in Corning, New York.
1975	Scientists predict the eruption of Mount St. Helens.
1976	Chatfield Dam is built to protect Denver.
1978	Treaty signed to return Panama Canal and adjacent land to Panama.
1980	Mount St. Helens, Washington, erupts.
1982	Bear Creek Dam is built to protect Denver.
1990	U.S. Census shows that seven of the eight largest metropolitan areas are adjacent to an ocean.
1991	U.S. military forces involved in Operation Desert Storm.
1992	Hurricane Andrew devastates south Florida.

1996	Hurricane Fran strikes North Carolina and moves inland.
1997	Floods in Northern California and Pacific Northwest.
1999	Panama Canal and adjacent lands scheduled to be returned to Panama.

BIBLIOGRAPHY

Albright, Harry. *Pearl Harbor: Japan's Fatal Blunder*. New York: Hippocrene Books, 1988.

American Association of Petroleum Geologists. *Explorer* 17 (1): (January 1996).

American Heritage Pictorial Atlas of United States History. Edited by Hilde Heun Kagan. New York: American Heritage, 1966.

American Geological Institute. *Earth Science Education for the 21st Century: A Planning Guide*. Alexandria, Va.: National Center for Earth Science Education, 1991.

American Institute of Architects. *Architects and Earthquakes*. Washington, D.C.: AIA Research Foundation, 1975.

Appleman, Daniel E. "James Dwight Dana and Pacific Geology." In *Magnificent Voyagers*, edited by Herman Viola, and Carolyn Margolis, 88-117. Washington, D.C.: Smithsonian Institution Press, 1985.

Arana, Luis Rafael, and Albert Manucy. *The Building of the Castillo de San Marcos*. St. Augustine, Fla.: Eastern National Park and Monument Association, Castillo de San Marcos National Monument, 1977.

Arnold, Caroline. *Coping with Natural Disasters*. New York: Walker, 1988.

Ballantine, Betty, and Ian Ballantine, eds. *The Native Americans*. Atlanta, Ga.: Turner, 1993.

Ballard, Robert D. *The Discovery of the Titanic*. Toronto: Madison, 1987.

———. *Exploring the Titanic*. Toronto: Madison, 1988.

Barhydt, Frances Bartlett, and Paul W. Morgan. *The Science Teacher's Book of Lists*. Englewood Cliffs, N.J.: Prentice-Hall, 1993.

Bascom, Willard. *Waves and Beaches*. Garden City, N.Y.: Anchor Books, 1980.

Brantley, Steven R. *The Eruption of the Redoubt Volcano, Alaska, December 14, 1989-August 31, 1990*. U.S. Geological Survey Circular 1061. Washington, D.C.: U.S. Government Printing Office, 1990.

———. *Volcanoes of the United States*. Washington, D.C.: U.S. Geological Survey, 1994.

Brogdon, N. J. *Galveston Bay Hurricane Surge Study, Report 1, Effects of Proposed Barriers on Hurricane Surge Heights*. Technical Report H-69-12. Galveston, Tex.: U.S. Army Corps of Engineers, 1969.

Brown, Billye Walker, and Walter R. Brown. *Historical Catastrophes: Hurricanes and Tornadoes*. Reading, Mass.: Addison-Wesley, 1972.

Brown, Richard. *Voyage of the Iceberg*. New York: Beaufort Books, 1983.

Callahan, Steven. *Adrift: Seventy-Six Days Lost at Sea*. Boston: Houghton Mifflin, 1986.

Canby, Thomas Y. "Water: Our Most Precious Resource." *National Geographic* 158 (1980): 144-79.

Catalano, Peter. "Hurricane Alert." *Popular Science* 247 (1995): 3.

Clague, David A., and G. Brent Dalrymple. "The Hawaiian-Emperor Volcanic Chain." In *Volcanism in Hawaii.* U.S.G.S. Professional Paper 1350, edited by Robert W. Decker; Thomas L. Wright; and Peter H. Stauffer, 5-54. Washington, D.C.: U.S. Government Printing Office, 1987.

Claiborne, Robert. *The First Americans, the Emergence of Man.* New York: Time-Life Books, 1973.

Clark, Thomas H., and Colin W. Stearn. *The Geological Evolution of North America.* New York: Ronald Press, 1960.

Clottes, Jean, and Jean Courtin. "Neptune's Ice Age Gallery." *Natural History* 102 (1993): 64-70.

Coachman, L. K.; K. Aagaard; and R. B. Tripp. *Bering Strait: The Regional Physical Oceanography.* Seattle: University of Washington Press, 1975.

Coch, Nicholas K. "Geologic Effects of Hurricanes." *Geomorphology* 10 (1994): 37-63.

——. "Hurricane Hazards Along the Northeastern Atlantic Coast of the United States." *Journal of Coastal Research* Special Issue No. 12 (1995): 115-47.

Corcoran, Thom. *Mount St. Helens: The Story Behind the Scenery.* Las Vegas, Nev.: KC Publications, 1985.

Corning Glass Works. *The Flood and the Community.* Corning, N.Y.: Corning Glass Works, 1976.

Dabney, Virginius. *Virginia, The New Dominion.* Garden City, N.Y.: Doubleday, 1971.

Dane, Michael. "Icehunters." *Popular Mechanics* 170 (10): 76-131 (1993).

Davie, Michael. *Titanic; The Death and Life of a Legend.* New York: Alfred A. Knopf, 1986.

Davis, Lee. *Natural Disasters.* New York: Facts on File, 1992.

DuVal, Miles P. *And the Mountains Will Move.* Stanford, Calif.: Stanford University Press, 1947.

Eaton, J. P.; D. H. Richter; and W. U. Ault. "The Tsunami of May 23, 1960, on the Island of Hawaii." *Bulletin of the Seismological Society of America* 51 (2): 135-57 (1961).

Fenster, J. M. "A World in the Middle of the Ocean." *American Heritage* 47 (2): 96-116 (1996).

Flerow, C. C. "On the Origin of the Mammalian Fauna of Canada." In *The Bering Land Bridge,* edited by David M. Hopkins, 271-80. Stanford, Calif.: Stanford University Press, 1967.

Fox, R. Steve. *Water Resources Development in Louisiana.* New Orleans, La.: U.S. Army Corps of Engineers, New Orleans District, 1993.

Foxworthy, Bruce L., and Mary Hill. *Volcanic Eruptions of 1980 at Mount St. Helens: The First 100 Days.* Geological Survey Professional Paper 1249. Washington, D.C.: U.S. Government Printing Office, 1982.

Funk, Ben. "Hurricane." *National Geographic* 158 (1980): 346-79.

Gannon, Robert. "What Really Sank the Titanic?" *Popular Science* 246 (2): 49-83 (1995).

Gardner, Martin. *The Wreck of the Titanic Foretold?* Buffalo, N.Y.: Prometheus Books, 1986.

Garriott, E. B. "The West Indian Hurricane of September 1-12, 1900." *National Geographic* 11 (1990): 384-92.

Gray, W. M. "Strong Association Between West African Rainfall and U.S. Landfall of Intense Hurricanes." *Science* 249 (1990): 1251-56.

Hale, John R. *Great Ages of Man; Age of Exploration.* New York: Time, 1966.

Hammond's Historical Atlas. Maplewood, N.J.: C. S. Hammond, 1960.

Hayes, Miles O. *Hurricanes As Geological Agents: Case Studies of Hurricanes Carla, 1961, and Cindy, 1963.* Report of Investigations Number 61. Austin, Tex.: Bureau of Economic Geology, 1967.

Hays, W. W., ed. *Facing Geologic and Hydrologic Hazards.* Geological Survey Professional Paper 1240-B. Washington, D.C.: U.S. Government Printing Office, 1981.

Heyerdahl, Thor. *The Ra Expeditions.* Garden City, N.Y.: Doubleday, 1971.

Holmes, Arthur. *Principles of Physical Geology.* New York: Ronald Press, 1965.

Hughes, Patrick. *American Weather Stories.* Washington, D.C.: National Oceanic and Atmospheric Administration, 1976.

————. "The Great Galveston Hurricane." *Weatherwise* 43 (4): 190-98 (1990).

Hunter, Henry. "The American Isthmus and the Interoceanic Canal." *Engineering Magazine.* February, March, 1899.

Ihinger, Phillip. "Mantle Flow Beneath the Pacific Plate: Evidence from Seamount Segments in the Hawaiian-Emperor Chain." *American Journal of Science* 295: 1035-57 (1995).

International Ice Patrol. Washington, D.C.: U.S. Government Printing Office, 1993.

Isthmian Canal Commission. *Report for 1899-1901.* Washington, D.C.: U.S. Government Printing Office, 1904.

Jahns, Richard H. "Geologic Jeopardy." In *Limitations of the Earth: A Compelling Focus for Geology,* edited by Richard H. Jahns, 69-83. Austin, Tex.: Bureau of Economic Geology, University of Texas, 1967.

Jones, William C., and Kenton Forrest. *Denver: A Pictorial History.* Boulder, Colo.: Pruett, 1985.

Kachadoorian, Reuben, and George Plafker. *Effects of the Earthquake of March 27, 1964 on the Communities of Kodiak and Nearby Islands.* U.S.G.S. Professional Paper 542-F. Washington, D.C.: U.S. Government Printing Office, 1967.

Keegan, John. *The Price of Admiralty.* New York: Viking Penguin, 1989.

Kenney, Marianne, and Lori Morrow. *Mapping out a Standards-Based Framework for Geography: The Colorado Geography Curriculum Framework.* Denver, Colo.: Colorado Department of Education, 1995.

Kent, Deborah. *The Titanic.* Chicago: Childrens Press, 1993.

Kimball, Lieutenant W. W. *Special Intelligence Report on the Progress of the Work on the Panama Canal During the Year 1885.* U.S. House of Representatives, Miscellaneous Document 395, 49th Congress, First Session. Washington, D.C.: U.S. Government Printing Office, 1886.

Kopper, Philip. *The Smithsonian Book of North American Indians.* Washington, D.C.: Smithsonian Books, 1986.

Kreitler, Charles W. *Faulting and Land Subsidence from Ground-Water and Hydrocarbon Production, Houston-Galveston, Texas.* Research Note 8. Austin, Tex.: Bureau of Economic Geology, 1978.

Lander, James F., and Patricia A. Lockridge. *United States Tsunamis 1690-1988.* Publication 41-2. Boulder, Colo.: National Geophysical Data Center, 1989.

Latham, Jean Lee. *The Chagres; Power of the Panama Canal.* Champaign, Ill.: Garrard, 1964.

Leet, L. Don, and Sheldon Judson. *Physical Geology.* Englewood Cliffs, N.J.: Prentice-Hall, 1971.

Legrand, Jacques. *Chronicle of America.* Mount Kisco, N.Y.: Chronicle Publications, 1989.

Levy, Matthys, and Mario Salvadori. *Why Buildings Fall Down.* New York: W. W. Norton, 1992.

Lockridge, Patricia A. "Historical Tsunamis in the Pacific Basin." In *Natural and Man-Made Hazards*, edited by M. I. El-Sabh, and T. S. Murty, 171-81. Dordrecht, Netherlands: D. Reidel, 1988.

Lord, Walter. *A Night to Remember.* New York: Bantam Books, 1955.

Lott, Arnold S., and Robert F. Sumrall. *Pearl Harbor Attack; An Abbreviated History.* Annapolis, Md.: Leeward Publications, 1977.

Luling, Virginia. *Aborigines.* London: MacDonald Educational Limited, 1979.

MacLeish, William H. *The Gulf Stream.* London: Hamish Hamilton, 1989.

Maddocks, Melvin. *The Great Liners.* Alexandria, Va.: Time-Life Books, 1982.

Malahoff, Alexander. "Geology of the Summit of Loihi Submarine Volcano." In *Volcanism in Hawaii.* U.S.G.S. Professional Paper 1350, edited by Robert W. Decker, Thomas L. Wright, and Peter H. Stauffer, 133-45. Washington, D.C.: U.S. Government Printing Office, 1987.

Maxtone-Graham, John. *The Only Way to Cross.* New York: Collier Books, 1972.

Mayor, Adrienne. "Derelict Ships." *Mariner's Weather Log.* (National Oceanographic Data Center, Washington, D.C.) 36 (1992): 4-10.

McComb, David G. *Galveston: A History.* Austin, Tex.: University of Texas Press, 1986.

McCullough, David. *The Johnstown Flood.* New York: Simon & Schuster, 1968.

———. *The Path Between the Seas.* New York: Simon & Schuster, 1977.

McEvedy, Colin, and Richard Jones. *Atlas of World Population History.* New York: Facts on File, 1979.

McGee, W. J. "The Lessons of Galveston." *National Geographic* 11 (1900): 377-83.

McPhee, John. *The Control of Nature.* New York: Noonday Press, 1989.

Melham, Tom. "Earthquakes: Global Tremors, Drifting Continents." In *Powers of Nature*, edited by Robert L. Breeden, 6-47. Washington, D.C.: National Geographic Society, 1978.

Mersey, Lord. Shipping Casualties (Loss of Steamship "Titanic."). *1912, The Final Report of the British Investigation into the Sinking of the Titanic.* Published by His Majesty's Stationery Office, London.

Miller, Francis Trevelyan. *History of World War II.* Washington, D.C.: Community Home Sales, 1947.

Morgan, W. Jason. "Convection Plumes in the Lower Mantle." In *Plate Tectonics and Geomagnetic Reversals*, edited by Allan Cox, 659-61. San Francisco: W. H. Freeman, 1973.

Morton, Robert A. *Shoreline Changes on Galveston Island (Bolivar Roads to San Luis Pass): An Analysis of Historical Changes of the Texas Gulf Shoreline.* Geological Circular 74-2. Austin, Tex.: Bureau of Economic Geology, 1974.

Morton, Robert A., and J. H. McGowen. *Modern Depositional Environments of the Texas Gulf Coast.* Austin, Tex.: Bureau of Economic Geology, 1980.

Nance, Raymond L. *Water of the World.* Washington, D.C.: U.S. Government Printing Office, 1977.

National Academy Press. *National Science Education Standards.* Washington, D.C.: National Academy Press, 1996.

National Geographic Society. *The Making of America, Northern Approaches,* map supplement to the *National Geographic* 167 (2): 208a (February 1985).

National Oceanic and Atmospheric Administration. *Johnstown, Pennsylvania Flash Flood of July 19-20, 1977.* Natural Disaster Survey Report 77-1. Rockville, Md.: U.S. Department of Commerce, 1977.

National Park Service. *Bering Land Bridge National Preserve.* Washington, D.C.: U.S. Government Printing Office, 1992.

———. *Johnstown Flood National Memorial.* Washington, D.C.: U.S. Government Printing Office, 1993.

Nichols, D. R., and J. M. Buchanan-Banks. *Seismic Hazards and Land Use Planning.* U.S. Geological Survey Circular 690. Washington, D.C.: U.S. Government Printing Office, 1974.

"On Thin Ice." *Denver Post,* March 16, 1995, p. 2.

Pewe, T. L., and David M. Hopkins. "Mammal Remains of Pre-Wisconsin Age in Alaska." In *The Bering Land Bridge,* edited by David M. Hopkins, 245-65. Stanford, Calif.: Stanford University Press, 1967.

Phalen, W. C. *Geologic Atlas of the United States, Johnstown Folio.* Folio Number 174. Washington, D.C.: U.S. Geological Survey, 1910.

Rappaport, Ed. "Hurricane Andrew—A First Look." *Mariner's Weather Log* (National Oceanographic Data Center) 36 (1992): 16-25.

Repenning, Charles A. "Palearctic-Nearctic Mammalian Dispersal in the Late Cenozoic." In *The Bering Land Bridge,* edited by David M. Hopkins, 288-311. Stanford, Calif.: Stanford University Press, 1967.

Richardson, P. L. "Drifting Derelicts in the North Atlantic 1883-1902." In *Essays on Oceanography.* Progress in Oceanography, Volume 14, edited by J. Crease, W. J. Gould, and P. M. Saunders. Oxford: Pergamon Press, 1985.

Richardson, Philip L. "Derelicts and Drifters." *Natural History* 94 (1985): 6, 43-48.

Riegel, Robert Edgar. *The Story of the Western Railroads.* Lincoln: University of Nebraska Press, 1964.

Russell, Loris S. "Mammalian Migrations in the Pleistocene." In *Problems of the Pleistocene Epoch and Arctic Area,* edited by G. R. Lowther, 48-55. Montreal: McGill University, 1962.

Sarna-Wojcicki, Andrei M.; Susan Shipley; Richard B. Waitt Jr.; Daniel Dzurisin; and Spencer H. Wood. "Areal Distribution, Thickness, Mass, Volume, and Grain Size of Air-Fall Ash from the Six Major Eruptions of 1980." In *The 1980 Eruptions of Mount St. Helens, Washington,* edited by Peter W. Lipman, and Donal R. Mullineaux. U.S. Geological Survey Professional Paper 1250. Washington, D.C.: U.S. Government Printing Office, 1981.

Small, Charles S. *Rails to the Diggings.* Railroad Monographs, 1981.

Souza, D. M. *Powerful Waves.* Minneapolis, Minn.: Carolrhoda Books, 1992.

Spaeth, M. G., and S. C. Berkman. *The Tsunami of March 28, 1964.* Rockville, Md.: U.S. Department of Commerce, 1965.

Steinbrugge, Karl V. *Earthquakes, Volcanoes and Tsunamis.* New York: Skandia America Group, 1982.

Stewart, R. W. "The Atmosphere and the Ocean." *Scientific American* 221 (3): 76-86 (1969).

Stommel, Henry. *The Gulf Stream*. Berkeley: University of California Press, 1958.

Tannehill, Ivan Ray. *The Hurricane Hunters*. New York: Dodd, Mead, 1961.

Thomas, David Hurst. "The Long Span of Time." In *The Native Americans*, edited by Betty Ballantine, and Ian Ballantine. Atlanta, Ga.: Turner, 1993.

Tilling, Robert I. *Eruptions of Mount St. Helens: Past, Present and Future*. Washington, D.C.: Superintendent of Documents, 1985.

Tope, Gregory. "Alaska-Siberia Bridge." *Popular Mechanics* 171 (1994): 56-58.

Trefil, James. *Meditations at Sunset*. New York: Charles Scribner's Sons, 1987.

———. *A Scientist in the City*. New York: Doubleday, 1994.

United States Army Corps of Engineers. *The Galveston Seawall*. Galveston, Tex.

———. *Galveston's Bulwark Against the Sea; History of the Galveston Seawall*. Galveston, Tex.: U.S. Government Printing Office, 1981.

———. *The Tri-Lakes Project, Colorado*. Omaha District. Washington, D.C.: U.S. Government Printing Office, 1992.

United States Senate. *"Titanic" Disaster; Report of the Committee on Commerce*. Report 806, 62-2. Washington, D.C.: U.S. Government Printing Office, 1912.

Vangengeim, E. A. "The Effect of the Bering Land Bridge on the Quaternary Mammalian Faunas of Siberia and North America." In *The Bering Land Bridge*, edited by David M. Hopkins, 281-87. Stanford, Calif.: Stanford University Press, 1967.

Villiers, Captain Alan. *Men, Ships and the Sea*. Washington, D.C.: National Geographic Society, 1973.

Walden, Don. "Raising Galveston." *American Heritage of Invention and Technology* 5 (1990): 8-18.

Warfield, Ronald G.; Lee Juillerat; and Larry Smith. *Crater Lake, the Story Behind the Scenery*. Las Vegas, Nev.: KC Publications, 1982.

Weast, Robert C., ed. *Handbook of Chemistry and Physics*. Boca Raton, Fla.: CRC Press, 1986.

Wilcox, Del. *Voyagers to California*. Elk, Calif.: Sea Rock Press, 1991.

Williams, S. Jeffress; Kurt Dodd; and Kathleen Krafft Gohn. *Coasts in Crisis*. U.S. Geological Survey Circular 1075. Washington, D.C.: U.S. Government Printing Office, 1991.

World Almanac and Book of Facts. New York: Pharos Books, 1992.

Wright, Thomas L., and Thomas C. Pierson. *Living with Volcanoes*. U.S. Geological Survey Circular 1073. Washington, D.C.: U.S. Government Printing Office, 1992.

Young, Louise B. *Sowing the Wind*. New York: Prentice-Hall, 1990.

INDEX

About the Author

Craig A. Munsart is a former energy industry geologist, educational programs manager at a children's museum, and middle school science curriculum writer. He has taught at the university, high school, and middle school levels and has presented to elementary school students and teacher groups. He holds bachelor degrees in geology and architecture and a master's degree in geology. He is presently a science educator in the Denver area and a secondary school teacher in Jefferson County, Colorado. His previous works are *Investigating Science with Dinosaurs* (winner of the Dinosaur Society 1994 Book Award), and *Primary Dinosaur Investigations* (with Karen VanGundy).

From *Teacher Ideas Press*

SOCIAL STUDIES READERS THEATRE FOR YOUNG ADULTS:
Scripts And Script Development
Kathy Howard Latrobe, Carol Casey, and Linda A. Gann

Introduce readers theatre as a means to link literature to social studies with these 16 reproducible scripts from YA classics in world literature. An overview of readers theatre techniques and outlines (including introduction and script for the narrator) are given for readers theatre scripts based on contemporary YA novels that have been chosen for their interest level and historical accuracy. **Grades 7–12**.
ix, 189p. 8½x11 paper ISBN 0-87287-864-3

CIVIC MATHEMATICS: Fundamentals in the Context of Social Issues
Terry Vatter

"What has math got to do with my life?" If you've ever heard that protest from your students, this book may provide the answer. Presenting mathematics in the context of social issues makes it relevant and helps students learn how to apply math skills appropriately.
Grades 6–10.
xvi, 169p. 8½x11 paper ISBN 1-56308-435-X

GREAT MOMENTS IN SCIENCE: Experiments and Readers Theatre
Kendall Haven

Significant moments and characters in the history of Western science come to life in 12 scripts that are linked with student experiments. These parallel or simulate the actual experiments in the stories, so that students can discover and learn the concepts for themselves. **Grades 4–9**.
xii, 227p. 8½x11 paper ISBN 1-56308-149-0

INVESTIGATING SCIENCE WITH DINOSAURS
Craig A. Munsart

Chosen for the Dinosaur Society's Recommended Reading List in 1994, these reproducible, hands-on activities offer students the opportunity to experience authentic learning about science and scientific subjects (e.g., mechanics, skeletal systems, radiometric dating, plate tectonics, fossils). **Grades 4–12**.
xiii, 249p. 8½x11 paper ISBN 1-56308-008-7

NATURE PUZZLERS: Thinking Activities from the Natural World
Lawrence E. Hillman

Bring a little intrigue into the classroom with these puzzling anecdotes from the real world of nature. Written to encourage critical-thinking and problem-solving skills, they serve as springboards to activities across the curriculum—from active discussions to research projects to brainstorming to creative writing and much more. **Grades 6–12**.
xiv, 152p. 8½x11 paper ISBN 0-87287-778-7

MYSTERY AND DETECTION: Thinking and Problem Solving with the Sleuths
Jerry D. Flack

Turn your classroom into a real Scotland Yard! This unique resource ties in dozens of problem-solving and enrichment activities with mystery and sleuthing. It is divided into topical chapters on language arts, art, social studies, future studies, and crime and punishment. **Grades 5–9** *(Adaptable to other grades)*.
Gifted Treasury Series; Jerry D. Flack, Ed.
xx, 246p. 8½x11 paper ISBN 0-87287-815-5

For a FREE catalog or to order these or any Teacher Ideas Press titles, please contact:

Teacher Ideas Press
Dept. B32 • P.O. Box 6633 • Englewood, CO 80155-6633
Phone: 1-800-237-6124, ext. 1 • Fax: 303-220-8843 • E-mail: lu-books@lu.com